GRAC
DISGRACE

Dr Neil Ormerod is a lecturer in Systematic Theology, St Paul's National Seminary, Sydney, and Theology Editor for *National Outlook* Magazine. He is the author of *Introducing Contemporary Theologies* (E.J. Dwyer).

GRACE & DISGRACE

A THEOLOGY OF SELF-ESTEEM, SOCIETY AND HISTORY

NEIL ORMEROD

E.J. DWYER

DEDICATION

to my dearest Therese,
my lifelong companion in the life of grace

First published in 1992 by
E.J. Dwyer (Australia) Pty Ltd
3/32–72 Alice Street
Newtown NSW 2042
Australia

National Library of Australia
Cataloguing-in-Publication data

Ormerod, Neil.
Grace & disgrace: a theology of self-esteem, society and history.

Bibliography.
Includes index.
ISBN 0 85574 428 6.

1. Sin, Original. 2. Sin, Original – History of doctrines.
3. Grace (Theology). I. Title.

233.14

Distributed in Canada by:
Meakin and Associates
Unit 17
81 Auriga Drive
NEPEAN, ONT K2E 7Y5
Ph: (613) 226 4381

Distributed in Ireland and the U.K. by:
Columba Book Service
93 The Rise
Mount Merrion
BLACKROCK CO. DUBLIN
Ph: (01) 283 2954

Distributed in the United States by:
Morehouse Publishing
871 Ethan Allen Highway
RIDGEFIELD CT 06877
Ph: (203) 431 3927

Cover designed by Rex Turnbull
Typeset in 11/12 Garamond by Graphicraft Typesetters Ltd, Hong Kong.
Printed by SRM Production Services Sdn. Bhd.

CONTENTS

PART B: ORIGINAL SIN

PREFACE

This book has grown out of a course I teach at St Paul's National Seminary, Kensington. The overwhelmingly positive response of the students has encouraged me to undertake the task of writing the material in a form which will make it accessible to a wider public. The book is aimed at such an undergraduate theology audience, though it should be readable by anyone who is interested in the topics of grace and original sin. It requires no previous theological knowledge and is relatively self-contained.

This book attempts to present a synthesis of the theologies of grace and original sin. As an exercise in systematic theology, I have not attempted to give a detailed historical account of the developments of the doctrines involved, though I have included some historical material on the history of the doctrine of original sin. I felt this was necessary since there is no readily available account of the doctrine for a general readership. For the history of the theology of grace, Roger Haight's *The Language and Experience of Grace* (Gill and Macmillan, Dublin, 1979) is an excellent and accessible source.

The structure of the chapters perhaps requires some comment. Each chapter contains a main text, which is meant to deal with the issue at hand. In general I thought it better not to clutter up this text with detailed references or accounts of current theological debate. Thus I have included notes at the end of each chapter which comment on current theology, or expound on issues which may have disrupted the flow of the text. I have also made use of a limited number of footnotes. In general these are meant to indicate sources and provide justification for stances I have taken. Sources are generally idiosyncratic, drawing on a wide body of psychological, theological and philosophical writings. Where I have felt some necessity to justify a particular stance I have tried to use references which are commonly available to theological students, such as biblical commentaries and theological dictionaries.

As with my first book, *Introducing Contemporary Theologies* (E.J. Dwyer, Sydney, 1990), this work has drawn heavily on the foundational work of Bernard Lonergan. I hope I have been faithful to his spirit, though I have not been slavish with regard to his terminology. I would also like to express my appreciation of the work of Sebastian Moore, whose thought has been so seminal in many of my researches. I hope I have done justice to his ideas.

In a more immediate sense there are many I would like to thank with regard to this project. Firstly, there are the students who have borne with me in the development of the thought contained in this work. Their wholehearted response to the material has assured me that there is something worthwhile in this whole project. Secondly I would like to thank Fr Michael Fallon MSC, who first showed me that there really is something to theology. Thirdly I would like to thank E.J. Dwyer for their commitment to theological publishing and their decision to go ahead with this book. Fourthly I would like to thank Rev. Dr John Chryssavgis of St Andrew's Greek Orthodox Theological College, Redfern, for the timely inclusion of material giving a Greek Orthodox understanding of what we in the West have called "original sin". Fifthly I would like to thank Denis Edwards for his many helpful comments and criticisms of an initial draft of this work. Finally I would like to thank my wife, Therese, for her companionship and love. In all I write, she is my first and most valued critic.

ACKNOWLEDGMENTS

The author gratefully acknowledges the use of material from the following, which are used with the permissions of the publishers or copyright holders:

The New Jerusalem Bible, published and copyright 1985 by Darton Longman and Todd Ltd and Doubleday & Co Inc, and is used by the permission of the publishers.
The Fire and the Rose Are One, Sebastian Moore, published 1980, Darton Longman and Todd Ltd (London) and Harper Collins, New York.
Let This Mind be in You, Sebastian Moore, published 1985 by Darton Longman and Todd Ltd (London) and Harper Collins, New York.
"Original Sin, Sex, Resurrection and Trinity", Sebastian Moore, published in *Lonergan Workship*, Vol. IV, Fred Lawrence (ed.), Scholars Press, 1983.
The Passionate God, Rosemary Haughton, published 1981, by Darton Longman and Todd Ltd (London).
Method in Theology, Bernard Lonergan, published 1972, by Darton Longman and Todd Ltd (London).
Grace and Freedom, Bernard Lonergan, published 1971, by Darton Longman and Todd Ltd (London).
Luther's Works, (Vol. 25) copyright 1972, Concordia Publishing House. Reprinted by permission from CPH.

The Desires of the Human Heart, V. Gregson, (ed.) published and copyright 1988, Paulist Press, NY.
"Our hearts of darkness: Original Sin revisited", Stephen J. Duffy, *Theological Studies*, 49 (1988), pp. 597–622.
Infallibility, Peter Chirico, published 1983, Michael Glazier.
Christ: The Christian Experience in the Modern World by Edward Schillebeeckx. English translation copyright © 1980 by The Crossroad Publishing Company. Reprinted by permission of The Crossroad Publishing Company.
"Totem and Taboo", Sigmund Freud, in *The Origins of Religion*, Vol. 13, The Pelican Freud Library, 1985 (trans. James Strachey), copyright Sigmund Freud Copyrights.
Original Sin: Two Major Trends in Contemporary Roman Catholic Reinterpretation, G. Vandervelde, Rodopi, Amsterdam, 1975.
"Original Sin — An Orthodox Perspective", by John Chryssavgis, by permission of the author.

Every effort has been made to contact the copyright holders of significant text material used within. The author and publisher apologise in those cases where this had proved impossible.

Some Standard References

The New Jerome Biblical Commentary, R. Brown, et al. (eds), Prentice Hall, New Jersey, 1990, referred to as *NJBC*.

The New Dictionary of Theology, J. Komonchak, et al. (eds), Gill & McMillan, Dublin, and Michael Glazier, Wilmington, 1987, referred to as *TNDT*.

The New Jerusalem Bible, H. Wansbrough (ed.), Darton, Longman & Todd, London and Doubleday, NY, 1986, referred to as *TNJB*.

Enchiridion Symbolorum Definitionum et Declarationum de Rebus Fidei et Morum, Denzinger, referred to as *DS* (this is a standard source for Catholic Church pronouncements).

PART A

Grace

CHAPTER ONE

AN OVERVIEW

It does not take the most astute powers of observation to note that something is terribly wrong with the human condition. The world is torn by wars, famines, massive global poverty, sufferings which find their origins not just in the fickleness of nature but in a hardness of heart, an inability, an unwillingness to do little more than maintain the status quo. Yet it is this very status quo which gave rise to the problems in the first place. The question which confronts us all is "How do we get out of this mess? Where can we turn for help?"

In general one could say that there are two types of solution for this human condition, both sharing a common premise that our present situation is the result of a massive misuse of human freedom. Evil occurs when the human heart freely turns from its proper good and becomes perverted in its goals. Yet the two solutions are vastly different. The first sees human freedom as the basic problem. The solution then is to do away with freedom. Such an abolition of freedom is achieved through a total, unquestioning, automatic obedience to a designated authority. People must simply do what they are told to do, and if they fail they must be expelled from human society. The second solution recognizes that freedom is the cause of our problems but it also recognizes that when freedom is drawn to evil, it is freedom itself which suffers. The solution to this problem is not less freedom, but more freedom, the freeing of a freedom which has become trapped, enslaved in patterns of unfreedom. While the first solution despairs in the human condition, the second rejoices in what is essential to human dignity, the full flowering of human freedom.

Sadly we have seen too many attempts to implement the first solution. The totalitarian excesses of Stalin and Hitler have given us ample evidence that this solution easily falls into the demonic. Yet there are many who would still see it as viable, if only we could find the right person or group to obey. Some even suggest the Church as the right group, that the solution to the human condition would lie in absolute obedience to the authority of the Church. However, as the teaching of the Second Vatican Council has made clear, not even the Church can undermine the dignity of human freedom.[1] When it attempts to do so, it too finds itself no longer the agent of God but of dark forces which destroy true humanity. As Lord Acton once commented, "Power corrupts, absolute power corrupts absolutely".

While many have identified Christianity as offering a solution of the first type, this is a misreading of the Christian tradition. In his letter to the Galatians Paul exclaimed, "For freedom Christ has set you free . . . do not submit yourself to the yoke of slavery once more" Galatians 5:1. At the heart of the Christian faith is a story of one man's remarkable freedom, a freedom which was willing to take on the powers of darkness, of sin and death. It was a freedom which was not diminished by its closeness to the divine, but was empowered in a way which no other human freedom has experienced. Such a freedom could not be contained by the powers of darkness but bursts forth again in the resurrection, bringing the gift of freedom to all who will travel with him.

In a sense this is what this book is about. It is the human story of freedom and its empowering by the mystery which Christians have called grace, and its enfeebling by the sadder mystery of sin. All of us are caught up in these elements of the human condition, not just as individuals living our private lives, but as societies, communities caught up in the historical sweep of grace and disgrace, struggling to find meaning and direction in a world of conflict which still yearns for peace, a world of corruption which still longs for justice, a world of environmental devastation which still aches for a renewed creation.

While the mystery of grace finds its ultimate explanation in the sovereign freedom of God, the mystery of evil and sin remains hidden, not in light but in darkness. Many attempts have been made to make sense of evil. Some have sought to explain evil by appealing to an anti-God, an evil being equal but opposite to God. While some Christians appear to fall into this dualism, it is not really the Christian answer to the problem. Some, such as the

Swiss psychologist Carl Jung, have sought to explain evil by locating it in God's own being. Evil is just part of creation and we must seek to right balance between competing forces of good and evil. Again such a solution is incompatible with a Christian faith which sees in God only light, with no darkness at all.

The problem of the origin of evil remains however, and the Christian tradition has attempted to grapple with it. Its answer, at least traditionally, has been to see evil as originating not in some cosmic source, God or an anti-God, but to see evil originating in human history, in some ancient calamity, a fall or original sin, which forever blights human existence. This fall sets a seal of tragedy on human history, a tragedy which is only turned around through the death and resurrection of Jesus.

This simplistic account has come under increasing attack and growing incomprehension in recent years. Matthew Fox, in his book, *Original Blessing* (Bear & Co., New Mexico, 1983), sets up the notion of creation as originally blessed in opposition to the traditional notion of original sin. Fox traces most of the problems associated with Christianity to this misunderstanding, with Augustine of Hippo being the main culprit. The popularity of Fox's writings show that he has struck a responsive chord in many people, yet critics have questioned whether Fox honestly addressed either the tradition or the problem of evil.

Fox's writings are not the only source of growing incomprehension. The formulation of the doctrine of original sin took place in a world whose cosmology was much simpler than our own. The simple three-tiered universe of heaven, earth and hell has been replaced by an evolving cosmos billions of years old, billions of light years across. A simple creationist account has been replaced by the evolution of species, including the human species. The biblical story of Adam and Eve in a beautiful garden cannot stand up to such scrutiny. The problem for many has been that the theological formulations of the doctrine of original sin have been so closely tied to a world view which can no longer be sustained, that the only option appears to be the rejection of the doctrine.

The situation is not helped by those who, in seeking to affirm the truth of the doctrine, demand assent to such outmoded cosmologies. The whole doctrine of original sin requires a restatement in a way which is more compatible with modern scientific understandings of the origins of the human species. If this is not possible, if the doctrine really is incompatible with modern scientific theories of the origins of the human species, then perhaps the most honest option would be to reject the doctrine and start again.

However, one has to be clear about what one would be rejecting. The doctrine of original sin does not stand in some splendid theological isolation in the Christian view of the world. Indeed it stands in profound relationship to theologies of grace and redemption. To reject the doctrine of original sin would be to call into question much of Christian faith and theology.

Perhaps the thing which would be most up for question would be how we are to understand the death and resurrection of Jesus as the primary saving event. This again is an issue which critics feel is not faced adequately by Matthew Fox. However it is also an issue which the tradition itself has found problematic. Whatever may have been available in the rich theological tradition of the Church, for many the death of Jesus has been presented as a bloody sacrifice which appeased God for the sins of humanity. This, and a number of other unsatisfying theological explanations, such as the ransom theory, have done little to clarify the significance of the death and resurrection of Jesus. The poverty of our soteriologies (theologies of salvation) has had a feedback effect on the doctrine of original sin. If we do not understand salvation, we will not understand what it is we are being saved from, namely original sin.

Yet the Christian tradition remains unequivocal, that the death and resurrection of Jesus IS the central saving event. Every Easter the Church proclaims it anew. A proper theological understanding of this is a pressing necessity for the Church today and in every era. Further, every advance in our understanding of salvation will in turn effect our understanding of original sin, and as we grow in understanding of original sin, we shall deepen our understanding of the mystery of salvation. Here a special mention must be made of the various theologies of liberation which have raised significant soteriological questions for our contemporary world.

This then, in broad outline, is the aim of this book. It is about human freedom caught in a tension between grace and disgrace, a tension which is personal, social and historical. It is about trying to make sense of this human condition in the light of the doctrines of grace, original sin and the saving mystery of Jesus' death and resurrection. I have not tried to say everything on these questions, but I hope that what follows will, at the very least, shed some light on the matters at hand.

It will be evident to the reader at this stage that this book is written very much in a Catholic context. I have not felt it my task, nor would I feel competent, to spell out the interesting historical twists and turns which led to various Catholic doctrines or the controversies they generated, particularly in the area of grace. I have, however, felt it necessary to give some historical information on the doctrine of original sin. Most of this, I admit, is from scholarly secondary sources, but little is available on this history in accessible non-scholarly form. The history is there to alert the reader to the issues and to place the doctrine into a more open-ended historical context.

BASIC THEOLOGICAL STANCE

The theologically literate reader will note that there is little significant engagement with or exposition of current debate in the theology of grace. It is clear to all that Karl Rahner has contributed more to a contemporary Catholic theology of grace than any other theologian, though my main inspiration has been drawn from the writings of Bernard Lonergan and Sebastian Moore.[2] My purpose has not been exposition of Rahner's or others' work, nor, I hope, has it been a polemic critique of still others. My concern has been to present a synthesis built upon a few basic building blocks. I hope that as a synthesis it stands on its own merits. This has also allowed me to focus on issues which are of particular interest to me, in particular the relationship between grace and freedom and the social and historical dimension of these. I would like, however, to spend some time spelling out the theological positions which will inform this study. In this way my indebtedness to others will become more evident.

GRACE AND NATURE

In line with mainstream Catholic thinking I accept the distinction between grace, as a strictly theological concept, and nature. Along with thinkers such as Rahner and Lonergan, I find the distinction more theoretical than actually realized in the concrete human situation. The distinction is necessary to preserve the gratuity of grace, yet in the concrete all human living is affected by both grace and sin so that we have no direct access to any presumed neutral state of nature.

In particular I find helpful the scholastic axiom that grace completes and perfects nature. This perspective helps resolve any conflict that might seem to exist, for example, between grace and freedom. To explain an action by reference to human freedom does not undermine nor deny that it can also be explained by reference to God's grace. Grace provides a higher level explanation which does not deny the lower, but places it within a fuller context.

METAPHYSICS OR PSYCHOLOGY

A traditional theology of grace—even as found in some contemporary writers such as Karl Rahner—is presented in basically metaphysical terms. While such an approach has its validity, it makes it particularly difficult for the reader unversed in metaphysics to tackle. Even the distinction between grace and nature, mentioned above, is basically metaphysical and is likely to puzzle a contemporary reader.

For this reason I have not attempted to give a metaphysical account of grace. The account within is largely psychological in nature, drawing on psychological categories such as self-esteem in order to clarify the human experience of grace. Thus there are far more references to authors in the psychological field, such as M. Scott Peck and Gerald May, than there are to traditional theological authors.[3] I hope this experiential focus more easily lends itself to a broadening of the horizon to include social and historical questions which were often neglected by traditional metaphysical approaches.

EXTRINSICISM OR INTRINSICISM

Of course, in adopting the language of psychology I have already opted for an intrinsic understanding of grace against a theological extrinsicism. One of the disadvantages of a metaphysical analysis of grace is that it makes it difficult to locate grace in human experience. Out of this tradition grew a theological extrinsicism which basically argued that grace simply was not part of human experience. It was more like a deposit into some heavenly bank account, unrelated to any experience here and now, or like a lump of gold in the stomach—clearly of value but not doing anyone any real good![4] One of the major achievements of a modern theology of grace has been the overcoming of this extrinsicist understanding of grace, largely through the efforts of Karl Rahner. Many authors, such as Denis Edwards in his *Human Experience of God*, have helped clarify the very real human experience of God which we call grace. I hope that what I write will further clarify this experience.

NATURE, SOCIETY AND HISTORY

The other difficulty associated with a metaphysical account of grace is that it focused largely on grace and the individual. Metaphysical categories tend to abstract the individual from his or her concrete social and historical circumstances, so that these circumstances are seen as purely accidental to a theology of grace. Together with an extrinsicist understanding of grace this leads to an individualistic piety cut off from any serious engagement with the world.

Contemporary theologies, in particular political and liberation theologies, have rightly called into question such an approach. It is simply not adequate to analyze the human subject in terms which ignore his or her social and historical constitution. Human existence is a social and historical existence and any theology of grace must address these aspects of living. Each of us is shaped by family, friends, community and culture often in ways which we do not appreciate. Marx sought to uncover the "false consciousness" of capitalism, while Freud attacked the repressed sexuality of a Victorian era. In our own era consumerism ruthlessly promoted by the mass media subtly shapes our feelings, thoughts and decisions through its subliminal influences. No man is an island, no person is isolated from these myriad powers. A contemporary theology of grace must address such issues.

MEDIATION AND UNIVERSALITY

A Catholic theology of grace has always stressed the mediated or sacramental quality of grace. In this life we simply do not experience a direct, immediate experience of the divine. Grace is always mediated through people, through relationship, through symbol and action. It is not enough to say that grace is always available to anyone at any time, that all they have to do is turn to God in some individualistic isolation. To the drug addict lying in the gutter grace is unlikely to be available until someone reaches down and offers love and acceptance.

While accepting such a mediated view of grace, it is important to recognize the difficulties it creates. These difficulties are highlighted by the classical axiom—outside the Church there is no salvation, *extra ecclesiam nulla salus*. The strength of this axiom is that it reinforces the mediated nature of grace, a mediation which takes place through the Church and its sacraments. The negative aspect is that the mediation of grace could be seen as restricting grace to one particular group of people, to the exclusion of all others. To this extent, emphasis on the mediational aspects of grace can undermine confidence in the universal salvific will of God as expressed in the First Letter to Timothy:

> . . . [God] wants everyone to be saved and to reach full knowledge of truth (I Timothy 2:4).

From this scriptural verse it would seem that any attempt to limit salvation, and hence grace, to a particular historical community or some particular set of rites, must come under question. St Augustine, a proponent of the classical axiom above and aware of this text, engaged in an imaginative "exegesis" of the text which understood it to refer to "all the predestined, because every type of mankind is among them".[5] This does not stand up to a critical examination.

There remains, however, an undeniable tension between a claim that grace is always mediated and seeking to hold onto God's universal salvific will. The most common solution given to this problem today is one which invokes Karl Rahner's theology of the "supernatural existential" and his concept of "anonymous Christianity".[6] Without denying the importance of Rahner's approach in this regard, I shall adopt a slightly different approach here. It will be based on a universally efficacious divine providence. In this way the universal offer of saving grace is made concrete through God's providential ordering of creation. Here it is belief in an efficacious divine providence which holds together the two poles of mediation of grace and the universal offer of salvation.

As a final word on the matter of mediation of grace, I note that Edward Schillebeeckx has consistently spoken of mediated immediacy.[7] This seemingly paradoxical language is in fact quite meaningful, and I hope to be able to illustrate it at a later stage. It helps capture something of the reality of grace.

CONCLUSION

In this chapter I hope to have set the stage for the ensuing material. The task, as I see it, is to bring together the concerns of a world crying out for salvation and a Christian tradition which claims to be a bearer of good news for humankind. The resources of that tradition are profound, yet they have too often been expressed in ways which obscure rather than enlighten. I hope that I have been a faithful listener both to the world and to the tradition and that this book will be able to communicate something of that tradition to men and women who feel trapped by feelings of powerlessness in a human history which frequently seems to teeter on the brink of disaster. Only grace and the active cooperation of free people can turn human history around, from a history of disgrace to the flowering of grace in God's kingdom.

1 In the *Declaration on Religious Dignity* it is argued that one "must not be forced to act contrary to his conscience. Nor must he be prevented from acting according to his conscience" para.3.
2 *See* the select bibliography for more detailed references to the writings of these authors.
3 *See* the select bibliography for more detailed references to the writings of these authors.
4 The image is taken from Joseph Donceel, *The Searching Mind*, p.110.
5 Quoted in J.N.D. Kelly's *The Pastoral Epistles*, Adam & Charles Black, London, 1963, p.62. Cf. also *TNDT*, p.817.
6 *See* Rahner's "Anonymous Christians", *Theological Investigations*, Vol.6, pp.390–8.
7 *See* for example his most recent work, *Church, the Human Story of God*, SCM, pp.66–72. See also Bernard Lonergan, *Method in Theology*, p.77.

CHAPTER TWO

GRACE AND FREEDOM

As I observed at the beginning of the previous chapter, at the heart of the human condition lies the problem of freedom. While many agree that freedom is essential to human dignity there is no clear agreement as to what freedom is. Differing views of freedom have profound consequences, both personally and socially, in the political sphere so it will be important for me to clarify what I mean by freedom, and what I don't mean! Corresponding to different understandings of freedom will be different understandings of the relationship between grace and freedom. These differences have had historical consequences particularly at the time of the Reformation. It was as much Luther's understanding of freedom which caused problems then as his understanding of grace. Be that as it may, here I will be content to give a positive account of freedom, its dignity and its limitations and how it can relate to the divine initiative we call grace.

FREEDOM

Of course the question of the nature of freedom is quite difficult and convoluted. There is no shortage of those who would even deny the reality of freedom, saying that what appears to us as freedom is really the outcome of some lower form of determinism. For example the French mathematician, Simon Laplace (1749–1827), sought to reduce everything to a mechanistic determinism. He claimed that given the positions and velocities of all the particles in the universe, one could predict all future events. More recently sociobiology has sought to reduce freedom to a biological determinism with all our actions controlled by "selfish genes". And of course Sigmund Freud sought to reduce freedom to a psychic determinism. This is not the place to enter into such debates. All such attempts alert us to forces which condition our freedom but in the end they fall over into some form of reductionism. Here I shall take the reality of freedom as given. It is the presupposition of all moral, legal and even political debate, and most would see it as a presupposition of the Christian message. Paul's frequent exhortations in letters to early Christian communities are unintelligible without it. However, while accepting the reality of freedom, it is not at all clear what it actually means. So the first task will be to clarify what is meant by freedom.

In our own western society freedom is a much used and abused term. We are told that "freedom is the power over money", or that "freedom of choice is the basis of our way of life". It is clear that we highly value freedom—"give me liberty or give me death!". We see the deprivation of freedom as a severe punishment and we chastise the immoral on the basis that they have misused their freedom. We all long to be free. But free from what? Free to do what? Freedom from responsibilities or freedom for them? What is this freedom we all so strongly desire?

In order to clarify the concept of freedom we first need to clear away a trivial notion which sees it in terms of "arbitrary choice". Such a notion would see freedom in terms of choosing what breakfast cereal you eat! Freedom is then increased by multiplying the number of options one has. The more different brands of breakfast cereals there are on the shelves, the more freedom we have. While the availability of options is, of course, important to freedom, the reduction of it to some arbitrary choice is a fatal error into which our consumerist society has tended to fall. Indeed one could argue that a multiplicity of basically meaningless choices does nothing but drain the person of the energy needed to make really important decisions. For the least important decisions we have too much choice, for the most important decisions we have too little! Twenty types of breakfast cereal but two dominant and often indistinguishable political parties!

It has to be acknowledged, however, that this trivial notion of freedom dominates our social dialogue and also has profound socio-political consequences. It is a freedom basically without responsibilities. It is a freedom based on an ideology of individualism. Where freedom is seen basically as arbitrary choice then the mere existence of other people and of society is seen as limiting one's otherwise unlimited freedom. I cannot do just what I choose because it might impinge on the freedom of others. On such an analysis the existence of other people and society is the cause of resentment since they limit my freedom just by being there. A society which actively promotes such an understanding of freedom is in deep internal contradiction which can lead in the end to social disintegration.

Nor is freedom primarily about a choice between good and evil, as is often said. While such an understanding adds an essential moral dimension to the discussion, to state it as such would be to imply that we are finely balanced between the two, with the way we fall being almost arbitrary. In fact the ability to choose between good and evil is not essential to the notion of freedom. God is clearly free, indeed totally free, yet God is not able to choose evil. Freedom is already directed towards the good, not balanced between good and evil. Freedom is freedom to do good. When we do evil it is not simply the use of freedom, but its misuse. While our freedom will involve such decisions between good and evil it is not an essential part of the meaning of freedom.

In contrast with a concept of freedom as "freedom of choice", I would like to consider freedom in terms of "self-determination". The term "self-determination" has a twofold sense. In the first and most obvious sense the self determines particular courses of action. The self, freely and responsibly, decides to act or not to act in a particular way. While self-determination includes the making of choices between simple options, its more basic sense is the determination of a way of living, a way of relating to the world. Here it is perhaps significant that many oppressed people, including those in eastern Europe, while cautious about a western concept of freedom as "freedom of choice", speak openly of the right to self-determination.

There is another sense to the term "self-determination". It is not only the self which determines, it is also the self which is being determined. Through my decisions I not only affect the world, I also affect myself. I determine who I am to be. Through my decisions I make myself who I am; I shape my character from which future decisions and actions will spring. It is this aspect of "self-determination" which is most often neglected in popular discussion about freedom. And it is this aspect which makes freedom an essentially moral concept, for it is within the subject that the basic norms of human action reside. Freedom is primarily about the self-determination or self-constitution of the human subject.

The normative direction of freedom can be seen in the following way. In as much as I choose the good I increase my ability to do good in the future. An act of generosity makes future acts easier to do until goodness becomes a habit. By increasing my ability to do good I have, in fact, increased my freedom which is directed towards the good. On the other hand, the choice of evil contracts my freedom. Indeed it is evil precisely because it undermines my freedom. This contraction is not in the obvious sense that every decision will mean closing off various options. Rather my actions no longer spring from my freedom but from a compulsive force within which distorts my perception of the world and myself.

THE LIMITS OF FREEDOM

Here I would like to clarify this question of the limitations of freedom. For many, freedom takes on some absolute sense. Either I am totally free or I am not free at all. However, it would seem clear that freedom has its relativities. In fact human freedom is never absolute. It is always a relative and conditioned freedom. I come into a world which is as it is. I may work to change it, but its initial givenness is beyond my freedom to change. All my decisions are made against a backdrop of circumstances which are not of my making. It is my freedom to act within these circumstances. This is not a denial of freedom but a simple recognition of its limits. This is in contrast with God's freedom which is sovereign and total.

To further clarify the limits to freedom I shall introduce the concept of an individual's *horizon* and the distinction between *essential* and *effective* freedom. As a visual metaphor my horizon is determined by the limit of my vision. My horizon is determined by the limits of my imagining, knowing, valuing and doing. Within my horizon lies what I know and value and the actions I can readily do. Actions which I can readily do we call habits. Such habits, whether it be my choice of clothes or the generosity with which I donate money to the needy, are a concrete expression of my freedom, "where I am at" at the present moment. At the limit of my horizon are the "known" unknowns, the recognized but unappreciated values, the actions which are not yet part of my "habitual" make-up, the limit of what I am able to do easily and freely. My horizon marks the concrete effective limit of what I am *now* able to know, value and do. Within my horizon I exercise my effective freedom. With this effective freedom I may act freely within my horizon. I may extend (or contract) the boundaries of my horizon and in this way shape my future horizon. However, the effect of my essential freedom is generally incremental, one step at a time. Only occasionally will I be confronted with a decision which radically alters the structure of my horizon, either through a conversion or a moral breakdown.

Apart from my effective freedom, there is also my essential freedom which is the ground of my effective freedom. I am a free person even if I am imprisoned and my effective freedom is severely limited. Such an essential freedom is part of my constitution as a human subject. Without it I would simply not be human, I would be something less than human. It is part of my essential dignity, something which marks me as being in the image and likeness of God. Whereas I have spoken of an effective and an essential freedom, Rahner would speak of a categorical and a transcendental freedom. Further, he would note that these are not two freedoms but two poles of the one basic human reality.[1]

An idealistic understanding of freedom tends to focus mostly on the essential freedom of a person. However, one must recognize the real limits which can be placed on effective freedom. One could note, for example, that a smoker is essentially free to give up cigarettes but many smokers have simply found themselves unable to do so. While they freely chose to take up smoking and while they freely light up each individual cigarette, they cannot find the freedom to stop. They have come up against a real limit to their effective freedom.

While this example of the smoker is amusing and instructive, it has a much more serious side. An ancient axiom of St Augustine stated that a sinner was *non posse non peccare*—not able not to sin. Sinners may be essentially free to stop sinning, but may at the same time, effectively be unable to stop. Each time they sin, they sin freely, but through their action they have shaped their own character to the extent of not being able not to sin. This is the notion of the moral impotence of the sinner. It is for this reason that we react with such fear at the news of some random killing or rape. We know deep within us that criminals are most likely to do it again and again until they are caught. Such criminals, when caught, often speak of the power of the compulsion within them. Sin has a compulsive component, be it the compulsion of violence or sexual misconduct, or the more pervasive and acceptable compulsion of consumerism. Indeed, it is this compulsive component of sin which tells us that it is immoral. Sin is immoral because it undermines my project of self-determination by undermining my freedom. Compulsion is the opposite of freedom since it is no longer I, but some power within me which is in charge of my life.

Thus Paul, in speaking of the struggle against sin, speaks of our human incomprehension of our own actions:

> . . . I am a creature of flesh and blood sold as a slave. I do not understand my own behaviour; I do not act as I mean, but do things that I hate . . . so it is not myself acting, but the sin which lives in me (cf. Romans 7:14–23).

In this regard it is interesting to note the title of a recent book by Gerald May, *Addiction and Grace*. May sees addiction, a compulsive undermining of our freedom, as of basic concern to the human condition. Addiction is an inordinate attachment to something, anything, which then dominates my actions.[2] Addiction undermines my dignity, my self-esteem, and unless overcome can lead to personal destruction, as in the case of serious drug or alcohol addiction.

From this we can see that although essential freedom is part of the essential make-up as a human person, effective freedom is in a process of development and *cannot be taken for granted.* Through my moral development or lack thereof, I shape my effective freedom, I make myself who I am. If I act in such a way as to undermine my effective freedom, I remain responsible for my later compulsive behavior, just as the drunken driver is responsible for the life of his victim, even though at the time of driving he was not so responsible! Of course this is not to say that I am solely responsible. Human freedom is always limited. Other factors, such as a violent or deprived family background, or the structural violence of political and social discrimination, can also limit my horizon, can reduce my options, can lead to compulsive choices. In any individual case it is almost impossible to untangle the threads to where responsibility really lies. Fortunately we can generally leave this problem to God and bear in mind—"Do not judge, that you yourself be not judged, for the judgment you give out will be the judgment you receive" (Matthew 7:1)!

GRACE AS FREEING FREEDOM

This discussion does raise an important question. If I am at the limits of my effective freedom, then the question has to be asked, what can I do? In fact *I* can do nothing. If I could do something, I would not be at the limits of my effective freedom! One could argue that such a situation never occurs but the evidence, even in simple cases of those addicted to cigarettes, would seem to indicate that it does occur and occurs regularly. When it does occur something or someone needs to act on me from without, needs to help me break out of the cycle of compulsion which has caught me. This is not in opposition to my freedom, but is necessary to free my freedom, for it is my freedom which has been compromised. Such an action helps me to break the limits of my effective freedom, to get in touch with the deeper resources of my essential freedom.

While I have argued that grace is not opposed to freedom, where freedom is understood as self-determination, it may be that grace can be in opposition to a freedom conceived of as "freedom of choice". Indeed grace may "limit" my freedom in that the object of my compulsion no longer holds me in its sway and I will no longer desire it. Moreover I am no longer "free" to accept grace AND choose the object of my compulsion. The two are incompatible.

We shall discuss further the nature of this action in a later chapter. For the moment we should note that this action must come from the *free initiative* of the other. There are, of course, many ways in which a person caught in compulsive behavior can manipulate others, manipulate them in such a way as to appear to be seeking their help and even appear to be receiving it.[3] In the end such "help" does not help since its origin is still within the closed horizon of the manipulator. Help, if it is to come, must come freely, almost unexpectedly, from the other to break down the blocks which have been built up. It can come, say, in the form of an unexpected and undeserved offer of forgiveness, an offer of unconditional support and love. But it must come freely from the other if it is to overcome the limits of freedom.

From this discussion we can push a little further in determining our concept of grace. Now we can think of grace as such an initiative, a divine initiative. God operates in such a way as to free my freedom, so that I am no longer a "slave of sin" but may become a "slave of God" (cf. Romans 6:15–23). Here a greater dependence on God does not limit freedom but allows for greater and greater freedom. Hence Paul can exclaim "For freedom Christ has set us free ... do not submit to the yoke of slavery once more" (Galatians 5:1). Again this is not freedom as some power of arbitrary choice, but a power of self-determination to become more fully human. We can think of grace as a higher principle (or explanation) than freedom, within which freedom operates, just as freedom is itself a higher principle of human actions. Such a higher principle does not contradict or undermine freedom. It is simply one factor, though certainly the highest, of many which determine the conditions of freedom, a freedom which is always relative. In fact it is a factor meant to safeguard and protect freedom, to free it from the unfreedom of sin which is compulsion. Thus God's grace is never in opposition to freedom but completes and perfects it.

This notion of a divine initiative freeing my freedom is what was meant by the Thomistic concept of *operative grace*.[4] As it is the prior principle which conditions my freedom it does not depend on my freedom. It is, as Paul says, "the love of God which has been poured into our hearts through the Holy Spirit which has been given to us" (Romans 5:5). We cannot manipulate God into giving it to us since God is absolutely free. Neither can we earn it. Nor do we "deserve" it in any way. It is simply given. The question as to why it seems to be given to some and not to others, of the limits, if any, of the divine initiative, raises other difficult questions, of the nature of divine providence and the thorny issue of predestination. I shall consider these again in Chapter 5.

Finally I would like to sound a note of warning. As I pointed out earlier in this chapter, freedom has a social and eventually an historical dimension. Freedom, while highly personal, is not a private, individualistic notion. Freedom is not just a moral and legal category. It also has a political content which impinges on society and history. It is not just my personal psychological background which shapes my freedom, but also my cultural, social and political situation. Our horizon is the product of other forces, what Paul might call principalities, thrones and dominations (Colossians 1:16), what we might call ideologies, myths and symbols which are cultural and political in origin. In their own ways these may help mediate grace by helping to free my freedom, or they may work to bind my freedom, locking me into compulsive behavior, blinding me to truth and value. We shall consider this again in Chapter 4.

CONCLUSION

To summarize, in this chapter we have studied the nature of freedom and its relationship to grace. I have distinguished between effective and essential freedom and developed the notion of a horizon. I have used this to give a more precise determination of the concept of grace as a divine initiative to break open a horizon and expand the limits of effective freedom. Viewed in this way grace is a solution to the moral impotence of the sinner. In the next chapter I shall attempt a more precise, if somewhat speculative, determination of the nature of grace.

CHAPTER NOTES

1. The notion of freedom used in this chapter draws heavily on the writings of Bernard Lonergan. I have not tried to maintain his precise terminology but have tried to remain faithful to his insights. See for example, B. Lonergan, *Insight*, pp.619–24.

2. While the *non posse non peccare* might sound like a good piece of Augustinian pessimism the underlying psychology seems well attested. For a fine psychological account of people so trapped see M. Scott Peck, *The Road Less Travelled*, especially pp.32–4. The most common example of compulsive behavior undermining freedom would be compulsive substance abuse, be it alcohol, cigarettes, heroin, or even food. Many people caught up in such compulsions have found help in self-help groups such as Alcoholics Anonymous. The starting point for AA, and groups which model themselves on AA, is to admit one's inability to deal with one's problem and to recognize one's dependence on God if one is to overcome it.

3. The bold assertion of God's operation within the sinner lies at the heart of a Thomistic theology of grace. As Lonergan notes, it is "the elegant and very simple solution taught by St Thomas" to the problems posed by grace and freedom.[5] Such a solution maintains both human freedom, since grace is not opposed to freedom, and divine sovereignty. It also requires a fully developed position on providence and divine transcendence if it is to avoid the problem of a double predestination cf. Chapter 5.

---

1 Cf. *Foundations of Christian Faith*, pp.35–9.
2 G. May, *Addiction and Grace*, gives an account of someone addicted to nose drops, cf. p.9, 22ff.!
3 In professional circles such a situation is called co-dependency, cf. G. May, op. cit., pp.50–2.
4 On the concept of operative grace see Lonergan's *Grace and Freedom*, pp.136–7, where the connection is made with conversion. The connection is also made in *Method in Theology*, pp.107, 241.
5 Cf. *The Desires of the Human Heart*, p.178.

CHAPTER THREE

SELF-ESTEEM, CONVERSION AND SANCTIFICATION

This chapter is the central one in our investigation of grace. Here I shall attempt to formulate, in a relatively systematic way, what we mean when we talk about grace and the nature of the human experience of grace. So far I have spoken of grace as a divine initiative which operates to free our freedom from the compulsion of sin. To push further will require a more precise determination of the principles of human freedom and the horizon in which freedom operates. I should like to stress at the outset that what is proposed here is speculative, in the manner of a speculative systematic theology. It seeks to give an account of the human experience of grace within a systematic understanding of the human person, an account which makes sense of a Catholic theological tradition of grace and of human experience. Its value, if any, lies in its ability to make sense of that long tradition.

HORIZONS, VALUES AND SELF-ESTEEM

In the previous chapter I discussed the notion of a horizon. One's horizon is determined by the limits of one's attention, questioning, judging, valuing and doing. Is it possible to focus in upon something within one's horizon which conditions all the rest? Firstly I would argue that a basic principle which structures one's horizon is one's set of values. What I value tends to determine what I attend to, what I find intelligible, what I find good and a possible path of action. Thus when I read the newspapers I attend to those sections which interest me, the sport, the financial news or whatever. When I seek to understand some other person's actions I do so in relation to the set of values which I hold. If I can see how those actions conform to values which I hold then I find such actions intelligible. For example, I can understand the actions of Mother Teresa since they conform to my Christian values, yet I cannot understand an act of suicide based on a Japanese code of honor which may require a person to commit suicide rather than lose face. Clearly my values determine what I judge to be good and also what courses of action I find acceptable for myself. This does not explain how or why I adopt a particular set of values. That is a different matter and clearly depends on parental and social factors as well as a personal apprehension and appropriation of values through personal experience. One should note, however, that my set of values remains fairly stable. While my knowledge may change and increase frequently, there is an overall stability about my values. Changes in values can often be quite traumatic events.

Is there something within my set of values which plays a preeminent role, a determining role for all others? Here I follow the investigations of Sebastian Moore. In his own cryptic way Moore notes that "the self, feeling, is the self felt".[1] What does this mean? The self, feeling, is myself turned towards the world as evaluating the world. Through my feeling I respond to the goodness (and evil) of the world, vibrating like a tuning fork in resonance. However, such an image is too passive, as if I have no contribution to make. While my feelings are my response to the values I find, they are still *my* response. They are filtered through me, in particular they are filtered through my self as felt. My own evaluation of myself, my self-feeling or self-esteem, is the prism through which the world's values are refracted. And so I propose that *human self-esteem is the basic determining principle of a subject's horizon.*

Here I am taking self-esteem as the spontaneous feeling of self-worth experienced by a person. It is immediate and unreflective unlike, say, a self-concept which one might deliberately develop. As spontaneous and immediate it is a constant part of my conscious living, shaping and being shaped by my actions, thoughts and other feelings. While one might describe self-esteem in terms of such immediacy it is also a highly mediated experience. The feeling I have for myself is also mediated to me by the world around me, by parents, by society, by the history of grace and disgrace to which I belong. I feel myself as reflected in the eyes of others. If I am a black person living in South Africa I cannot help but have my self-esteem undermined by the social and historical reality of apartheid. Thus when speaking of self-esteem it would seem quite valid to use the category of mediated immediacy, as proposed by Schillebeeckx.

At a superficial level we all have experienced how, when we feel good, the whole world glows and when we feel bad, the world is under a cloud. We all feel drawn to activities which build us up with success and avoid those which pull us down with failure. Most significantly when we experience the exhilarating thrill of being loved by another, when we see ourselves esteemed in the eyes of another, we are over the moon and we want to take the world with us. More negatively, the repeated experience of psychology is that damaged self-esteem is a major cause of psychological and behavioral problems for people. The more severe the damage the more severe the problems, leading to violence, promiscuity, depression and neurosis. Many of those we label as criminals come from a long history of abuse, particularly in their earliest years.

In a sense we may think of our self-esteem as our basic question to the cosmos—am I worthwhile? Is my existence meaningful? My life's quest is to find an answer to this question, an answer which I seek from parents, from friends and lovers, through careers and financial success, through a happy and rich family life. Ultimately I seek the answer from God who is the very source of my existence. All the answers I hear, or think I hear, all the truth and lies from all these sources leave an almost indelible mark on my character, shaping me, forming me, for better or worse. All the evidence indicates that the most significant source is my parents, the proximate cause of my being. If my parents love and nurture me then I develop a bedrock of self-esteem which lasts a lifetime. If my parents, the people who are the source of my life, neglect me, if I am not of value to them then the damage done can be irreparable in human terms. If those who made me do not love me, then I must at heart be unlovable! Experience shows how even children who suffer the most serious neglect from their parents will still seek them out in some desperate hope of a kind word or some grudging affirmation.

Where self-esteem has been so damaged there are a variety of strategies which can be developed to bolster it. Some seek to bolster it through a single-minded commitment to a career. Some seek to bolster it by putting other people down—"I must be good because I'm so much better than them"! Such self-righteousness, particularly religious self-righteousness, is a common problem. The parable of the Pharisee and the publican is a classical example (cf. Luke 18:9ff.). Some try to bolster their self-esteem by seeking public office which carries prestige, such as priesthood or political office. All such strategies are short-term solutions. They work for a while but soon the demon within requires a greater satisfaction. Then such strategies can easily fall over into despair, "I really am worthless after all". Hatred turns inward in endless patterns of self-destruction, drugs, violence, sexual irresponsibility, severe de-ession. For some suicide seems the only way out. To counter such a grim scenario we all need an affirmation which goes right to the heart of the matter, a truly unconditional love, something which affirms our existence without qualification, without reserve. Such is the solution offered by grace.

Here it is interesting to recall Jesus' commandment, "You must love your neighbor as yourself" (Mark 12:31). Many forget the last bit, *as yourself*. Many try to love their neighbor while at the same time hating themselves, with disastrous consequences for all concerned. In fact there is something of a truism in Jesus' saying since we cannot love our neighbor more than we love ourselves. To do a proper job in loving our neighbor we must love ourselves. Otherwise what we are doing is not loving our neighbor but seeking ways of manipulating them so that we can get the love and attention we crave. Until my self-esteem finds a satisfying answer it will dominate my consciousness, driving me on, restless and seeking. As Augustine said "Our hearts are restless, O God, until they rest in you"![2]

CONVERSION AND GRACE

Given this understanding of the place of self-esteem in the constitution of my horizon I can now define what I mean by CONVERSION. We have all experienced people with vastly different horizons from our own, so different that we come to quite opposite conclusions on the same basic questions. Thus what one finds meaningful the other finds unintelligible. What one finds good the other finds bad. In public life good examples of this are the opposed positions on nuclear power[3] or on abortion. Such horizons are called dialectically opposed.[4] *Conversion* can then be thought of as *a radical change in one's horizon, from one horizon to a dialectically opposed horizon, from a horizon determined by inadequate, false and distorted self-esteem to one determined by proper, undistorted true self-esteem.*

In a sense this description of conversion begs the question—what is a proper, undistorted, true self-esteem? What is the real value of a human person? Does their value reside in what they can do, in what they can achieve or have achieved? Or is there something more basic than this? Here the Christian tradition has always promoted the unique and irreplaceable value of every human person. Each and every person is created by God, literally loved into being. An earlier metaphysics stated that "to be is to be good". In this it affirmed the central Christian belief that all of creation is, first and foremost, good. Genesis tells us "God looked on all that he had made and indeed it was very good" (Genesis 1:31). A proper, undistorted and true self-esteem takes as its starting point this unassailable goodness of the human person. Such a goodness is "unconditional" and is perhaps most commonly experienced in the self-esteem boosting event of falling in love with another person. Here I experience my value in the eyes of another, unconditionally, totally.

Moreover, the question arises, if I have a distorted self-esteem, what can I do about it? All my actions, all my evaluations, spring from this distortion. While I may engage in a variety of strategies to build myself up, all such strategies are flawed, since they are subject to the constant undermining that they are *mine*. Yet who am I, what value do I have? It would be like pulling myself up by my bootstraps. Since such strategies are mine they are subject to the same basic distortion. I would argue that a distorted self-esteem represents a real limit to my effective freedom, something which can only be overcome by the free initiative of another who mediates to me an experience of my value, whose love for me frees me from my lack of self-esteem.

The experience of myself as made by God and hence of an unconditional goodness, while a foundational event for my self-esteem, is still not what I think is meant by grace. Such an experience of itself is "natural", in the sense of the distinction between grace and nature. It is what I deserve, of my nature, to experience. As God's creature I am good, I am loved unconditionally by him and it is appropriate that I feel such a goodness about myself. While it may in fact be the case that I am robbed of such an experience by neglectful parents or other social and historical circumstances, it seems to me that the experience of grace will involve something more than an experience of my own true value no matter how significant such an experience may be to me.

Thus, I would suggest that to experience grace is to experience not just one's own value, but to experience divine, transcendent value, God's value. It is, as St Paul states, "the love of God poured into our hearts by the Holy Spirit which is given to us" (Romans 5:5). Exegetes have debated whether Paul is referring to God's love of us or our love of God.[5] When I experience transcendent value I am drawn into loving a value which is the source of all goodness, drawn to love God. However the experience of divine value includes the experience of God's value for me. I experience God valuing my value in my experience of God's value. In this experience divine value does not destroy or undermine my self-esteem but introduces something new and distinct. It puts my self-esteem on a new basis, preserving and carrying it forward to a fuller realization within the richer context of divine value. As a summary I shall say that divine value *sublates* my self-esteem as the central value which structures my horizon.[6] It becomes the "higher principle" which frees my freedom. As the Scholastics would say, it is the love of God above all else.

As with self-esteem it is useful to consider grace under the category of mediated immediacy. Grace concerns immediacy since it becomes the spontaneous, consciously felt, if unanalyzed, principle of my horizon. However, this felt principle within my horizon does not spring from nowhere. It, like my self-esteem, is mediated to me through people, events, symbols and actions which convey to me an experience of transcendent value. Such people, events, symbols and actions mediate to me firstly an experience of my own value, but that experience becomes, through God's sovereign freedom, something more, a concurrent experience of transcendent value.

While such an experience of transcendent value sublating my self-esteem can do wonders for my self-esteem giving me the experience, however briefly, of my own unconditional goodness, it does not necessarily mean that all the hurt and damage done by previous denials of my value are suddenly gone. The full restoration of my self-esteem may take a lifetime to occur. The healing of past hurts may seem long and tedious but, in the experience of grace, these other hurts become less important. The injuries may heal but the scars remain. They simply become less significant and dominating in life. In her remarkable book, *Breaking Through*, Cathy Anne Matthews notes regarding her own childhood sufferings:

> It was a poignant revelation to me that after Christ's resurrection, he still had the physical scars in his hands (p.220).

Under the influence of grace, past scars can become openings into the suffering of others so that the once-wounded person becomes a mediator of healing for others.

Before moving on to explore some of the consequences of this analysis I would like to make some pertinent points. In the first place, I would say that what I have suggested above is simply a systematic account of the twin commands of Jesus "You must love the Lord your God with all your heart, with all your soul, with all your strength, and with all your mind, and your neighbour as yourself" (Luke 10:27). It is the experience of God's love, in that of transcendent value, which gives my self-esteem a secure anchor, enabling me to reach out in love to others.

Secondly, such an analysis rejects the Augustinian opposition between love of God and love of self. To oppose the two is to undermine human self-esteem, something which can only end in disaster. Spiritualities which seek to belittle or humiliate the person through an excessive focus on sin and weakness do not come from God. Too often we have seen such spiritualities turn people, whose sense of their own dignity has been totally undermined, into willing puppets of cult leaders who serve not God but Death. The most graphic example in our own time was the disaster at Jonestown, where hundreds of people committed suicide at their leader's insistence.

This supposed opposition between love of God and love of self leads to confusing statements such as "despair is the absolute extreme of self-love"![7] Typically, people caught up in despair will describe their situation not in terms of self-love but in terms of feelings of negative self-esteem, a lack of self-worth. While they may be excessively absorbed with themselves, to describe this as love when it is coupled with such poor self-esteem is only to confuse the issue.

Thirdly, I would like to indicate how this suggestion above can be interpreted as the indwelling of the Holy Spirit. Aquinas' psychological analogy for understanding the Trinity, three persons in one God, Father, Son and Spirit, Son proceeding from the Father and Spirit from Father and Son, has the following elements. The Son is thought of as the inner Word of the Father, the Word which gives expression to the Father's infinite understanding. The Spirit is then thought of as the affective response of the Father to the value affirmed in the Word who is Son.[8] In his interpretation of this Thomistic analogy, Lonergan describes the Holy Spirit as "the dynamic presence of God in God". Commenting on this dynamic presence, T.C. O'Brien describes the Spirit in terms of an "*affective* harmony" and as a "*felt* presence".[9] Just as the Son is the Word of God, so this analogy might lead us to think of the Spirit as the Feeling of God. It is this Feeling of God which is present in the experience of transcendent value. Moreover such an experience of transcendent value is an "uncreated grace", not just a created effect in me.

This indwelling of the Holy Spirit, who is grace, draws us into the life of the Trinitarian God. Just as the center of Jesus' life is the Spirit of his love for the Father, so too as the Spirit becomes the center of our lives we become adopted sons and daughters of the divine Father. As the Son was divine, we too are divinized by the "dynamic presence of God in God" dwelling within us. Through grace we truly share in the divine nature (cf. 2 Peter 1:4).

Fourthly, this analysis allows us to find at least a speculative answer to the question concerning Jesus' relationship to the Holy Spirit.[10] While we have no direct account of Jesus' experience, the synthesis above might help us understand how Jesus' experience might differ from ours. Whereas in us, transcendent value sublates our self-esteem, becoming the new and higher principle of our freedom, it could be argued that transcendent value *is* Jesus' self-esteem. Jesus feels himself to be of transcendent value ("The Father and I are one" John 10:30), feels himself to be of ultimate significance for us all ("If it is by the finger of God that I drive out devils, then the kingdom of God has indeed caught you unawares" Luke 11:20). Jesus speaks with an authority and power even to forgive sins, which goes beyond the experience of his listeners (Mark 2:1–12). From his first conscious moments it would seem that Jesus has an unshakeable sense of his own goodness, affirmed by the love of the Father. This is probably what is meant in theological discussion by Jesus possessing the beatific vision. It is this powerful sense of his own value which frees Jesus to stand up against the powers of the world, secure in the fact that it is not their estimation, but God's that is important (cf. Luke 16:15). Moreover this freedom is contagious, spreading to his disciples and into the early Church.

CONSEQUENCES OF CONVERSION

Now we can explore some of the consequences of the experience of grace in the human subject. Such a divine affirmation both makes necessary and creates the conditions for the possibility of a repudiation of past sins and failings. Such a repudiation is necessary since the new horizon is dialectically opposed to the old. The old ways and values are to be rejected as incompatible with the experience of grace. Such a repudiation is also made possible but without the experience of grace it would simply be a further attack on self-esteem, a further undermining of self-value, leading in turn to further sins and failings. Repudiation is only constructive in the context of affirmation. We have all experienced the "helpful" person who tells us to "get your act together" without at the same time affirming us. The result is simply to push us further into despair.

This does not mean, of course, that the experience of grace is all sweetness and light. Coupled with the previous domination of sin and self-disvalue from the past, the experience of grace can be one of desolation, of smallness in the light of God. This is a common part of religious experience and is constantly reflected in the Psalms. However it always takes place within a broader context of affirmation and love.

It is in affirming transcendent value as true, in saying yes to God, that we respond in faith to the divine initiative. In doing so we respond freely to that which has been given, to that which has freed our freedom so we are able to respond. This is a justifying faith, an affirmation of and commitment to the divine value. Such faith involves conforming oneself to the consequences of this new value, such as taking on board a whole new set of values which one has received in grace. This task of faith is our *cooperation* with the *operative* grace given in the act of conversion, given as a free initiative from God.

In the above analysis I have taken the experience of conversion as the paradigm for the experience of grace. It should not be taken in an exclusive sense, however. While conversion is a peak and a paradigm experience of grace, this does not mean that it is the only such experience of grace. Other experiences are of grace in as much as they lead up to or reinforce and further the process of conversion. They may be experiences of prayer, of love between a man and a woman, a spectacular sunset, or listening to beautiful music.[11] Such experiences are also part of God's kairos, God's providential moments, which we cannot force or create for ourselves but occur as pure gift, at God's choosing.

This notion of grace is far and away from the notion of some extrinsicist heavenly bank account. Grace cannot be stored up like money put away for a rainy day. Grace is an active presence, related dynamically to the values which I hold, challenging and transforming them, leading me on to greater freedom and committed action. If I am not changed, or if changes which have already taken place are not reinforced and furthered, then grace, which may have been present as an offer, is rendered ineffective.

SANCTIFICATION

Conversion and other peak experiences are not the norm of Christian living. Just as in a marriage it would be wrong to expect to be able to maintain the highs of the first years throughout one's married life, so too in Christian living one should not seek to maintain the peak experiences of conversion. To seek to do so would indicate some lack of trust in the process of development that needs to take place. The peak experience of conversion sets a new agenda which needs to be followed. One must move on or one is not being true to the original experience. This is one of the problems faced by Pentecostalist and charismatic groups when they continually seek to recreate the peak experience of conversion.

Conversion leads to the creation of a new horizon, rich in potentialities, but still largely unformed. While the old person has been put off, the new person is still in the process of formation. Human freedom, in cooperation with the experience of divine value, must work to develop the new horizon, to explore its potentialities and consequences. Here we can speak of a process of *sanctification*, a greater realization of the divine value which one has experienced, affirmed and committed oneself to. Traditional Christian wisdom has affirmed that such a process will pay great attention to the moral and ethical development of the converted person. Edward Schillebeeckx notes the experience of the early Church:

> In time, however, in New Testament Christianity the experience of the Spirit becomes more and more a sober, real and yet intensive ethical emotion.[12]

Further:

> This enables us to understand the tendency of many religious people today to regard ethics ... as a criterion of religious authenticity. A religious attitude can in fact be suspect of being an ideology if it is socially, politically and personally neutral in the ethical sphere.[13]

This is what St Paul calls "faith working itself through love" (Galatians 5:6). Here the new organizing principle of divine value acts as a cooperative grace since it is in cooperation with human freedom that particular acts of love are carried out. Such acts are the product of both the divine principle of grace and the human principle of freedom. These are not in opposition but stand in relationship to one another as higher to lower.

In this account of grace, conversion and sanctification I hope that I have been able to avoid the extremes of both the Pelagian and the Lutheran position.[14] Pelagius affirmed the self-sufficiency of human freedom to deal with the problem of moral impotence. This arises from a superficial human psychology. Luther, on the other hand, could find no place for human freedom, seeing it simply as the source of sin. He could not see grace and freedom as different levels of explanation. It was either one or the other. In the end such a position is destructive of human dignity, seeing what is essentially human as essentially the problem! Catholic doctrine has sought the middle course, affirming both the dignity, necessity and radical insufficiency of human freedom. Further, it has seen the fruits of grace as shown in a real active *caritas*, a love of neighbor as oneself, effective in the social, political and personal spheres.

CONCLUSION

In summary then, I have argued for an understanding of grace as an experience of transcendent value which sublates my self-esteem as the principle which structures my horizon. This can be seen as an indwelling of the Holy Spirit. Its principle effect is conversion which is a movement across dialectically opposed horizons. It is further effective in the process of sanctification in which the consequences of my initial conversion are worked out in my life. One sign of this is a commitment to action on behalf of others. In the next chapter I shall expand this point of view to include its social and historical dimensions.

CHAPTER NOTES

1. The philosophical anthropology in this chapter is drawn largely from the writings of Bernard Lonergan as found in *Method in Theology*, in particular the notions of horizon and sublation. The role and significance of self-esteem was first brought home to me by the writings of Sebastian Moore. His basic stance on this has been confirmed for me by all the psychological reading I have done since. If there is anything new in the chapter it is the bringing together of these two viewpoints into a systematic whole.

2. For a compelling account of the consequences of child-abuse and its effects of self-esteem and the subsequent effects on human living see *Breaking Through: No longer a Victim of Child Abuse* by Cathy Ann Matthews. The question as to the effect of abuse on self-esteem will also be considered later when considering original sin.

3. The classical source for material on the human experience of grace is *The Varieties of Religious Experience*, by William James. James classifies religious experience into two types, the religion of "healthy mindedness" (the once born), and the religion of

the "sick soul" (the twice born). In the end he concludes that the second type is more profound since it is more realistic about the problem of evil (cf. p.141). Many so-called "new age" faiths fall into the first category.

4. The process of transcendent value sublating self-esteem is probably what is symbolized by the decentering of the Ego and its replacement by the *Self*, as discussed in Jungian psychology. Sebastian Moore, in *The Crucified [Jesus] is no Stranger*, sees Jesus as the true Self, who is crucified by the Ego. Healing comes in the realization that this crucified Jesus is in fact our true self, and in making this true self the center of our lives, rather than our ego.

---

1 Cf. *Let This Mind Be in You*, p.17ff.
2 Cf. *The Confessions*, Bk.1, Chap.1.
3 For a chilling analysis of this debate see R. Haughton, *The Passionate God*, p.108ff.
4 On the concept of dialectically opposed horizons, *see* Lonergan, *Method in Theology*, p.247ff.
5 Most now favor that Paul is speaking of God's love for us, cf. *NJBC*, p.844.
6 On sublation, *see* Lonergan's *Method in Theology*, p.241.
7 Cf. Thomas Merton, *Seeds of Contemplation*, Anthony Clarke, Wheathampstead, 1972, p.140.
8 B. Lonergan, *Verbum, Word and Idea in Aquinas*, p.203.
9 *See* Appendix Two, *Summa Theologiae*, Blackfiars Edition, Vol.7, pp.257–8.
10 James Dunn, *Jesus and the Spirit*, SCM, London, 1975, is primarily concerned with this relationship.
11 Cf. Denis Edwards, *The Human Experience of God*, for a fuller account of such experiences, pp.27–38.
12 *See* his *Christ*, p.474.
13 Ibid, p.660.
14 I am using the term "Lutheran" here, perhaps unfairly, as a type. In recent years Catholics and Lutherans have come much closer on the issues involved concerning grace and human freedom, cf. *Justification by Faith: Lutherans and Catholics in Dialogue VII*, H.G. Anderson et al. (eds), Augsburg Publishing, Minneapolis, 1985.

CHAPTER FOUR

SOCIAL AND HISTORICAL DIMENSIONS OF GRACE

So far in this book I have been focusing on the personal experience of grace, an experience of transcendent value which sublates self-esteem as the basic determining principle of one's personal horizon. While such a focus is valid as far as it goes, it runs the risk of privatizing grace, making it something purely individual with no links or consequences for others. Such a risk is particularly high if the person is not seen as fundamentally social in nature.[1]

Where such an individualism is present, the result is a dualism between the private and public spheres, a dualism which is basically alienating. Grace and religion in general are then seen as belonging to the private sphere, a private thing between a person and God. While such a view is indeed prevalent it runs counter to the communitarian nature of Christian faith and the communitarian depths of the mystery of the Trinity.[2] To help overcome this danger I shall now consider some of the social and historical dimensions of grace.

SOCIAL DIMENSIONS OF CONVERSION

In this book grace has been primarily conceived of as conversion, a movement from one horizon to a dialectically opposed horizon, from a horizon dominated by a false, distorted and inadequate self-esteem to a true and well-based self-esteem sublated by transcendent value. Where a false, distorted and inadequate self-esteem is present people will develop a strategy of neurotic self-justification, rationalization for their behavior which conceals its true source in anxiety, guilt or self-hatred. Thus the rapist will blame his victim: "she had it coming", "she led me on". Racists will justify their oppression of other races on the grounds of their "obvious" inferiority. Through these strategies such people seek to justify themselves and their actions. Opposed to this is the situation of the converted person, someone who graciously receives his or her justification from God through the experience of transcendent value. For such people their existence is justified by God; they are freed from the neurotic cycle of anxiety, guilt and self-hatred and graciously receive the source of their life from the divine Other.

The strategies of self-justification are not just a private matter. They also have a social dimension. As we enter the world, there are already in place a variety of justifications for the ways in which the social and political environment is ordered. Such justifications may be grounded in the truth, but they may also act in such a way as to conceal the truth. For example, as noted above, previous generations justified the treatment of the black peoples by believing them to have an "obvious" inferiority. Women have fought long and hard to have their equality within the political and economic system recognized. Oppression of women was justified by their oppressors on their alleged irrationality and weakness.

Even more sad is the way in which millions of people around the world are condemned to poverty and death while the people of the rich nations justify the expenditure of billions of dollars on weapons whose sole purpose is to destroy human life. Indeed when we look at the suffering and evil in the world we see that a great deal more occurs because of such social evils than because of individual acts. The amount of evil done by individuals may be small indeed. Few of us would contemplate murder or even lesser forms of violence. Yet often we more or less willingly participate in the benefits of social, political and economic systems which perpetuate massive violence on large portions of the world's population. In general we prefer not to think about such things and if we are forced to recognize our situation, we simply feel powerless to do anything about it—*non posse non peccare*! Grace must speak to such a trapped human situation.

In sociological terms such systems of justification are called ideologies. Through various dominant social ideologies we justify the way things are, we justify the social and political order which favors those in power and justifies the suffering of the weak. It is not as though we take on board such ideologies through a process of responsible deliberation. For most of us they are part of the air we breathe. They shape our consciousness before we are even able to exercise any personal responsibility in our lives. They have become part of our habitual mental furniture, part of our horizon, part of the way we find meaning in our lives. We often could not even imagine the world as operating in another way.

In as much as we take on board such ideologies and use them to justify our own positions, we need to repent and be converted away from them. They produce a distortion of one's basic self-esteem, since the source of one's personal value is found in adherence to a particular social or political structure. Such ideologies are a basic distortion of the values revealed in the experience of transcendent value and must be negated.

It might be helpful to list and analyze some of the dominant ideologies which are prevalent in our societies and consider how they distort basic self-esteem.

Racism justifies the oppression of one race by another. It claims that I am only of value in as much as I belong to the superior race. Otherwise I am worthless. The consequences of such a distortion can be seen in the Holocaust or apartheid in South Africa. Sexism justifies the oppression of women by men. It claims that I am of greater value if I am male rather than female. The consequences of such a distortion can be seen in the repeated denial to women of access to economic independence and political power. Nationalism justifies the placing of my national rights above those of other nations. It claims that I am of greater value because I belong to my nation. The consequences of such a distortion can be seen in the political and economic colonialism of the modern era. Militarism justifies the "might is right" syndrome. It claims that the greater my weaponry, the greater my value, the more important I am. The consequences have been endless wars and the destruction of human life and culture. Economic consumerism justifies the wasteful and unjust distribution of economic goods around the world. It claims that my value is determined by my disposable income. The consequences have been massive distortion in the systems of production, massive global poverty and destruction of the natural environment. None of us can claim to be untouched by these ideologies and all run counter to the life of grace.

The distortions which these ideologies cause in the self-esteem of the beneficiaries of ideological systems are nothing compared with the destruction of self-esteem inflicted upon the victims. The dominant ideologies shape the consciousness of all, not just the beneficiaries. Soon the victims of ideologies begin to accept the descriptions given of themselves as lazy, weak, primitive, irrational or whatever. They not only accept these descriptions, they begin to live up to them, thus adding further justification to the ideological system. Living up to these descriptions only undermines an already weakened self-esteem, pushing the victims further into cycles of violence and despair. Too often the violence of the poor and suffering, so abhorred by the middle class, is little more than the predictable outcome of an ideology which justifies the existence of both groups.

As was mentioned above, ideologies tend to justify the way things are within a society. In particular they tend to justify the victors over the victims, oppressors over oppressed. One strategy of the process of justification is to erase the voices of the victims from the social memory, even from the history books. Just as an individual may suppress the memory of a childhood wrongdoing so, as a society, we suppress the memory of suffering caused. In my own country of Australia this process of suppression, in regard to our treatment of the Australian Aborigines has been quite thorough. Lost was the memory of resistance offered by Aborigines to the invasion of their land by the white people. White history books simply made no mention of it. To ensure the further suppression of the memory, Aboriginal communities were broken up, children separated from parents and family so that the memory could not even be carried in their own hearts. The end result has been a people who have been in danger of losing any sense of their own value, threatened with destruction by alcohol abuse, violence and poverty. It is a picture which has been all too common among the indigenous populations of North and South America, Australia and South Africa.

On the other hand, the social dimension of grace and conversion demands an attention to the voices of the victims, a calling to mind of dangerous and subversive memories. By attending to the voices of the victims the hidden biases that we have taken on board are challenged. It is the cries of the poor, heard by the Lord, which break through our ideological defences and call for our conversion. Such a conversion asks for a faith which is not a leap into irrationality but "into reason away from the biased irrationalities of dehumanizing and depersonalizing social and historical bias".[3] From this we can see that the so-called "preferential option for the poor" is central to the life of grace, an important part of the process of conversion. The preferential option for the poor is first of all a listening to the voices of the victims. It involves a change to what we give our attention, a change in our imagination. We must learn to attend to voices we prefer not to hear and so begin to imagine new possibilities for social and economic structures. It is only a beginning, but a necessary beginning.

Here we may also reflect on the situation of Jesus. The New Testament sees Jesus' death as a consequence of a dominant ideology. Caiaphas states, "... it is to your advantage that one man should die for the people, rather than the whole nation perish" (John 11:50), it is better that one innocent man die than that the whole nation be put at risk by the Roman forces.[4] Caiaphas represents the voice of the dominant party, those enjoying the privileges of the present system. They believed such privileges were theirs by divine right, the worst form of self-justification, and they could not be put at risk by this upstart, Jesus. Indeed Jesus' life was sacrificed in a futile attempt to maintain these privileges. Eventually the nation was destroyed and Jerusalem razed.

At the heart of the Christian liturgy is the dangerous memory of this life sacrificed—"on the night before he died ... do this in memory of me". On that night, in the breaking of bread and the drinking of wine, Jesus identified himself with all victims, everywhere and for all time. Jesus became the Victim, whose death was to signal the end of all future victimization. The death of Jesus calls into question all ideologies, all justifications for the organized suffering of peoples. In the resurrection God raises up Jesus, proclaiming to the world that God stands at the side of all those who have been victimized. Christians, in particular, have special reason to be sensitive to the issues of the social dimensions of conversion!

GRACE AS HISTORICAL

The social dimensions of grace and conversion imply that grace has a history, that it has a concrete, if hidden, unfolding in human history. It is a history of progress and decline, of success and failure. It is a history of wars, of suffering, of reconciliation and forgiveness between individuals and nations. It is a history of grace and dis-grace writ large in nations, cultures, societies, peoples. In this history, grace is mediated or hindered not just through personal decisions but through social institutions and historical realities. As one Latin American bishop once commented "While it is true that a saint may come from a slum, we do not build slums to create saints!". Regions with histories of suffering and violence such as, for example, the Middle East, cannot be expected to be effective mediators of grace. Violence begets violence, human life is counted as nothing, human self-esteem of no consequence. In less clear-cut situations it may be more difficult to make judgments about the "grace-fullness" or "dis-grace-fullness" of a particular situation or institution, but all contribute to or hinder grace, all contribute to the promotion or neglect of conversion.

Indeed the whole of the Old Testament can be read as an ongoing story of the history of grace and disgrace for the Jewish people. From the call of Abraham, through the Egyptian captivity, the Exodus, the entry into the Promised Land, the establishment of a kingship, the Babylonian exile and the second exodus, all the events in the life of the nation are read as a dialogue of sin and forgiveness between the people and God. The prophets were God's faithful interpreters, reading out of events God's providential plan, both punishment and promise.

For the Christian this dialogue of grace and dis-grace reaches a definitive climax in the person of Jesus. Jesus is the mature fruit of the long and careful cultivation of grace initiated in Abraham. Jesus is God's definitive contribution to the dialogue, saying "Yes" to all the promises made by God (cf. 2 Corinthians 1:18–19). In his own body, Jesus bears the suffering inflicted by an equally long history of disgrace, dying unjustly at the hands of evil men. Yet from the cross Jesus speaks words of forgiveness (cf. Luke 23:34, 39ff.), showing once and for all that there are no limits to the divine mercy. Vindicating Jesus' stance, God raised up Jesus who then poured out his Spirit to create the Church. For the Christian these events are of decisive historical significance, for the Church exists to carry on *in history* the mission of Jesus, the mission of mediating the love and forgiveness of God.

More generally, all sincere religious traditions are attempts to fulfil the role of being historical mediators of grace in human history. By orienting their adherents towards the transcendent, by calling for moral righteousness, by seeking to promote conversion, all religions seek to mediate grace in the lives, the history and culture of their people. Indeed all the major religions have had profound effects on the history and culture of their peoples. It is also clear that these effects are not unambiguous. All religious traditions, even (some might say especially) Christian ones, have not only mediated grace but also dis-grace. From holy wars (a contradiction in terms?) to the petty power-mongering of religious hierarchies, all religious traditions are in constant need of reformation.[5] To label something or someone as religious is never without its ambiguities. No religion can claim to mediate grace like some divine automatic teller machine. Grace is mediated only where there is a constant openness to conversion and constant cooperation with grace in working out its concrete consequences.

In identifying religions as mediators of grace it is important not to limit grace to the religious. It is simply to identify religion as one area which is particularly concerned with the mediation of grace. Many non-religious groups and movements have in our own day sought to mediate grace, to promote conversion. The peace movement has, through its many efforts, sought to promote a conversion which challenges the ideologies of militarism and nationalism. The environmental movement has challenged the ideologies of economic consumerism and has to a little extent produced the beginning of conversion among sections of society. Similarly the women's movement has challenged the distortions created by sexism. Again to claim that such movements have mediated grace does not mean that they are unambiguous, that everything they do or say is correct. As with religious traditions they share in the ambiguity of human existence.

To speak of religions and other movements as mediators of grace should not be seen in purely personal terms. While it is true that these mediate grace to individuals through the promotion of conversion, of equal importance is the challenge they present to social structures. There are at least three ways in which they can operate to promote the conversion, not just of individuals but of societies and cultures.

In the first place they can present critiques of the dominant ideologies which are used to support existing social structures. They can point out the inconsistencies between such ideologies and truly human and transcendent values. In Christian terms this means preaching the Gospel, using the Gospel as a critical principle in analyzing society. In recent time the Catholic Church has kept up a steady flow of social teaching which has been critical of the dominant ideologies of consumerism, militarism, economic liberalism, colonialism and communism.

Secondly, they can work to establish alternative structures of human relationship, for example communal and non-domineering lifestyles. Thus, in the Acts of the Apostles, we find the early Christians living in new ways, selling all they owned and sharing with those in need (cf. Acts 2:42–47). The establishment of such alternatives is not meant to say that everyone must live in this way. What it does show to people is that alternatives are possible. They liberate our imagination so that we can break the bonds of the dominant ideologies. Throughout the ages people have developed new and varied forms of religious life, religious orders and monastic life which gave real alternatives for living.

Thirdly, they can work for the many victims of the dominant ideologies. The victims are many and their needs are great, be they starving people in Africa, dis-spirited indigenous races, or abused children caught in a cycle of violence. When we consider the miracles of Jesus it is important to see in them not just nice things to do for people. The sick and the lame were not just ill. They were subject to religious criticism—was it this man or his parents who sinned? (cf. John 9:1ff.)—and often reduced to poverty, begging simply to live. Through his miracles Jesus sought to restore justice to a broken social and religious culture. Throughout its history the Church has held up as saints those who have worked to alleviate the suffering of, and sought justice for, the victims of such forces. These activities are not peripheral but simply the social dimension of the grace which the Gospel reveals. This was stated succinctly in the statement of the Synod of Bishops, *Justice in the World* (1971), when they said:

> action on behalf of justice and participation in the transformation of the world fully appear to us as a constitutive dimension of preaching the Gospel (para.5).

In engaging in such activities we are all helping build up the Kingdom of God. In the Lord's Prayer we say "your kingdom come ... *on earth*", yet often those who do engage in such activities are seen as subverting the "spiritual" ends of religion. The Kingdom of God is concerned with the concrete events of human history, though this history is always ambiguous. There is not only the Kingdom of God in the land but also forces of darkness which seek to subvert the Kingdom. Even the devil himself may appear to some as an angel of light. Discernment is always difficult. Finally, the certainty of victory does not mean that we can look forward to easy sailing into the promised land. To reach the resurrection Jesus first had to die. Evil may, in the end, seem to have won the day but out of the jaws of defeat God's final victory is assured.

CONCLUSION

In this chapter I have sought to outline the social and historical character of grace. The experience of grace and conversion, while highly personal, is not individualistic. It has consequences which touch all aspects of our living, including social, political and economic aspects. Grace demands a conversion away from ideologies which distort our sense of personal value. In living out the consequences of conversion we are caught up in historical processes, a historical dialectic of grace and dis-grace. The end of this dialectic process is assured in God's victory in establishing God's Kingdom, though this may only be achieved through great cost. I shall return to this issue in Chapter 8. In this chapter I considered the role of religious traditions as historical mediators of grace. In the next chapter I shall consider God's universal providence as grounding confidence in the hope that, despite the many failures of grace in history, the mediated offer of grace remains a concrete possibility for all.

CHAPTER NOTES

1. It is clear that in this chapter I have been highly influenced by contemporary political theology. The works I have found most helpful in this area are *Faith in History and Society* by Johann Baptist Metz (Burns and Oates, London, 1980), *Solidarity with Victims* by Matthew Lamb (Crossroads, NY, 1982) and *The Praxis of Suffering* by Rebecca Chopp (Orbis, NY, 1986). For a more detailed account of the nature of political theology and its relationship to liberation and feminist theology, see my *Introducing Contemporary Theologies* (E.J. Dwyer, Sydney, 1990).

2. There is no common agreement as to the meaning of the term "ideology" in the social sciences. Sometimes it is used as a purely descriptive and value free term and simply denotes a total social world view. At other times it is used in a negative sense, as a fundamentally distorted world view. I prefer to use it in the second sense. It seems to me that this is more in keeping with common usage, and can also be systematically defended once the normative viewpoint of Chapters 2 and 3 is adopted.

---

1 Cf. *Gaudium et Spes*, n.12.
2 Cf. for example, Leonardo Boff, *The Trinity*, Burns and Oates, esp. pp.148ff.
3 Cf. M. Lamb, *Solidarity with Victims*, Crossroads, NY, 1982, p.140.
4 Cf. The footnote for this verse in *TNJB* notes that "Caiaphas means that Jesus must be executed to save the nation from *political* extinction" [emphasis added], p.1771.
5 In *Lumen Gentium*, the Church speaks of itself as "at once holy and always in need of purification" Sect.8.

CHAPTER FIVE

GRACE AND PROVIDENCE

Asserting the divine operation within the subject may be an elegant solution to the question of the relationship between grace and freedom (cf. Chapter 2). However it raises other questions with greater urgency. If grace comes from a free divine initiative, if it is not some automatic dispensing machine, how can we be sure of the universality of the concrete offer of grace (cf. Chapter 1)? If grace is not simply our transcendental relationship with God, but requires mediation through contingent events and persons, how can we be certain that events and persons will form into the right constellation leading to an offer of grace and conversion? Is God in that sort of control, like a master puppeteer, or is the hope of a concrete offer of grace nothing more than wishful thinking?

Such questions remain even if we acknowledge Rahner's notion of supernatural existential. For even such a supernatural existential requires specification within the historical sphere. The event of operative grace leading to conversion, as outlined in Chapters 2 and 3, occurs within the story of my life; actual events, and experiences, which change my life—a special person, a holy place, a text of scripture and so on. How do we account for such events?

A fine example of this type of event is given by Augustine in his account of his own conversion in *Confessions* (Book 8, Chap.11). Here Augustine recalls hearing some children singing a children's song , "tolle, lege", "take and read". He rushes inside to open the scriptures, by chance on a text of St Paul which mediates the next stage of conversion. Perhaps all of us have had such events. It could be the chance meeting of a person which opens up new and unexpected opportunities. It could be the tragic death of a loved one which causes us to re-evaluate the direction and purpose of our life. It could be spotting someone in the act of prayer and being taken up in the other's holiness. Grace may be found in any such circumstance, tragic, joyous, mystical. Something within us rebels at the suggestion that events so meaningful are just chance, just the toss of the coin. To see in such events something more than chance we need to explore the concept of divine providence.

It is quite easy to dismiss the sort of events which we are discussing as *chance*, that is, random events which occur with a certain statistical frequency but which otherwise have no special significance. The problem is, of course, that such events are significant, highly significant in a very *personal way*. The people who experience such events recognize them as highly meaningful. Is such meaning really "present" or is it just the product of a fevered imagination? Sometimes it might be. However, it has to be said that to explain such events by invoking chance is simply not to explain them at all. Too often it merely says that no other explanation is forthcoming.

Traditionally such events were accounted for by the term PROVIDENCE. They were seen as part of God's providential care and concern for each and every person. Belief in such a concern is deeply imbedded in popular piety, reflected in a never-ending stream of simple prayers of petition. Jesus himself said "every hair on your head has been counted" (Matthew 10:30). His own prayer, the Lord's prayer, is a collection of petitions—"may your name be held holy . . . your kingdom come . . . your will be done . . . give us today our daily bread . . . forgive us our debts . . . do not put us to the test . . . save us from the evil one" (Matthew 6:9–13). St Paul further stated "We are well aware that God works with those who love him . . . and turns everything to their good" (Romans 8:28). Indeed the Old Testament writers see the whole of Israel's history as under the sway of God's providential love and guidance.

While such a view may have been plausible in the compact, three-levelled cosmos of the Bible, can it survive a modern expansive cosmology of billions of galaxies, all teaming with billions of stars? Does God really have a personal interest in each and every one so that every hair on our heads is counted? And can that concern be reflected in concrete events of our life, not just as chance, but as a real "operation" of God's freedom? Or is God no more concerned about the events of our life than in the motions of countless stars?

THE DIVINE TRANSCENDENCE

The simple trust of piety is sadly not enough for a theological analysis. To answer these questions we need to consider the broader question of God's relationship to the created world. My starting point will be the divine transcendence. Such transcendence means that God is wholly other than creation, is not dependent upon it for God's being, could exist without it without any detriment to God's being. While some contemporary philosophies, such as process philosophy, have called this into question, it seems a valid starting point within a Catholic tradition.[1]

Such a transcendence is not to be conceived in the manner of the Deists of the eighteenth century. The God of the Deists was an infinitely remote God. For them creation was like a giant clockwork mechanism, with God the almighty clockmaker. Once having made the clock, God winds it up and departs, leaving it to its own devices, making occasional forays to miraculously repair its broken workings. Such a position was inspired by the successes of Newtonian science which sought to explain all natural phenomena in mechanical terms and gave rise to a mechanistic determinism. The transcendence of God was thought of in terms of an almost spatial quality. Thus God was beyond space by being in some imagined, still larger, space! Here when I speak of transcendence I do not mean that God is beyond space but that God is totally other than space. We cannot imagine what this is like since our imagination always works in spatial terms.

If we take seriously God's transcendence from the world then we see that God's existence is strictly eternal, that is, timeless. Modern science tells us that space, time and matter are strictly correlative. To have space means there will be time and matter, and so on. This is a consequence of Einstein's theory of general relativity and modern theories of quantum mechanics. When God created the universe, space–matter–time was created. God's own existence is strictly non-spatial, non-material and non-temporal. To be any one of these would imply the others. And so God's existence lies outside the temporal flow of events which constitute the world. God's creative act is not within time, but creates time. God never stops creating, since for God creation is a single timeless act. As a single act, *all of creation, past, present, future (for us) is immediately present to God*, not as successive acts for God, but as elements of a single act for God. God does not foresee the future in the sense of seeing a future event in the present. God sees it in a divine timeless present, as future for us but present to God.

And when I say "all of creation" I mean all, from the cataclysmic events of the "big bang" to the tiniest movements of electrons around an electric circuit. All is held in being by God who understands and esteems intimately the place of each and every element of the universe. Of the whole sweep of creation, human history is a brief but infinitely valuable part. Indeed some cosmologists have argued that the vast magnitudes of space and time would have been necessary even if human beings were to be the only intelligent beings in the universe. Small changes in initial conditions at the beginning of the big bang would have created a universe in which no such life would have been possible.[2]

Process philosophy has protested that this view of the transcendence of God makes God too remote, too distant, not in a spatial sense but in the personal sense of not being able to respond and feel for creation. On the contrary, I would argue that it is only a position of strict transcendence which allows God to be totally immanent in creation. Only a God who is totally transcendent can be totally and personally present to all creation, no matter how dark, no matter how deep the incursions of evil. To compromise the transcendence of God is to run the risk of God being ultimately powerless in the face of evil. While it might seem terrible to talk of the presence of God in the Holocaust, it is even more terrible to speak of God's total absence.[3] What hope then for the divine redeeming power? A transcendent God is the ultimate ground of hope since God's immediate presence to all of creation is a guarantee of the presence of divine redeeming power.

Another danger is that if we lose sight of the transcendence of God then God becomes the "world-soul", the merely immanent principle of the world. God becomes identified with nature and God's will is read into the events of nature. Earthquakes and other disasters such as epidemics are read to be God's will, a divine punishment of a sinful humanity. To fight the illness of an epidemic is then to fight God who sent the disease. Many have spoken in this way with regard to the AIDS virus. In the end such a position falls over into a pantheist solution to the question of God's relationship to the world.

The other question which God's transcendence raises is the problem of the origin of evil—*unde malum*? Whence comes evil in the creation of a transcendent and good God? Again this is a difficult question for theodicy on which one could write a book. Here I will be content with a simple analogy for God's creative activity which recognizes the possibility of evil. Later in the section on original sin we shall consider again the question of the origin of evil.

GOD AS THE DIVINE ARTISAN

We are perhaps all familiar with the work of creative artists who, in a single creative act, grasp in its totality the whole of a work of art, and must then make their material conform to what was grasped. It is said, for example, that Mozart and Beethoven held entire symphonies in their heads, and simply wrote them down with virtually no changes.

Now imagine God as such a creative artist, writing a symphony. In God's creative grasp, however, there is not only the entire score of the symphony, but also the instruments to be played and the musicians to play them. God creates it all from nothing—*ex nihilo*. We can extend the analogy even further. Since God creates the players God knows them intimately, all their strengths and weaknesses, where they will play well and where they will simply fall away. God even knows that some will try to disrupt the score by throwing in discords. God does not stop them since God has created and respects their freedom, but, in the divine creative grasp, God places every discord into a greater harmony, even incorporating various deliberate errors. The whole of creation is God's symphony. God is "in control" as the composer and conductor, writing the score and inspiring us to play our best. We all have our part to play but no matter how difficult it becomes, the final harmony is assured since, for God, the creative grasp is in fact completely creative, with no intervening steps. In the divine grasp it already is. This is God's omnipotence and omniscience.

This analogy should not be read as saying that evil is just part of life and that we have to take the good with the bad. Sin is a deliberate attempt to depart from the score. Given human freedom God cannot prevent it happening in some mechanical way, reducing us to mere automatons. God can only prevent evil by enlisting our freedom, not destroying it. However, given that it does happen, God the Artisan works the disharmony into an even greater harmony and so overcomes evil from within. Thus God provides not a theoretical solution to the problem of evil, but a practical solution revealed in the Incarnation, seen in the power of self-sacrificing love to overcome evil.

We have to be careful here not to speak as if the musical score is some type of divine plan which we are bound to at some future time, something which would make our freedom merely the appearance of freedom and not a reality. Nor is it a set of moral imperatives, or "maker's instructions", which God establishes for the smooth running of human living. The whole symphony, in its concrete reality, is held and created in a single divine act. Such an understanding does not deny or undermine our freedom, since for God the totality of all our free acts past, present and future (for us) are known by God in one single act of creation.

And so we can see that providence is not a plan in the sense of a mechanistic determinism. God is not like some master mechanic, but more like a creative artist. Part of that artistic creativity results in us, free human subjects, whom God invites to join in a divine artistic collaboration. We have a real and free contribution to make. Our task is to make of our own lives a work of art.

From our perspective, then, there is real chance, real contingency in the cosmos. However these events can be, and are, meaningful within the providential creative power of God. When asked whether this strong notion of providence undermined contingency and freedom in the world, St Thomas Aquinas answered: "what providence intends to be contingent will inevitably be contingent".[4] In the end we are saying the same thing about God's providence and creation as we said about grace and freedom. Providence is a higher principle, as is grace, which does not deny lower order explanations, but simply completes and perfects them by putting them into a fuller context.

One conclusion which is worth bearing in mind from this discussion—the ultimate responsibility for the universe is God's; while humanity is co-responsible, humanity is ONLY co-responsible. It is important to recognize the limits of human responsibility, whoever and wherever we are. It is just as out of place to feel responsible for things which are not our responsibility, as it is to not feel responsible for things we should! To feel overly responsible is usurping the role of God, and so succumbing to the temptation of the serpent (Genesis 3:5).

Further, we can see that a strong belief in divine providence is necessary if we are to hold the following position: *the offer of saving grace is made to everyone at some time, in and through their concrete life situation*. It is belief in divine providence which allows us to maintain both the mediated nature of grace, mediated through concrete historical circumstances in the events of our lives, and the universality of God's saving will (I Timothy 2:4).

PREDESTINATION

Apart from the problem of evil, the greatest difficulty with regard to this view of a universal providence is the question of *predestination*.

If the whole drama of salvation is played out in relation to God's saving grace within God's providence, does not God's offer of grace, in the mysterious divine purpose, determine who is saved and who is damned? Is not God, then, the author of both salvation and damnation? This was the conclusion made by Calvin in his doctrine of double predestination. On the other hand, could we not argue with equal validity that if God's will is universally salvific then indeed everyone is saved? This would be a form of universalism. In general a Catholic theology of grace has not accepted either of these two solutions to the problem of predestination. It has held that no-one is predestined to damnation, while still maintaining that such damnation is a real possibility.

A partial solution to this dilemma is to recognize that grace and freedom are different levels of explanation. Even without grace human persons are still free and responsible for their actions—each time sinners sin, they sin freely, even if they are not free not to sin! Each time the smoker lights up, he does so freely, yet he is not free not to smoke. So too our freedom may be diminished, but we have often allowed that diminution to happen. Personal destiny remains a personal responsibility.

Grace or its absence does not do away with this truth. Grace and providence subsume this truth into a higher context, one which does not deny the validity of the lower. Thus Catholic doctrine does speak of the predestination of the elect, those who in God's providence are brought to redemption. However it never speaks of a predestination of those who are lost. People are lost solely through human responsibility, *while God does everything possible to prevent it*. Everything, that is, short of destroying our freedom. Belief in the universal salvific will of God (I Timothy 2:4) gives us confidence that all are offered sufficient grace for salvation, though the person remains free and responsible within the context of that offer.

CONCLUSION

In this chapter we have considered the concept of providence. As I have argued, a strong notion of providence, based on the transcendence of God, is a necessary element in a theology of grace. It is necessary if we are to maintain both the mediated aspect of grace and the universality of the offer of grace. A strong notion of providence allows for a real operation of divine freedom, acting through the events of the world. This is especially important when we consider the nature of the sacraments in the next chapter.

CHAPTER NOTES

1. This discussion of divine providence has been influenced by Lonergan's treatment of the work of Thomas Aquinas in his study *Grace and Freedom*. In particular the notion that providence is a higher order explanation, to quote Lonergan:

> The Thomist higher synthesis was to place God above and beyond the created orders of necessity and contingence: because God is universal cause, His providence must be certain; but because He is a transcendent cause, there can be no incompatibility between terrestrial contingence and the causal certitude of providence.[5]

According to Lonergan, the heated debate between the Banezian (named after the Dominican, Dominicus Banez, d.1604) and Molinist (named after the Jesuit, Louis Molina, d.1600) schools lies in the failure of both sides to understand the nature of divine transcendence. The Banezian position stressed the transcendence of God, but could not see it as offering a higher level explanation. It thus needed artificial constructions to account for the reality of human freedom. The Molinists, on the other hand, failed to comprehend the divine transcendence and so located God within a temporal frame with divine knowledge of the *futuribilia*, possible future events (ibid, pp.144–5).

The dispute between Banezian and Molinist camps raged for generations, both seeking to have the other position condemned. It was ended, at least in public, by the Pope who threatened both sides if they did not desist![6]

2. In using an artistic metaphor for understanding God's creation I have been influenced by Gibson Winter's *Liberating Creation* (Crossroad, NY, 1981). Winter contrasts organic, mechanistic and artistic metaphors for understanding creation. As discussed above, the organic corresponds to a pantheistic and the mechanistic to a Deist understanding of creation. Gabriel Day also speaks of using artistic metaphors for creation in his *Creation and Redemption*. Neither of these authors provides a critical grounding for the metaphor. Such a critical grounding can be found in the work of Robert Doran, especially his *Psychic Conversion and Theological Foundation* (Scholars Press, Chico, 1981).

3. The problems of suffering and evil are profound and difficult. The first difficulty is to distinguish between the two.[7] I prefer to use the term "evil" when talking about a moral failing and so distinguish it from the problem of suffering. The problem of suffering is more straightforward. Suffering occurs when a finite

being reaches its limits. Thus I break my arm when I exceed the physical limits of my bone, or I become ill when various microbes exceed the limits of my body to deal with them. I think it is impossible to conceive of[8] a creation of finite beings in which there is no such suffering. It is either that or not create at all!

Evil, on the other hand, is not straightforward. A classical ontology saw evil as having no being, no substance, no cause. In modern terms we would say that evil is meaningless. Evil is a mystery which lacks ultimate intelligibility, even to God. Even God does not understand why we sin, though given that we do sin, God does something about it. There can be no theoretical solution to the problem of evil, only a practical one. To find a theoretical solution will eventually be to fall over into a dualism, opposing and equal principles of good and evil, or to locate God as the source of evil. Neither of these solutions is compatible with Christian faith.

4. On the Catholic doctrine on predestination we have the following statements:

> The omnipotent God wills to save all people without exception (I Timothy 2:4) even though not all are saved. In the case of those who are saved, salvation is a gift, in the case of those who are damned, damnation is their own fault (DS 623, Synod of Quiercy, 835 AD).
>
> If anyone shall say that it is not in man's power to make his ways evil, but that the works that are evil as well as those that are good God produces, not only permissively but properly and in itself, so that the treason of Judas is no less his own proper work than the vocation of St Paul—*anathema sit* (DS 1556, Council of Trent).
>
> If anyone shall say that the grace of justification is shared by those only who are predestined to life, but that all others who are called are called indeed but receive not grace, as if they are by divine power predestined to evil—*anathema sit* (DS 1567, Council of Trent).

5. On Catholic Teaching on providence we have the following statements:

> God protects and governs by his Providence all things which he has made, "reaching from end to end mightily, and ordering all things sweetly" (Wisdom 8:1). For "all things are bare and open to his eyes" (Hebrews 4:13) even those which are yet to be by the free actions of creatures (DS 3003, Vatican I).

Correctly, this teaching on providence comes after a strong affirmation of the transcendence of God:

> who, as being one, sole, absolutely simple and immutable spiritual substance, is to be declared as really and essentially distinct from the world, of supreme beatitude in and from himself, and ineffably exalted above all things which exist, or are conceivable, except himself (DS 3001, Vatican I).

---

1 *See* in particular, the declaration of Vatican I, DS 3002, 3025.
2 *See*, for example, J. Barrow and J. Silk, *The Left Hand of Creation*, Unwin, London, 1985, pp.204ff.
3 For a discussion of the presence and/or absence of God in the Holocaust, *see*, P. Fiddes, *Past Event and Present Salvation*, pp.210ff.
4 Cf. *Grace and Freedom*, p.108.
5 Ibid, p.79.
6 Cf. E. Schillebeeckx, *Church, the Human Story of God*, p.89.
7 Scott Peck notes the spontaneous identification of the two in *People of the Lie*, p.45.
8 The use of the term "conceive of" is deliberate here. Conceiving involves having grasped a meaning or intelligibility. It may be possible to *imagine* a world of no suffering. But an *image* is different from a *concept*, which involves an intelligent grasp of a possibility.

CHAPTER SIX

GRACE AS SACRAMENTAL

In Chapter 1 I mentioned the type of theology which saw grace as strictly mediated through the sacraments of the Church. In such a theology other occasions could be experiences of grace but the normal, expected means of grace were the sacraments instituted by Jesus. In this book I have argued for a broader understanding of grace, while still maintaining the mediated nature of grace. In this way grace continues to have a sacramental character in that it is seen as mediated by concrete situations, events, relationships and so on. Now I would like to turn our attention to those specific rites belonging to a religious tradition which we call "sacraments".

SACRAMENTS AND THE SYMBOLIC

In the broadest terms, sacraments and sacramental liturgies are a combination of words, symbols and actions which seek to mediate the presence of transcendent value to a religious community. Through sound and smell, touch and taste, through symbol and affect, sacraments seek to make present key religious values, recall the significance of life events, or invoke the memory of key figures of the tradition. All religious communities have their sacraments and we should be slow to see them as ineffective or meaningless. Where Thomas Aquinas could see a sacramental efficacy in the rites of the Old Testament, so we too should see an efficacy in the rites of all religious groups. It is important to see the Christian sacraments as fitting into this broader, anthropological context while noting, however, that they are not reducible to such a context.

Wherein lies the power of sacraments? Psychologically symbols used in sacraments can act so they allow for a negotiation of the blocks and biases within consciousness which cut us off from true understanding and values. In this way symbols can play a vital role in the promotion of conversion. On the role of symbols Lonergan claims that:

> [The] need is for internal communication. Organic and psychic vitality have to reveal themselves to . . . consciousness and, inversely, . . . consciousness has to secure the collaboration of organism and psyche. Again, our apprehensions of values occur . . . in feelings: here too it is necessary for feelings to reveal their objects and, inversely, for objects to awaken feelings. It is through symbols that mind and body, mind and heart, heart and body communicate.[1]

Through such internal communication the biases that block a true apprehension of meaning and value can be confronted, overcome and removed. Hidden griefs, guilts and anxieties can be uncovered and dealt with, restoring people and freeing their energies for the business of life. A most striking account of the power of symbolic mediation is given by Ainslie Meares in his book *The Door to Serenity*.[2] Meares reports the case of a schizophrenic woman who was brought to him at a psychiatric clinic for treatment. The woman was in a state of almost complete withdrawal. She had been living alone for several years, only venturing out of her rented room at dusk to buy provisions at the local shop. In her initial sessions she was almost totally incommunicative. Meares would simply sit in silence with her, asking occasional questions. He feared that no progress would be made.

Without warning during one session the woman produced a painting, a bizarre, tormented painting. It was the first of several paintings to be produced by the woman. These were not the paintings of a deliberately self-directed artist but the spontaneous products of a tortured psyche, nightmares reproduced immediately onto paper. Through the series of paintings Meares was able to discover that the woman had experienced a sexual assault by a trusted figure when she was a child. As is frequently the case, this gave rise to a tremendous guilt in the woman, who saw herself as being possessed of an evil and terrifying sexuality. These tremendous feelings of guilt so distorted her consciousness that she was unable to do anything but withdraw from the world.

In the atmosphere of trust and acceptance created through the sessions, the paintings became a therapy. Meares narrates how, through the symbolic mediation of the paintings, he was able to alleviate the guilt that the woman had experienced. As the treatment progressed her painting changed from tormented nightmares to beautiful and evocative images of serenity. Through this symbolic mediation, the woman's condition was eased to the point where she was able to return to a normal existence.

In their use of symbols, sacraments are not simply signs of grace but seek to actualize grace through their symbolic power. This is not to posit a magic power, but more a recognition of a psychic structure which correlates with the processes of a sacramental grace. Nor is it an attempt to provide a "naturalistic" account of a sacrament. It is simply to note that level of "nature" on which grace seeks to build in a sacramental situation. The presence or absence of transcendent value in such a situation is solely dependent on God's freedom, not on human manipulation of symbols. While noting the role which symbols play, Christian faith ultimately takes its stand on God's fidelity and graciousness to his people, as expressed in the sacraments.

Now the symbols effective in the sacraments of a religious tradition are not the solely personal symbols which are often so important in a psychotherapeutic context, as in the example above. Sacramental symbols are of necessity public and communal in nature. They are symbols which arise out of the common history of the religious community, for example the Exodus and Passover meals for the Jewish people, and perhaps even the common history of humanity, for example, symbols of birth and death, suffering and reconciliation. The shared nature of such symbolism indicates that the key issues addressed in religious sacraments are communal ones. Inasmuch as grace is the experience of transcendent value and such an experience is for the sake of conversion, the sort of conversion addressed is one which touches on the communal life of the religious tradition.

CHRISTIAN SACRAMENTS

Within the Christian Churches the mediation of grace is brought about through an *anamnesis*[3] or recollection of the life, death and resurrection of Jesus. A people is formed through a common memory. In this memory the central meanings and values of the community are celebrated, reinforced and passed on to the succeeding generations. Thus in the USA, Thanksgiving is celebrated, in Britain, Guy Fawkes Day, and in Australia, the Anzac story. Without such a memory the identity of a people is lost and communal dissolution follows. Thus, to the Christian people, what is central is the memory of Jesus, the memory in particular of his suffering unjustly at the hands of men, his death on the cross and his subsequent vindication in his resurrection by the Father.

Indeed, in a very real sense Jesus is himself the primary Christian sacrament. He is the Incarnate Word, the living symbol of the Father's love for the world, who goes about doing his Father's work. When a Christian community gathers "in the memory of Jesus" it is not just a matter of their own memory of Jesus, precious as that might be, that is central to their faith. It is also a matter of Jesus' "memory" of them, that Jesus is faithful to his promise to always be with his people. In particular in the eucharist Jesus re-members, that is, brings together the members, of his body the Church, drawing them again into his presence, to recall his passion, death and resurrection. It is this resurrection which reminds us that Jesus remains an active and free agent in the history of the world through his Body the Church. It is the fidelity of Jesus' love and commitment to his Church which gives the Christian confidence in approaching the sacraments.

The key sacraments of baptism and eucharist are replete with symbols drawn from the memory of this passion. In baptism we die with him that we may rise with him. Being drowned (baptized) with water allows us to participate in Jesus' own baptism unto death on the cross. Yet we live to rise out of the waters as Jesus rose from the tomb (cf. Romans 6:1–5). In the eucharist we explicitly recall Jesus' passion—"on the night before he died". We recall Jesus' own symbols of bread and wine and the meaning he gave to his death—"a new covenant for all". Such symbols are grounded in Jesus' passion and it is from these that Christian sacraments draw their power.

Moreover, it is again becoming clear that Christian sacraments are not just privatized events between me and God or Jesus. Sacraments find their proper setting within the Church *community*. For a time the sacramental piety of the Church made the sacraments a private, intense, almost mystical experience so that even an obviously communal rite such as the eucharist became more a collection of individuals in touch with the "divine" rather than a religious community celebrating its identity in the memory of Jesus' death and resurrection. Cut off from its grounding in the Christian community, such a piety correlated with an extrinsicist understanding of grace. One stored up graces simply by frequent attendance at Mass and participation in the sacraments, like making deposits in a bank account.

Under such an extrinsicist view the question "Have I received grace in this sacrament?" could be answered almost automatically "Yes". Yet this is simply not the case. The question needs to be met with the further question, "Have you experienced conversion, had your conversion deepened, your appreciation of its consequences furthered?" Grace is always grace directed towards or furthering conversion, it always seeks a response. While the offer of grace is secure in the fidelity of God's graciousness, its reception can never be automatic for this would reduce us to automatons.

Again it is important to highlight the communal dimensions of the sacraments and the social dimensions of grace and conversion. Grace is addressed to us not only as individuals but also as a community. Thus, for example, baptism is not some magic rite for the removal of an imagined stain on the soul called original sin (more can be found on the connection between baptism and original sin in Chapter 17). Baptism is primarily entry into the Christian community. As such, it is effective only in as much as the baptized person and the baptizing community incarnate the mutual rights and responsibilities which such entry entails. If baptized people never darken the church pews again in their life, or if the community, having baptized them, leaves them to their own devices, then the sacrament has been rendered ineffective.

Symbols of the sacrament and the conversion they seek to effect bring into question not only the self-justification of the individual but also the self-justifying ideologies of the community. I have already mentioned this in Chapter 4 concerning Jesus' status as the Victim. Any discussion of the Real Presence of Jesus in the eucharist cannot afford to forget the nature of that presence, the presence of a Victim. As the Victim who puts an end to all sacrifices, Jesus calls upon us to renounce all victimizations by which we justify the divisions within our community. Indeed we can see this illustrated in the eucharistic dispute within the Corinthian community (cf. I Corinthians 11:17–34).

The Corinthian community was being subjected to a number of disputes which threatened its basic unity. One dispute concerned the apostolic authority of its founding fathers, Paul and Apollos (cf. I Corinthians 3:1ff.). Others touched on the division between those who saw themselves as "spiritually strong" and those whose faith was "weak", (I Corinthians 8:1ff.). However, of far more serious concern was the dispute which threatened the eucharistic unity of the community. Paul notes that their celebration is more a cause of scandal than anything else. Indeed he claims that it is doing them "more harm than good" (v.17). Paul goes so far as to say "It is not the Lord's Supper that you are eating" (v.20)! What have they done wrong? Have they violated some liturgical canon, gotten their rubrics all wrong? Were they wrong perhaps on their eucharistic doctrine, some failing in orthodoxy? No. What undermines the gathering's identity as the Lord's Supper is that the rich are eating their fill while the poor are left hungry. "Surely you have enough respect for the community of God not to make poor people embarrassed?" he asks (v.22). While such divisions may exist in society and may be difficult to change, Paul will not tolerate their introduction into the community eucharist.

Starkly and forcefully Paul seeks to correct the Corinthians by recalling the actions of Jesus on his last night. Jesus is the victim whose death seals the new covenant. No more victims are needed, nor can they be tolerated. Whenever Christians victimize others, as Jesus was victimized, they are "guilty of the body and blood of the Lord" (v.27). Such people have classed themselves "among those who murdered Jesus".[4] For Paul the eucharist is not an occasion for an individualistic mystic union with Jesus, but an expression and reinforcement for the unity of the Body of Christ, the Church. Indeed a person who takes part in the eucharist "without recognizing the body, eats and drinks his own condemnation" (v.29). Here Paul is not talking about recognizing the presence of Jesus in the eucharistic species, but the body which is the Church. On this verse Murphy O'Connor notes that:

> This is the criterion by which believers must judge themselves. They must evaluate the authenticity of their relationships to other members of the body of Christ, a theme already known to the Corinthians (6:15) and mentioned in 10:17.[5]

Nothing undermines that unity more than the introduction into the life of the community of the same divisions, justified by the same ideologies, which are found in society at large. Such divisions render relationships inauthentic. When a Christian community gives itself over to such forces of darkness then they are no longer capable of celebrating the Lord's Supper.

A similar situation can be found in the Letter of St James; cf. James 2:1ff. While James does not explicitly refer to the celebration of the eucharist, he clearly has in mind the gathering of the community as a whole in the "synagogue" (it is not clear if this refers to a continued use of the Jewish synagogue or an extension of the term to a Jewish–Christian setting).[6] James is quite blunt. You cannot "combine faith in Jesus Christ, our glorified Lord, with the making of distinctions between classes of people" (v.1). Again the distinction which particularly annoys James is that between rich and poor (v.2–4). In making such "distinctions between classes of people, you are committing sin" (v.9).

THE CHURCH AS SACRAMENT

These comments reinforce what was stated previously in Chapter 4. The social dimensions of grace call for a questioning and a repudiation of ideologies which make "distinctions between classes of people". Part of the role of the Christian community is to create real alternatives to such social structures, to create new ways of relating which break down such divisions. Indeed in his letter to the Church in Galatia Paul proclaims that in the Christian community:

> There can be neither Jew or Greek, there can be neither slave or freeman, there can be neither male or female (Galatians 3:28).

These divisions between people simply have no place within the Church. The Christian sacraments, in particular the sacrament of the eucharist, are concrete ways of living out and symbolizing such new ways of relating. Where the world offers alienation, entry into the Christian community through baptism offers a loving home. Where the world offers hatred and bitterness, the Christian community offers reconciliation and forgiveness. Where the world offers division and oppression, the Christian community offers communion and solidarity with all victims and an end to all victimizations in the eucharist.

This setting up of alternatives does not imply an ethic of separation, however, where the Christian community cuts itself off from the world in order to maintain its own purity. The setting up of alternatives has a purpose other than the establishment of a pure and holy community. Its purpose is for the Christian community to be a sacrament to the world, a light to the nations. All the particular sacraments of the Church are grounded in the sacramental nature of the Church itself. Cut off from the world it no longer addresses the ambiguities present in the world. The world finds in it simply another harsh judge not a loving and challenging companion (one with whom we break bread!). Jesus himself did not hesitate to break bread with those publicly identified as sinners. This is a symbol of the reconciliation and communion later expressed in the eucharist.

Worse still, those who choose the separatist path too often carry with them their own unacknowledged ambiguities. Free from the questioning glance of the world their own biases and blindspots become dogmatic principles which cannot be challenged. We have seen the outcome of this far too often. Whether it be the separation from "racial defilement" as found in South Africa or a purity from the world as found in some Pentecostalist sects, such movements too often become blind to their own sinfulness in the very act of seeking to maintain their purity.

SACRAMENTS AND FAITH

Finally I should note that sacraments are faith events. Faith is neither intellectual assent nor a warm fuzzy feeling. It is a commitment, heart, mind and body to transcendent value and its consequences. The meaning and significance of the sacraments comes from the realities they represent grasped through such a faith. They are effective in as much as we are, through our faith, open to the transforming power of the symbols presented within the sacrament. Where faith is present the sacraments strengthen and renew that commitment. On the other hand if we partake of the sacrament without faith the power of the symbols may still break through, but it is far less likely. Sacraments generally presuppose and reinforce faith. They do not create faith.

CONCLUSION

In summary I have considered the nature of sacraments as words, symbols and actions which seek to mediate the experience of transcendent value. In part, the power of the sacrament lies in the way symbols operate within human consciousness, helping to free the blocks and biases which prevent an apprehension of meanings and values. Christian sacraments draw their symbolism from the passion of Jesus which is the founding event of the Christian community. As communal celebrations, Christian sacraments seek to address issues of conversion which affect the community as a whole and not just the concerns of the individual. This touches on the social dimensions of grace. In the next chapter we shall consider the completion of the life of grace in death.

CHAPTER NOTES

1. In his exposition of Lonergan's understanding of sacraments, Stephen Happel argues for the social dimensions of sacraments. He notes that:

> Christian sacraments are a virtuous remedy, not for private suffering and personal pain, but for the social decline created by human sins. Self-sacrificing love requires the public expression which overcomes the ... cycles of community-destruction ... Christian sacraments as the symbols of the community *redirect our social desires* [emphasis added].[7]

He further notes that sacraments:

> are the primary process by which the Church constitutes itself as social carrier of religious values. Through the message they enact, 'the self-sacrificing love that is Christian charity reconciles alienated [human beings] to [their] true being, and undoes the mischief initiated by alienation and consolidated by ideology'.[8]

2. On the eucharistic dispute within the Corinthian community see *A Body Broken for a Broken People, Eucharist in the New Testament*, by Francis Moloney, (Collins Dove, Melbourne, 1990), Chapter 6. In this book Moloney is concerned with what he sees as a distortion of the eucharistic practice of the Church which restricts communion to "those without serious sin". Drawing on New Testament practice Moloney sees the eucharist as given precisely to those who are broken.

---

1 Cf. *Method in Theology*, pp.66–7.
2 Ainslie Meares, Melbourne, Hill of Content, 1977.
3 The term *anamnesis* is derived from *an* (not) and *amnesis* (amnesia—forgetting). It implies not forgetting, which is stronger than simply remembering!
4 *NJBC*, commentary on I Corinthians by Jerome Murphy O'Connor, p.810.
5 Ibid.
6 Cf. *TNJB* footnote on this verse.
7 *The Desires of the Human Heart*, p.246.
8 Ibid, pp.247–8. The inner quote is from *Method in Theology*, p.364.

CHAPTER SEVEN

GRACE AND DEATH

Previously we discussed the nature of God's universal providence, his care and concern for each and every person expressed through the events of our lives and ultimately in the events of history itself. The focus in this chapter shall be upon the most mysterious of all the providential moments in human living, the moment of death. Death is part of the structure of human living as we experience it, though as many have noted, it is a part we often suppress.[1] How does grace relate to this most mysterious event? Is death the end of the life of grace? Or is it a fulfillment leading to greater riches? I shall now try to say something about the fulfillment of the life of grace in death.

If nothing else, we can say that death brings about a radical change in the nature of human existence. If there is continued human existence beyond this life, it is clearly not simply a continuation of our life at present. Indeed the very mystery and the ignorance of what comes with death can themselves fill us with fear. There are few among us who could go to our deaths without some trace of fear or hesitation. Death poses ultimate questions about the meaning of human existence and the nature of God. Is death the end of it all? Worse still, is God really the Angel of Death in disguise, not a god of life at all but a god waiting to throw us into eternal darkness? All may voice the questions in their own way but the answer comes to one and all in death itself, and from this there is no escape.

I have previously considered grace in terms of its relationship to self-esteem. Here it is important to recognize that death itself is a threat to my self-esteem, a powerful challenge to my search for meaning and significance. All the strategies I may have developed to promote and build my self-esteem come to nothing in the face of death. All my projects, all my achievements, what Ernest Becker calls my *immortality projects*, are a cold comfort when my body is laid in the ground. We can see something of the futility of such human projects designed to maintain some meaning to life, after death, in the ancestor worship of the East. Is my only hope that I shall be remembered in the future by my descendants? But what if they should forget?! And what will happen when the whole human race comes to an end?

On the other hand, the experience of transcendent value points to a meaning which goes beyond our spatial and temporal existence, beyond death. Here is a source of meaning and value which goes beyond the here and now, something born of eternity, something which can sustain my being beyond the limits of death. In the experience of grace I experience myself as valued, as loved with an everlasting love, and as that love will never die so there is at least the hope that death will not be the end of life.[2] Hence Paul can exclaim "Death, where is your sting?" (I Corinthians 15:54ff.). In the experience of grace we touch the hope that death is not the final word.

Sadly however, in this life the experience of transcendent value is always threatened, at risk, due to the continued possibility of sin. Whatever else we want to say about sin it is clearly incompatible with grace. Prior to conversion the state of the sinner is *non posse non peccare*—not able not to sin; after conversion it is *posse non peccare*—able not to sin. While the converted person is able not to sin, in order to remain free from sin there needs to be the cooperation of the person's freedom. Since our freedom remains capable of faltering, serious sin remains a possibility and, when realized, is incompatible with the experience of grace. Thus while the experience of grace gives us hope in the face of death, it remains a precarious hope, caught up as it is in human sinfulness.

These are the questions which death presents. How does my life of grace and disgrace relate to death? Is there in grace a source of meaning and value which can sustain me, can value me, beyond death? And if so what is the meaning of such an existence for me? What is the meaning of death itself? To address these issues I shall begin with a discussion on the nature of death.

DEATH AND THE FINAL OPTION

Two modern theologians, Karl Rahner and Ladislaus Boros, have sought to explore the mystery of death and its relationship to the life of grace.[3] They see death not simply as something which overtakes us as an impersonal force but as a final and total act of self-disposal, done in complete self-possession. Death is something which affects the whole person and involves the whole person at all levels of his or her being. While this aspect of death may remain hidden from us in the sudden and tragic deaths we encounter, we can catch something of it in the deaths of those who suffer prolonged terminal illnesses. It is a common experience for those dealing with the terminally ill that the afflicted can almost time their deaths, to come after some significant family event, a wedding or family reunion for example. While Rahner bases his conclusions on a metaphysical analysis of the meaning of death, we can catch something of the truth of what he says in such experiences.

If death is something which involves the whole person, if it is not something which simply overtakes me, then it will involve an act of the highest part of my nature, an act of my freedom. This will be so even in cases of tragic and sudden death where such an act may remain hidden. This has led Boros to speak of death as involving a final option, a final act of my freedom deciding for or against God.[4] Here it is important again to stress that freedom is not simply a matter of arbitrary choice, a matter of indifference like tossing a coin. Nor is my freedom an absolute freedom, but always a conditioned freedom, conditioned by my whole history of freedom (including the triumphs of grace and the failures of sin, of course) prior to that point. A final option is not a soft option but a final act of my whole person, summing up who I have become in my life. In fact, my final option is my personal judgment before God.

Many have criticized Boros for what they see as presenting us with a soft option, that somehow we are left to judge ourselves and we will all be too lenient. In fact this is at odds with the scriptural understanding. In the First Letter of John we find:

> My children, our love is not just words or mere talk, but something real and active; only by this can we be certain that we are children of the truth and *be able to quieten our conscience in his presence, whatever accusations it may raise against us*, because God is greater than our conscience (I John 3:19–20).

Here the author sees us as harsh judges of ourselves, our conscience raising accusations which only God can quieten. If it were not for the presence of God quietening our conscience, who of us would survive such a judgment? Would we not rather choose to flee from God in fear? Indeed a harsh judgment of oneself is all that is possible when one's horizon is dominated by a distorted and destructive self-esteem. Only grace can overcome such a harsh judgment.

This brings us to the second aspect of the theologies of Rahner and Boros. Death is not just a final option, a decision for or against God, it is also a moment of grace and an encounter with the Risen Lord. Even in death God does not abandon us, as death itself becomes God's final providential moment of grace, mediated through the presence of the Risen Jesus. Indeed for some who die after a brief but painful life of deprivation, could this not be their first real encounter with God's grace? The significance of such grace should not be underestimated. The purpose of grace is to free our freedom, to free it for the most important decision we ever make. Without such grace our decision is conditioned by our whole prior history of freedom and grace. Without such grace who would willingly see the face of God? With such grace we are freed to make a real option for life, for God.

Boros claims that there is no doctrinal support of this notion of final option and its concurrent grace. However one should note that the Council of Trent speaks of the "grace of perseverance", a perseverance unto the end (cf. DS 1541). One could argue that a grace of *final* perseverance, a grace not just prior to the end of life but at the moment of death itself, is precisely what Boros is talking about. Moreover, the role of grace is to free our freedom, and freedom is only necessary where a decision is to be made. Thus I would argue that Boros' position is supported by this teaching of Trent.[5]

DEATH AS DEFINITIVE

Another aspect of the theologies of Rahner and Boros is that they see death as initiating a new and definitive relationship with God and the cosmos. What can we say about the nature of the new and definitive relationship? St Paul tells us that in death we are finished with sin (Romans 6:7). In death, the experience of transcendent value is no longer at threat from sin. More importantly, for those who chose for God, the definitive state that is achieved in death is a fixity in the state of experiencing grace. Such a fixity in grace literally makes it impossible to sin—*non posse peccare*.

For those who see freedom simply in terms of the ability to choose between good and evil, the notion that it is impossible to sin sounds like a total denial of freedom. If we are not free to sin then surely we are not free. But, as I have previously argued, this is a misunderstanding of the nature of freedom. Freedom is not primarily about the ability to choose between good and evil but about self-determination. In a grace-filled death the self is determined in such a way that evil no longer holds any attraction, in fact is totally repulsive. Sin is simply no longer an option. This is not the denial of freedom but the definitive establishment of freedom—freedom to do good.

HEAVEN

Such a freedom must have its own proper goals. It is, as stated, a freedom to do good. But what good is there to be done? It seems to me a tragic collapse of the Christian imagination that the most common images we have of the afterlife are of clouds and harps. Ask many what they think of such a heaven and they say they think it will be boring! Put in other terms the only way we can think of a sinless existence is if there is nothing to do, no decisions to make, hence no opportunity to sin! Far from it. Heaven will be a place for the full flowering of human freedom. While we may not be able to imagine what this involves we can be sure it will be totally un-boring!

The New Testament presents us with a variety of images concerning this life with God—a heavenly banquet (Luke 14:15ff.), a new city (Revelation 21:9ff.), coming home to a heavenly mansion (John 14:1ff.); Paul talks about "seeing God face to face" (I Corinthians 13:12). The images, appropriate for the day, sought to express a joy and excitement at the prospect of heaven. Perhaps such images are no longer appropriate for our present times. Generally they represent a static world view where perfection is attained in some final unchanging state, be it a banquet or a homecoming. Such a static view does not fit well with our present understanding of a dynamic developing cosmos. Perhaps more appropriate images can be found in such cosmic process, a sharing in the excitement of a universe which continues to change, which is still directed within God's creative providence and purpose, culminating in a new heaven and a new earth. In death and particularly in the resurrection we still share a common interest in God's bounteous creation.

In his book, *Infallibility*, Peter Chirico contrasts the type of conception of the afterlife commensurate with a static world view, with the type commensurate with a dynamic world view. A static world view gives rise to the concept of a static unrestricted subject who:

> ... would be one whose self-differentiation would be conceived as totally developed in regard to the world in which he lived. Every capacity of this subject within that world would

> be developed to its fullest extent possible ... The static fully developed subject would live in a static world and would fully grasp himself and the world.[6]

On the other hand a dynamic world view gives rise to the concept of a dynamic unrestricted human subject who:

> ... would constantly be expanding within a constantly expanding world, a world whose intelligibility would be ceaselessly increasing.[7]

Chirico argues that the risen Jesus exists as such a dynamic unrestricted human subject. It seems to me that to speak of Jesus as such a subject is to speak of the possibility of an ongoing personal and active engagement in the world on the part of Jesus. Such active engagement is a personal act of Jesus' freedom, acting through his Spirit, through his eucharistic Body, through the Church which is his Body and in ways we may possibly never imagine.

The same sort of difficulty can be found in traditional statements about "degrees" of glory in heaven. Again much here depends on whether one has a static or dynamic understanding of continued human existence after death. Clearly a definitive possession of grace does not rule out growing depths of appreciation of that value. One need not assume that the depth of appreciation attained is a static thing. A dynamic state of continual transformation through further acts of cooperation cannot be ruled out. Indeed the Catholic doctrine of purgatory seems to assume that such is the case, for, though the final state of those in purgatory is assured, there is still a further process of development that needs to take place. If such change is truly personal it will involve the cooperation of our freedom, forging new ways of relating and so overcoming old and defective ways of relating.

Whatever the case, the definitive freedom of the person to do good must have some purpose! What that purpose is we may not know in any detail but we can be sure that it is far from boring. The Christian doctrine of the communion of saints would indicate that the dead are not cut off from the affairs of the world. In their continued existence they maintain an active relationship to the world, a relationship which is usually spoken of in terms of intercession. Such intercession cannot be based on an ignorance or lack of concern for the world, but must be based on real knowledge and love for the world and a continued freedom to act, in however mysterious a way, within the world. Such a continued freedom to act within the world seems to be central to the notion of resurrection.

HELL

Equally definitive, of course, is a decision against God. Can such a decision be possible? Well, there is certainly enough evidence that such decisions are made in this life every day. Can we extrapolate such instances into a final decision against God, an ultimate rejection of God's presence? We simply do not know. While Catholic doctrine talks about the reality of hell, it never claims to know of any person who is in hell (on the other hand the Church does make claims about people who have attained glory in heaven, the saints). This reticence is necessary since no one can claim to know the limits of God's grace and forgiveness.

What images might we have of hell? While the image of a fiery prison is common, it is not fully adequate. A prison is an extrinsic binding of my freedom. It seems to me that the binding of hell is not extrinsic but to do with freedom itself. In rejecting God we also freely reject our own freedom. The opposite of freedom is not a prison with nothing to do, but eternal compulsive action, action which arises not out of my freedom, but out of forces to which I have surrendered myself, out of my demons. It is this surrendering to demons in eternal compulsive behavior which is the suffering of hell. Even in this life we can see people caught in such compulsive behavior, trapped in their own hell. Scott Peck speaks of people who are

> ... [f]orever fleeing the light of self-exposure and the voice of their own conscience ... They live their lives in sheer terror. They need not be consigned to any hell; they are already in it.[8]

Often such behavior is at heart a form of self-punishment, a torment for failures real or imagined which one cannot flee. Indeed Scott Peck speculates that even those in hell are free to leave but they see the path out as even more painful than remaining where they are![9] It is not God's will that anyone live this way, in this life or the next. It is God's will that all be saved and it was to this end that Jesus came. God does not *send* anyone to hell. In the end those who go do so as a result of their own free choice. God does everything possible to save us from such a fate.

CONCLUSION

In summary, in this chapter I have considered the relationship between the life of grace and death. I have noted the position of some modern theologians that death can be and, with the mercy of God, is in its own way a real moment of grace, setting a final seal on our struggles with grace and disgrace. Finally I have considered some images of how this final seal is expressed in traditional doctrines of the afterlife.

CHAPTER NOTES

1. Above, reference is made to the work of Ernest Becker, *The Denial of Death*. Becker argues from a Freudian perspective that all human culture arises out of a variety of immortality projects that seek to prolong human meaning and value beyond the grave. For Becker human existence is tragic, caught between a need for affirmation from others, and death which puts an end to any possibility of such affirmation. Perhaps this would be an accurate account of human existence if it were not for grace. Becker does not seem to consider the possibility that death actually brings with it the potential for a full affirmation of our being through a living contact with the divine.

2. For a readable account of Rahner's and Boros' position see Boros' book *The Moment of Truth*. The position there developed on the final option is a significant development in a Christian understanding of death. The most thorough and readable attempt to develop a systematic study of death and eschatology in the light of this approach is that of Tony Kelly, *Touching on the Infinite* (Collins Dove, Melbourne, 1991). Kelly's approach is most congruent with the approach developed on grace and sin in this present work.

3. In my opinion, for what it's worth, Christian imagination on the afterlife has recently been too dominated by a Platonic dualism. This domination has starved the Christian imagination and isolated our imagined afterlife from any meaningful relationship to the cosmos. As a result many Christians, while affirming a bodily resurrection, see no sense in it at all. From a Platonic point of view a resurrection is madness, imprisoning the soul in a body once more. While the images of Dante and Milton may no longer inspire us, we need to recover images which do justice to Christian earthiness.

4. While I have not spoken at length of purgatory that does not mean that I do not agree with such a doctrine. Indeed it seems to me that such a doctrine makes perfect psychological sense. Jung once commented that "neurosis is always a substitute for legitimate suffering".[10] Even in death we are presented with such alternatives. Hell is neurosis eternally prolonged while purgatory is the legitimate suffering of conversion and repudiation of past sins.

1 A thorough discussion of this is given in Ernest Becker's *Denial of Death*.
2 This is how J. Ratzinger reads the growing Old Testament understanding of the possibility of the resurrection of the dead, cf. his *Eschatology*, CUA Press, Washington, 1988, p.80ff.
3 Cf. K. Rahner, *On the Theology of Death*, Herder and Herder, London, 1961; L. Boros, *The Moment of Truth*, Burns and Oates, London, 1962.
4 *TNDT* adopts Boros' position, cf. pp.272–3. Ratzinger finds Boros' position "elaborated in impressive style" but remains hesitant himself, *Eschatology*, p.208.
5 *See* P. Schoonenburg, *Man and Sin*, p.39. Schoonenburg also links the notion of a grace of perseverance with the notion of a final option.
6 P. Chirico, *Infallibility*, Michael Glazier, Wilmington, 1977, pp.155–6.
7 Ibid. p.156.
8 *People of the Lie*, p.67.
9 Ibid. Scott Peck is drawing on the writings of C.S. Lewis, *The Great Divorce*.
10 Cf. Scott Peck, *The Road Less Travelled*, p.17.

CHAPTER EIGHT

SIN, PERSONAL, SOCIAL AND HISTORICAL

So far in this book we have studied the nature of grace and its relationship to human freedom as expressed personally, socially and historically. In general it has been argued that grace has become a moral necessity, necessary to free us from a bondage to sin which captures us in its compulsive web. Yet so far I have not sought to analyze what it is that is meant by sin. Sin is clearly in opposition to grace. Just as grace has its personal, social and historical dimensions so too does sin. It will be important to clarify these before we enter into a discussion of that most mysterious of sins, original sin.

SIN AS PERSONAL

The starting point of this discussion is to recall the understanding of the human person given in Chapter 2. Here we studied the nature of the freedom of the human person as a process of self-determination. We noted that through our moral decision-making we not only affect the world, we make ourselves who we are. It is not only the self that determines but also the self that is determined through our decisions. Thus we are not unaffected by our moral decisions. If we were so unaffected, conversion, which involves a repudiation of and detachment from the past, would not be such a big deal.

The fact that my decisions affect me totally reflects the

physico–psycho–spiritual unity of the human person. At the first level my decisions affect my thinking, which in turn reaches down to shape my psyche. An easy conscience finds sleep a pleasant refuge while the tormented conscience finds in its dreams a further reminder of its guilt and anxiety. Reaching down further into my physical being, a tormented conscience contributes to physical stress and symptoms of anxiety—high blood pressure, digestive problems, heart problems and even cancer. This is not to say, of course, that all such symptoms are the result of a tormented conscience. Clearly there are other causes of stress and disease which have nothing to do with personal sin. However, it is important to recognize the unity of the person. The simplest application of this unity is the polygraph or so-called "lie-detector". A person cannot generally lie without giving off detectable physical symptoms of his or her action. Thus we can see that the decisions we make affect all parts of our being, our thinking, our dreams, even our health.

A denial of this physico–psycho–spiritual unity of the person usually takes some form of dualism. Such a dualism sees the person as made up of distinct substances of matter/body and spirit/soul. The spirit/soul is then the real person while the matter/body is simply a shell which is discarded at death. The morality which flows from such a dualism is usually of two types. The first would see any contact with or furtherance of the material world as sinful. For example, sex is sinful because it leads to the entrapment of more spirit in matter. This form of dualism leads to a path of renunciation from the world and contemplation of spiritual things. Christianity has often fallen prey to such dualism and at a popular level is often identified with it. Its most recent manifestation has been widespread Jansenism. The second type of morality goes in the opposite direction. Since my body and my spirit are distinct substances what I do with my body cannot affect my spirit. This leads to all sorts of licentious behavior. Both forms can be found in the Manichean sect with which Augustine flirted in his youth. The first path was for the elect, the second for the plebs!

The thing such a dualism misses is that my decisions not only reveal my values, they also, in some way, "constitute" my values. While it is clear that my decisions reveal my values in that I usually make my decisions on the basis of what is of value to me, the second statement is not so obvious. It is an assertion that through my decisions I *make* something a value for me whether I notionally hold such a value or not. Herein lies the power of those psychological treatments known as "behavior modification". By helping the subject modify his or her behavior, the psychologist helps to alter feelings and their associated values so that the subject may resume normal living. Through experiencing situations once seen as threatening, but now undertaken in a more relaxed frame of mind, the subject is enabled to change his or her feelings and hence his or her values.

The question remains, what happens if I act against values which I claim to hold? I have two options. Either I immediately renounce the new value incarnated in my action or I must find some justification for the new value and so make it my own. For example, in a fit of anger I may lash out and kill someone. If I do not repent my action then I must justify it to myself—he had it coming, life's cheap anyway! This process of justification will involve a restructuring of my value system, a reallocation of my preferences, a change in my horizon. Where such a change in horizon is a conversion its justification will be found in the peace and truth of an undistorted self-esteem. Where such a change in horizon is a breakdown its justification will be found in one of the many varieties of self-justification which build up so many lies about the true nature of my worth. Sadly, the most powerful form of justification is to repeat the act which led to the breakdown. If it was right once it must be right again. Hence arises the compulsive power of sin.

Thus, it is possible to see that through my decision I am able to displace transcendent value as the central principle of my horizon. Some decisions which I might make constitute "values" (really disvalues!) which are dialectically opposed to transcendent value. If they are dialectically opposed they are incompatible with it and so drive it out of my consciousness. To claim that there are such (dis-)values is not to claim some *a priori* way of identifying them. Human wisdom built on centuries of experience would indicate that things such as murder, rape, and serious distortion of the truth are all incompatible with transcendent value. They are denials of the value of life, of human dignity and truth which experience teaches are important consequences of transcendent value. Unrepented, such actions lead down a sorry path of violence, crime and even insanity. One can only note the difficulty we have in comprehending violent criminal acts as anything other than the acts of insanity. While the mad are not necessarily bad, in the long run the bad seem to us as mad![1]

If transcendent value has been driven out by such an action what am I left with? In the absence of transcendent value I must fall back on my self-esteem as the central principle of my horizon. Sadly however, it is self-esteem which has been seriously damaged by moral fault. Nothing is more damaging to my self-esteem than the doing of something which I had judged to be wrong. I see myself as less than human, of no value to anyone. I have failed both myself and God. I have made myself once again a slave to sin! "Who then can deliver me from this body of death? Thanks be to God through Jesus Christ our Lord" (Romans 7:24–25).

I have argued above that some sinful decisions will involve a distortion of values so as to move a person from one horizon to a dialectically opposed horizon. Such decisions incarnate dis-values opposed to transcendent value. The only way back to the previous horizon will be through a grace-filled conversion experience. However, it could also be argued that some other decisions will simply involve a contraction of my horizon rather than its radical transformation. Such decisions fail to explore potentialities within my horizon, they fail to make use of the freedom which has been restored by grace. For example, I may fail in some act of generosity well within my means. While it is true that some contraction has indeed occurred, through the exercise of my effective freedom, in a horizon which remains under the influence of grace, I am still able to recover lost ground.

Perhaps we can find in this distinction the classical distinction between mortal and venial sins? Mortal sins can be said to involve the breakdown of my grace-filled horizon into a dialectically opposed one which can only be restored by some future grace-filled conversion. Venial sins can be said to involve a contraction of or failure to expand the horizon, but not its breakdown. Such a situation is far more common and far less serious. Recovery is possible with the resources still available within the present horizon.

In this discussion sin has both a moral and religious dimension. It has a moral dimension in as much as it is a distortion of the self-determination of the human person. It is not only a misuse of my freedom, it also undermines that freedom. As a distortion of God's creation, a distortion of my very freedom wherein lies my special dignity, it is also a turning away from God and a rejection of God's design. It has religious dimension in as much as it involves a rejection of transcendent value, a rejection of that special divine intimacy which is made present in grace. This is much more than a simple turning away from God as found at the moral level. It is a fundamental break in relationship, a relationship established by God's own sovereign and gracious freedom. It is much more like the rejection of the intimacy of a lover than the disobedience to a superior found at the moral level. Despite such a lack of fidelity on our part God remains ever faithful, always ready to forgive, to offer us another chance, to renew us with his love.

SIN AS SOCIAL

Just as there are social and historical dimensions to grace, so too there are social and historical dimensions to sin. Personal sin does not just affect me, it also affects the community in which I live, the society as a whole, the culture, the economy, with consequences flowing on to history itself. As a social being I affect those around me, my family, my colleagues, my peers, those over whom I have responsibilities. My actions are emulated, admired, their consequences carried out by others. Through my personal sin I can create an ambience, an atmosphere in which sin is tolerated or worse still seen as the norm. The corruption of the police force may begin with a single bribe but end with corrupt dealings reaching to the very top.

Long tolerated, such an atmosphere becomes institutionalized. "This is the ways thing are and the way they have always been; don't rock the boat." Structures of inequality become reinforced by inequitable tax arrangements. The rich don't pay tax, they pay lawyers and accountants instead. Networks of cronies and former classmates exclude non-members from access to work. "It's not what you know, but who you know." Justice delayed is justice denied, but only for the poor who cannot afford adequate legal representation. At times of economic difficulty, social services are cut to the bone, affecting the poor and unemployed, while the well-off receive tax cuts and new "incentives" to "boost" the economy There are always good reasons to increase defense expenditure, while hospitals serving the needy scratch around for funds. Wealthy nations manipulate markets and currencies while the poorer nations sink deeper into debt. Injustice is not the exception, it becomes a way of life!

Not content with institutionalizing injustices we must then seek to justify them. As was discussed in Chapter 4, such justifications become dominant ideologies, complex ideational structures which seek to make such injustices not only acceptable but in fact right and proper, the essence of justice itself. Thus, the near extinction of the Australian Aborigines was justified by a social Darwinism which saw the Aborigines as no longer fit to survive in the face of a superior white race. Colonial expansionists everywhere have always debated whether indigenous peoples really had souls, whether they were really human. The poor are blamed for their indigence, women for being raped, particular races for being 'primitive', the sick for simply being inconvenient.

This is the world into which we are all born. If I am born on the top of the heap, through no merit of my own, I enjoy privileges gained through others' suffering. I enjoy the benefits of others' sins. If I am on the bottom, through no fault of my own, I suffer. Whether on top or bottom, my consciousness is distorted by ideologies which shape my imagination, my interests, my questions, my answers and most basically my values. I am born into a tainted world and it quickly taints me. What am I to do?

Clearly I am not responsible for the situation of my birth. At birth I am not responsible for the injustices of society and the lies that support them. Yet as I grow and develop morally I cannot remain simply a neutral observer. Unless some effort is made to the contrary I will become morally responsible for my cooperation with evil. I will slip into ways of thinking which reflect the distortions around me and eventually commit actions which are sinful in themselves. The social dimensions of sin create an undercurrent which must be combated, consciously, deliberately, lest I sink without trace.

Such a social dimension to sin does not fit into the neat categories of personal sin which always involves an element of my freedom. It catches me prior to any effective exercise of freedom on my part. However, since it helps shape my horizon I can quickly find myself unable not to sin—*non posse non peccare*. Either I am caught up in compulsive behavior sanctioned by the society (such as excessive consumption) or I become trapped in a feeling of powerlessness, of general malaise, knowing that the situation is wrong but feeling unable to do anything about it. As was stated previously in Chapter 4, this is a situation which grace must address.

Such social sin requires a social response. In instituting the Church, Jesus created a new society, an *ecclesia* (*ex-kaleo*—to call out of), those called out of the old and led into the new. This new "perfect" society is meant to empower us to break through the compulsive force of the old ways, to break through the feelings of powerlessness, by its effective mediation of the love of God made manifest in Jesus. Sadly however, Church communities too often simply reflect the dominant values of the society, except perhaps in areas of sexual morality.

SIN AS HISTORICAL

As societies are prolonged through history, so too sin has its own historical dimension. Sinful institutions develop a momentum, a drive to expand, to crush opposition, to find scapegoats. Evil people flourish and attain power while the good remain silent, trapped in a sense of powerlessness. The distortions created by sin begin to influence the course of history, reshaping societies, cultures, economies. Evil presses forward, planning future conquests, ignoring past failures, suppressing present dissent. With its own inexorable logic, sin moves towards destruction. Based on a failure to esteem oneself, it is ultimately unable to esteem anything else. Human life becomes cheap. Human achievements are counted for nothing. Self-hatred seeks more victims to feed the hellfires within. Only more and more destruction seems to satisfy the demon within until, in the end, there is nothing left.

In earlier days such orgies of destruction were limited to the local, the national, the regional. Eventually they burnt themselves out, literally destroyed themselves, but left those sufficiently far away untouched. In our own day technology has given us the weapons which are finally capable of destroying not just the local, the national, the regional, but all human life on the planet. At last evil has the means equal to its ends. Meanwhile this massive distortion of our human societies and economies has been justified by ideologies of conflict, of militarism and national supremacy, which have left the world a powder keg, a tinder box, as we all wait in fear for someone to strike the first match.

And as we slowly and hesitantly back away from this nuclear precipice, we find new dangers, ecological catastrophes, the products of our irrational commitments to unlimited economic growth and increased consumerism. The whole planet groans under our wastes, our poisons in the land, the air and the sea. We have turned fertile land into desert, clean water into dead lakes, fresh air into toxic clouds. No part of the globe is free from our destructive interference. Left unchecked we will render the planet uninhabitable.

Such is the historical "goal" of sin. The logic of sin is the logic of destruction, of nihilism. The end it has in sight is nothing less than the end of history itself. In our own day such an end has become a realistic possibility. There is no divine guarantee to human history that evil will not have its apparent victory. There is no guarantee that in ten, twenty or a hundred years all human life will not be gone, wiped out in a global cataclysm. It is important to bear in mind that the resurrection only came after the crucifixion, only after evil had seemingly achieved its goal. We need not expect anything more for history itself.

Such an awareness can be found in biblical apocalyptic literature. This literature sees history as a battleground between powerful forces of good and evil. The powers of sin and evil become personified in the mythical, apocalyptic figure of the Anti-Christ, the historical summation of a long and sorry history of evil. While it is not necessary nor even helpful to try to identify this figure with any particular historical figure, the intent of such a personification is clear. Unchecked, the historical forces of evil can and will manifest themselves in massive powers of destruction. We have seen the likes of this in recent times in Hitler and Stalin.

Apocalyptic thought always sees the forces of evil as having their day, of wreaking their destruction. The faithful remnant can only hold on in hope that the time will not be too long, that the end is not too far away. Indeed it sees evil as attaining such dominance that the only hope of salvation lies in God. Only God can bring about the final reversal and restore the world to justice. Only God can raise up a dead world, as he raised up Jesus, not snatched out of the jaws of defeat but in the very defeat itself.

This is not, of course, to counsel defeatism or a complacent attitude to the course of sin in history. Such complacency is always a danger in those with an apocalyptic bent, as found in some Pentecostal groups. Some have gone so far as to look forward to a nuclear holocaust, seeing in it the occasion of Jesus' second coming. The victory which we trust will be given by God does not justify the destruction that evil brings, nor does it glory in it. All are called upon to oppose the power of evil in history and if need be to put their lives on the line. Not, of course, by pitting against it an equal evil, but with the of power of truth and self-sacrificing love. The highest place in apocalyptic literature is given to the martyrs, those who have given their lives in the defense of truth, those who "have washed their robes white again in the blood of the Lamb" (cf. Revelation 7:14). Those who have accepted God's grace can never be complacent or defeatist in the face of evil. They have a hope which goes beyond the confines of this world, they know that final victory is theirs but that price they may need to pay is high.

CONCLUSION

In summary, in this chapter I have considered the notion of sin. Just as grace has individual, social and historical dimensions, so too does sin. I have explored the opposition between grace and sin on all these levels. While sin and its consequences are indeed terrible, it is always important to keep in mind that:

> however much sin increased, grace was always the greater; so that as sin's reign brought death, so grace was to rule through saving justice that leads to eternal life through Jesus Christ our Lord (Romans 5:20–21).

This concludes the account of grace. In the next section of this book we shall consider the nature of original sin. As we shall see this does not mean leaving behind what has been said, but it places it into the fuller context of redemption.

CHAPTER NOTES

1. The distinction between mortal and venial sins has declined in popularity in recent times among moral theologians. Many have noted that even in classical expositions, such as that of Thomas Aquinas, the distinction has difficulties. The distinction drawn here depends on the systematic framework which I have used in this study. While it makes sense within this framework, the validity of the framework itself depends on its adequacy for human experience.

2. In recent years there has been an increased interest in apocalyptic thought. Once dismissed as "either phantasy or gnosticism" by Karl Rahner,[2] it has become a significant element in the political theology of Johann Baptist Metz. Metz sees in apocalyptic thought a way out of the false dilemma posed by an immanentist eschatology and a purely futuristic eschatology. The immanentists stress the presence of God's kingdom in the here and now, while the futurists delay the coming of the kingdom to an endlessly expanding temporal horizon. Apocalyptic thought, on the other hand, takes history seriously even to the extent of contemplating the temporal end of history itself. Such an end to history is always a possibility while the history of dis-grace continues. It is the growing power of this history of dis-grace which apocalyptic thought acknowledges, something which many of us, especially those who indirectly benefit from it, would prefer to ignore. The phantasy elements in apocalyptic thought arise from its projection of the historical conflict between grace and dis-grace onto a cosmic setting. Most of those caught up in apocalyptic thought focus on this cosmic setting to the detriment of the historical realities.

3. In discussing the "end of the world", it is important to recognize that for the biblical writers there was no distinction between the end of human history and the end of the cosmos. In their simple three-tiered world the one implied the other. However, in our universe of billions upon billions of galaxies, billions of light years across, it is important to distinguish between the two. Human history could come to a swift and tragic end while the rest of the universe went on regardless. When considering the

biblical theme of the end of the world we have to decide what it is we mean, the end of human history or the end of the cosmos. My guess is that what we should mean is the end of human history. Such an end does not come about because of some extrinsic intervention by God. Rather it comes about as a result of powerful forces operating in human history, powerful but opposed forces of grace and sin.

---

1 In his study of the psychology of evil, *People of the Lie*, Scott Peck argues that evil should become a recognized psychiatric category, cf. pp.254ff.

2 *See* his article, "The Hermeneutics of Eschatological Assertions", in *Theological Investigations*, Vol.4, esp. p.337. Rahner states "the apocalyptic suggestion is either phantasy or gnosticism". Z. Hayes notes however that Rahner later modifies his position on apocalyptic, cf. *Visions of a Future*, Michael Glazier, Wilmington, 1989, pp.35ff.

PART B

Original Sin

CHAPTER NINE

THE CATECHISM APPROACH

In the first section of this book I presented an analysis of the human experience of grace and its consequences in the personal, social and historical spheres. We can now begin our discussion on the nature and reality of original sin. The two fit together well, for, as we shall see, grace comes to us precisely as a solution to the problem of original sin. They are intimately related as the dis-ease and the cure of the human condition. They are the two poles between which our concrete human existence oscillates. Having considered the one, we are now in a position to examine the other.

We are all aware, perhaps painfully aware, of the difficulties that this doctrine has in our modern setting, some of which I mentioned in Chapter 1. Few of the dogmatic traditions of the Church have been the subject of so much modern incomprehension as that of original sin. This incomprehension is not helped by fundamentalists of various persuasions who demand a near literal reading of the Genesis texts in order to defend the doctrine. Most are led to the conclusion that to reject a literalist reading of Genesis is to reject the notion of original sin. Since such a literal reading is contrary to the findings of modern science, then the doctrine of original sin must just be nonsense.

Now, as will become clear in the following chapters, it is not my belief that the doctrine of original sin is nonsense. In fact, it will become clear that I think it is one of the most basic of all Christian doctrines. However, at the same time I dissociate myself completely from those who would tie original sin to a literal reading of Genesis. While the mythological literary form of Genesis, particularly Genesis 3, can tell us much about the nature of original sin, it does not and was never meant to give us a literal account of "how things were". The task of any modern account of original sin is to achieve as much independence as possible from such fundamentalist readings, while preserving the depth and significance of the doctrine itself. To do this it will be necessary to use a variety of hermeneutical approaches.

A TRADITIONAL PRESENTATION

As a starting point it may be worthwhile considering what has been the fairly traditional presentation of the doctrine of original sin. Such a presentation is not concerned with the theological subtleties which were present in the tradition but with the way in which the doctrine was popularly perceived, its catechetical treatment and popular presentation in preaching. This may help us clarify what precisely are the difficulties which we experience when discussing original sin.

Does our belief in original sin derive from Genesis 3?

For most people the classical locus for the doctrine of original sin is Chapter 3 of the Book of Genesis. In Genesis 3 we find the account of Adam and Eve in a Garden, tempted by a snake to eat of the forbidden fruit of the Tree of the Knowledge of Good and Evil. Eve, and then Adam eat of the fruit and are subsequently expelled from the Garden for their disobedience. This sin is the first and original sin which is then transmitted to all their descendants.

For most people, their belief in the doctrine of original sin is tied in with a literal reading of these events. In 1909, the Pontifical Biblical Commission, established by Pope Leo XIII, declared that the literal and historical meaning of these texts could not be called into doubt (cf. DS 3514). While this ruling of the Biblical Commission was lifted with the issuing of the encyclical, *Divino Afflante Spiritu* (1943), which gave scripture scholars greater freedom in their research, further support for such a literal reading was given as late as 1950 by Pius XII in his encyclical, *Humani Generis*. However, most modern scripture scholars would now argue that a literal and historical reading of the text is a violation of the intention of the author, made possible only by a serious misreading of the text's literary form. Such a misreading was encouraged more by dogmatic concerns than by scriptural evidence.

This challenge to a literal, historical reading of Genesis 3 should not be seen as undermining the doctrine of original sin. In the first place Genesis 3 is not sufficient to establish it. Genesis 3 is also part of the Jewish scriptures but Jewish theology has no doctrine of original sin. In fact Jewish theology finds the doctrine quite anathema. How can the sin of one person affect another so powerfully, it argues? Original sin is a *Christian* doctrine and so requires more support than an Old Testament text.

Secondly, this re-evaluation of the significance of Genesis 3 has returned attention to the more important scriptural text of Romans 5:12–22. As we shall see this text from Romans has played, and continues to play, a more significant role in understanding the doctrine of original sin than Genesis 3. This is not to say that Genesis 3 is of no importance. It will remain significant but in a more secondary status.

Does the Church teach the existence of a historical figure, Adam?

Tied in with the literal reading of Genesis, but still independent of it, is the position that all the human race derives from a single set of first parents, Adam and Eve. This position is known as *monogenism* and stands in opposition to *polygenism* which would see the human race as descending from a number of first human beings. Monogenism is independent of a literal reading of Genesis since some would hold that even if we reject such a reading, the doctrine of original sin would still require us to believe in an original set of first parents, Adam and Eve. Though, of course, one could ask whether such a position would ever have developed without Genesis!

The theological argument takes its stand on the metaphysical and biological unity of the human race. If there is not such a unity then how can we be sure that all are affected by original sin? If some are not so affected then Jesus did not die to save us *all*! Indeed I once had a student, a native of the South Pacific islands, who told me that, in the folklore of his people, they were not descended from Adam and were thus free from original sin.

Dogmatic support for monogenism can be found in the previously mentioned encyclical, *Humani Generis*. There it was stated that:

> Christians cannot lend their support to a theory which involves the existence, after Adam's time, of some earthly race of men, truly so called, who were not descended ultimately from him,

> or else supposes that Adam was the name given to some group of our primordial ancestors. *It does not appear how such views can be reconciled with the doctrine of original sin* ... (DS 3987) [emphasis added].

It is clear from this that the concern for monogenism is intimately linked with preserving the doctrine of original sin. It is also important to note the qualifying phrase, "It does not appear how ...". What does not appear possible at one time may appear possible at another. Indeed it has been argued by Walter Principe that this qualification was added on the advice of Cardinal Bea to soften Pius XII's original intention to condemn polygenism absolutely.[1]

On the other hand there are many serious objections which can be raised against monogenism. In the first place the question of the biological origins of the human race seem more like a scientific question than a theological one. It is not clear that monogenism is compatible with modern theories of evolution. If the question of the biological origins of the human race is indeed an empirical, scientific question, then there are grave dangers in trying to settle it by dogmatic means. Such methods were tried with Galileo, much to the discredit of the Church.

Secondly, a related scientific concern raises the question of the size of the gene pool for the human race. A single set of original parents does not seem to provide for sufficient genetic diversity to sustain a viable human species. We are all familiar with the fact that too much inbreeding leads to serious genetic weakness developing in a species, even within a few generations. Given that such serious genetic weaknesses are not commonly present in the human race, monogenism does not seem at all likely.

Thirdly, monogenism raises some obvious moral dilemmas. If there were in fact only one pair of first parents, then the early generations of humanity can only have come about through multiple acts of incest or through sexual relations with creatures less than human. Both these alternatives would seem to be morally unacceptable. The Bible solves this problem by simply having a suitable wife for Adam's son, Cain, appear out of nowhere (cf. Genesis 4:17).

Monogenism thus has its problems. Any modern account of the doctrine of original sin would probably want to avoid taking monogenism on board, or to at least be independent of it. Indeed most modern theologies do not make monogenism integral to their account.[2] Finally, while the teaching of the Church has always presupposed monogenism, monogenism itself has never been the object of a definitive Church teaching.[3]

If Adam had not sinned, would he have lived forever, given that death is a punishment for original sin?

The notion that Adam's condition was significantly different from our own developed out of reflections on Genesis and was adopted as part of the theological and dogmatic tradition. The Council of Carthage (418 AD) condemned the position that Adam would have died if he had not sinned (DS 222). Theology spoke of Adam's supernatural elevation and his preternatural gifts. The most significant of these was the gift of integrity by which the desires of the soul were so ordered that they obeyed the commands of reason (Provincial Council of Cologne, 1860). Included as well was the gift of immortality. This derived from the Genesis discussion of the Tree of Life which Adam is denied the possibility of eating. The Council of Trent (1546) explicitly affirms that Adam lost his immortality because of his sin (DS 1511).

Again, this notion is hard to reconcile with contemporary reason. The theory of evolution would see the early condition of the human race as far different from the exalted state presented in this theological tradition. To modern science the first humans were primitive beings living in very primitive conditions. There is certainly no biological evidence to suggest that the first humans could have lived forever. Though of course one could argue that such evidence would have been lost because of the fall!

More seriously, the notion of such an immortality would seem to separate us biologically from the rest of creation. The cycle of birth and death is present in the whole of biological nature. Death is not a punishment for dogs and cats, so why should it be seen as such for Adam? All of the rest of biological creation experiences the pain of growing old, of life coming to its end. Moreover a life in which no-one ever died would also have serious difficulties, not least being the overcrowding of the planet.

Recently theology has moved away from the notion that if Adam had not sinned he would not have died. Rahner, in his work on the theology of death, has helped us understand that what sin brings is not death but a new meaning to death. This new meaning to death changes the reality of death so that death takes on qualities not present prior to sin.[4] Without sin death is a gracious return to the Father. With sin death becomes ambiguous. Is God really a God of life or is God simply the Angel of Death in disguise? Does death lead to God or to punishment? Death becomes something to fear, to repress. This is generally how the change which sin brings about is understood.

From an anthropological point of view there is also something of the "myth of the golden era" in this understanding of the "pre-lapsian" Adam. Many cultures have developed myths which speak of how things were better "in the beginning". I shall give more serious attention to this mythological element later.

Does God punish all people because of something that Adam did?

The effects of Adam's sin (interestingly, it is nearly always spoken of as Adam's sin, not Eve's) are not restricted to Adam alone, but they flow on to the whole human race. Thus, not only does Adam lose his original integrity and immortality, but all of us are punished similarly (cf. Second Council of Orange, DS 372, Council of Trent, DS 1512). All of us are punished for something which Adam did.

Scriptural support for this position was found in Romans 5:12. This was taken as saying:

> Wherefore as by one man sin entered into the world, and by sin death; so also death passed upon all men, in whom all have sinned.[5]

This was seen as implying that in Adam all men have sinned since all were somehow contained in him. Certainly scripture is not unfamiliar with such arguments, that future generations are contained "in the loins" of their ancestor and are affected by his actions. Indeed the Old Testament speaks of God's punishments being meted out generation after generation for the father's sins.

However, there are other strands in the Old Testament, particularly in the post-exilic prophets like Jeremiah and Ezekiel which stress individual, rather than corporate, responsibility and punishment. Jeremiah can proclaim:

> In those days people will no longer say: 'The fathers have eaten unripe grapes; the children's teeth are set on edge'. But each will die for his own guilt. Everyone who eats unripe grapes is to have his own teeth set on edge (Jeremiah 31:29–30, see also Ezekiel 18:2ff.).

There is something about the punishment of a person for someone else's sin which strikes us as particularly unjust. The doctrine of original sin seems to be saying that we have bought into a fixed game, with the rules stacked against us by God. How can God be just in punishing us for Adam's sin?

As a counterbalance, however, we are all too well aware that the sins of the father (and mother!) *do* have serious ramifications for subsequent generations, that, in fact, many can suffer for one person's sins. This is particularly evident in cases of child abuse where, unless something occurs to break the cycle of violence, abused children can become abusing parents.

Do all people share in Adam's guilt from the moment of birth?

This solidarity with Adam's sinfulness is not seen as something which we grow into, something which we pick up as we mature. No, it is something which affects us from our earliest moments. Augustine saw it as "transmitted" in the very act of sexual procreation. The Council of Trent condemned those who would deny the need for baptism for those "newly from their mother's womb" (DS 1514). Indeed such baptism is truly for the remission of sin, in their case original sin.

Such a position seems incongruent with a culture that so frequently talks about the "innocence of the newborn child". Those of us who have been parents know the innocent and open trust with which children enter the world. We also know how often we, as parents, betray that innocence and trust. For many, this perfect innocence of the child seems totally self-evident. How can we talk about the newborn being born guilty of original sin? Surely all God's creation is good. The doctrine of original sin seems to imply that something is wrong with God's most beautiful work, the newborn child.

Again we can get the sense that the game is rigged, that God is out to get us from the outset. God, it seems, has determined, by some arbitrary and unintelligible decree, that we are all guilty from birth. We are behind the eight-ball, precisely where God wants us and there is nothing any of us can do about it!

Such an impression, often conveyed by the way in which the doctrine of original sin is presented, must be wrong. There is nothing arbitrary or unintelligible about the way God acts. Any account of original sin must not end up being some subtle way of blaming God for our situation.

Does the Church teach the existence of a historical figure, Adam?

This is the crunch point. What happens to those not freed from this condition called original sin? Augustine did not shrink from the painful conclusion concerning unbaptized babies—they go to hell:

> This is the Catholic view: a view that can show a just God in so many pains and in such agonies of tiny babies.[6]

Further, the Council of Florence (1438–45) declared that:

> The souls of those who die in original sin as well as those who die in actual mortal sin go immediately to hell, but their punishment is very different (DS 693).

This "very different" punishment was later softened by theology to refer to limbo, the "outermost circle" of hell, in which those so contained enjoyed a "natural" bliss but were denied the vision of God.

Though such a position is no longer commonly accepted in theology,[7] it remains perhaps the most potent element in the popular imagination concerning original sin and its links with baptism. I have even heard an anxious mother ring up talk-back radio to complain about some priest who refused to immediately baptize her child. Her fear was that, without baptism, her child would go to hell if it died. This near superstitious stance which threatens to reduce baptism to some form of magic rite has had a long running in popular piety and has often been played upon by less scrupulous preachers.

Even within a traditional theology, the need for sacramental baptism was broadened to "baptism by blood" (martyrdom for the faith prior to baptism by water) or "baptism of desire". More recently the Church has been quite willing to speak of salvation being available to all, without any explicit reference to baptism at all. Hence at Vatican II the Church spoke of non-Christians who:

> . . . moved by grace, try in their actions to do [God's] will as they know it through the dictates of their conscience—these too may achieve eternal salvation (Lumen Gentium, para.16).

Perhaps we have more trust in God's boundless mercy than some of our predecessors. However the link between baptism and original sin does and must have some meaning. A proper theology of original sin must be able to say something intelligent about the connection.

At this stage we could present a "catechism" summary of the doctrine of original sin in the following terms:

> * the first man and woman were created in a state of happiness and integrity, free from suffering and death. Nonetheless they were tempted and sinned with the result that they were expelled from this state.
>
> * as a result of Adam's sin human nature was permanently damaged. This damage was passed on to all Adam's descendants. This damage means all are born guilty and inclined to sin. Thus, all sin derives from Adam's sin and all people are born under God's anger.

* because of his mercy, God promised Adam and Eve a redeemer (a classical misreading of Genesis 3:15[8]) and eventually sends his Son, Jesus, to save us and free us from sin through his sacrifice on the cross. Jesus himself is free from original sin and hence is a perfect sacrifice which turns away the anger of God.

* Jesus gives us the Church and especially baptism as a means of freeing people from original sin. Through baptism, people are freed from the guilt of original sin, though they still suffer from its consequences, e.g. the loss of integrity, mortality.

From this catechism summary it is clear that original sin is not simply a fringe doctrine, something which one could easily discard. Indeed it plays a central role in our whole understanding (or at least our imaging) of the process of salvation. It is like a key piece without which the rest of the puzzle falls apart. If we were to do away with the doctrine of original sin, then we would have to enter into a massive reconstruction of the whole of Christian theology. In particular, we would have to rethink the meaning of Jesus' death on the cross. It is not clear that at the end of such a reconstruction we would have anything even remotely recognizable to Christianity as it has traditionally been understood.

CONCLUSION

Such a position does not mean that there are no difficulties with the doctrine. The key question that needs to be asked is: how much of our difficulty lies in the formulation of the doctrine and how much with the claimed reality which the doctrine seeks to mediate? Pope John XXIII forcefully reminded us of the distinction between the doctrine and the way in which it is formulated. It would be a naive mistake to reject the doctrine because of such difficulties. On the other hand such difficulties need to be acknowledged and hopefully dealt with. At this stage I shall present a summary of such difficulties, some of which have been mentioned already above.

1. Monogenism or polygenism: were there really first parents?

2. If not how does everyone get "infected"? How and why does Adam's sin get "transmitted"—is it some type of metaphysical sexually transmitted disease?

3. In evolutionary terms the original state of happiness of Adam and Eve does not seem to make sense. What are we to make of the "myth of a golden era"?

4. Is original sin really just? Why do we need forgiveness for something we have not done, or is it just an arbitrary decision of God to make us all guilty from birth?

5. What has baptism got to do with original sin? Does the linking of baptism and original sin reduce baptism to a magical rite?

6. Most importantly, how does Jesus save us from original sin? And why are he and Mary free from original sin? If God could do it for them, why did he not do it for all of us and save a lot of mucking about?

How can we untangle such an unhappy theological mess? We must first go to the historical orgins of the theology. So where are the origins? In the next chapter I shall consider the original and creative contribution of Augustine.

CHAPTER NOTES

At a popular level no-one has done more to bring the debate about original sin to a head than Matthew Fox in his book, *Original Blessing*. By contrasting original sin with the notion of original blessing, Fox has called into question the Church's long-standing tradition on original sin and the theology of redemption which it underpins. Fox has stressed the underlying goodness of creation as more primary and original than any sin. He opposes this original blessing to the negativity and destructive tendencies which he sees as present in the doctrines of original sin and redemption.

While Fox's work has acted as a corrective to misuses of what has happened, it stands, in its own turn, in need of further correction. I shall make my own criticisms of the way in which the doctrines of original sin and redemption have operated in the life of the Church, but to attempt to do away with them altogether fails, in my estimation, to take seriously the problem of evil. Unless evil is taken seriously it cannot be overcome. Whatever their difficulties, the classical doctrines of original sin and redemption did seek to take evil seriously.

1 *See* his article, "When 'Authentic' Teachings Change", *The Ecumenist*, July–August, 1987, p.71.

2 A significant shift in the theological community came about when Karl Rahner publicly moved from his previous position of support for monogenism, cf. *TNDT*, p.444.

3 The conservative Church dogmatist, Ludwig Ott, does not consider monogenism as *de fide*, cf. his *Fundamentals of Catholic Dogma*, Tan Books, Rockford, 1974, p.96.

4 Cf. *TNDT*, p.273, entry on Death.

5 I shall deal in more detail with this controverted text in Chap.10. *See also* the appendix by John Chryssavgis.

6 Cited in Peter Brown's *Augustine of Hippo*, Faber, 1967, p.397.

7 Cf. *TNDT*, p.586, entry on Limbo.

8 The text has variously been read as saying "it/he/she will bruise your head, and you will strike its heel" depending upon whether read from the Hebrew, Greek or Latin text. The Greek "he" was taken to refer to Jesus and the Latin "she" to Mary. The original Hebrew text "it" simply refers to humanity in general, cf. the footnote for this verse in *TNJB*.

CHAPTER TEN

DID AUGUSTINE GET IT WRONG?

In the previous chapter I considered some of the difficulties which must be faced in connection with the doctrine of original sin. In order to help untangle some of these we can now turn our attention to its origins. Historically the doctrine has its origins in the controversy between Augustine and Pelagius. It was from this debate that Augustine gained his title as "Doctor of Grace". Note that this debate took place in the late fourth, and early fifth century. Prior to this time there was no strictly formulated doctrine of original sin. The early Greek Fathers had quite a different reading of the biblical texts and overall had a more optimistic view of the human condition which would not have meshed well with the Augustinian position. In many ways the doctrine of original sin is a creation of Augustine's own theology.

There are many difficulties associated with going over any debate in the early Church. Too often all we have of a particular viewpoint are the criticisms made of it by its opponents. History is always written by the victors! Thus it is difficult to know at this distance what it was that Pelagius taught. Most of what we know of his thought comes from the pen of Augustine and could well be exaggerated. Like so many "heretics" in the early Church, Pelagius has become a "type" rather than a real person. It is not my intention, nor am I equipped, to enter into detailed debates about the historical Pelagius. For the purposes of this study he shall remain, sadly, a type.

PELAGIUS AND AUGUSTINE

Pelagius was drawn into controversy with Augustine by his own reaction to Augustine's *Confessions*. In particular he was annoyed by the phrase "command what You wish, but give what You command" (*Confessions*, Book 10).[1] To Pelagius, this phrase undermined human morality since it seemed to state that the human person could not fulfill God's commands without divine help. If this were the case how could we be held responsible for our sins? And if we could not be held responsible for our sins, then all sorts of immoral behavior could be justified.

In response Pelagius developed his own theology of grace and sin. His concern was primarily moral, even moralistic. For Pelagius the Christian was a brave individual who stood up against the immorality of the world, putting in a total commitment to moral righteousness. It was this commitment that he saw Augustine as undermining. Pelagius believed in the perfectibility of human nature through such commitment. He believed that human nature was basically good and that it had complete freedom to do good. Broadly speaking he had an optimistic view of human nature, not unlike the Greek Fathers before him. This is not to say that he did not recognize sin. There was indeed sin, but it arose out of an imitation of other people's sin. We sin because we see others sin and get away with it. Jesus then saves us by providing a perfect example of sinlessness. If we want to be saved, we must imitate Jesus rather than Adam!

Augustine's position, in response to Pelagius, was more profound, more subtle. Augustine was not unconcerned with morality, but his concern was coupled with a profound sense of human weakness, perhaps out of his own personal experience. For Augustine, the Christian is forgiven, not perfect; the Church is not an army but more a hospital where we are nurtured back to spiritual health. In opposition to the perfectibility of human nature by its own efforts Augustine argued for our total dependence on God's grace. This was necessary because, while human nature had been created good, it had been corrupted by Adam's sin and was no longer capable of doing good — *non posse non peccare*. This pessimistic view saw sin not as a superficial imitation but as deeply personal, affecting the whole person *at depth*. Augustine had a much more subtle appreciation of the real limitations of human freedom than Pelagius.

Such dialectically opposed positions could not easily co-exist. Eventually Augustine sought the judgment of the Church in order to settle the matter. Before I consider the outcome of this, I

PELAGIUS (and followers) *vs*	**AUGUSTINE**
* perfectibility of nature	* necessity of grace
* human nature basically good	* nature basically corrupt
* optimistic	* pessimistic
* moralistic	* nurturing
* sin because of imitation	* sin deeply "personal"

shall look at some key elements in Augustine's argument, beginning with infant baptism.

INFANT BAPTISM

The Pelagians saw baptism as a brave step taken by adults, signifying their conversion to Christianity. Such a conversion involved a renunciation of their former sinful existence and a puritanical stance towards the world. It was often done in a situation which was seen as hostile to Christian morality and so was a public stand against lax "pagan" lifestyles which were often maintained by "nominal" Christians. For the Pelagians the Christian was a child of God in the sense of the Roman child who has attained adulthood and come into his/her inheritance. In this view infant baptism simply did not make sense. The infant had not undergone conversion, nor had it committed any sins which needed forgiveness.

On the other hand there had been a long-standing tradition of supporting infant baptism in the African Church, to which Augustine belonged. Among the supports was a popular miracle story of a child dying unbaptized, and being restored to life briefly so that it could be baptized and so avoid the sufferings of hell.[2] Such ecclesiastical support for infant baptism, it must be remembered, ran counter to the popular practice at that time of delaying baptism for as long as possible, even until one's death bed. Augustine relates in the *Confessions* how he was nearly baptized when a childhood sickness brought him close to death. He recovered and his baptism was put off till a later date!

In Augustine's view baptism was seen as a necessary, unique and unrepeatable event. This was the battle that Augustine had already fought and won with the Donatist schism, which had sought to set up a Church of the perfect. The axiom, *extra ecclesiam nulla salus* (no salvation outside the Church), had its origins in African ecclesiastical battles whose tradition Augustine had inherited. There was no salvation outside the Church and baptism was the only way into the Church, even for infants. In fact in many ways one could argue that baptism had taken on the aspects of a magical rite!

Augustine uses his understanding of infant baptism as a starting point for his reflections on original sin. The starting point is *orthopraxis*, the actual practice of his own African Church. From this practice he argues for the existence of an inherited sin of Adam. His argument, which goes as follows, has great logical simplicity:

* infants are baptized, therefore there must be a reason!

* following St Paul, baptism is for the remission of sins. Infants have no personal sin. Therefore they must be suffering from a different type of sin.

* hence they suffer from the sin of Adam, not a personal sin, but an inherited sin, original sin.

Thus Augustine provides a theological justification for the Church's practice of baptizing infants.

THE PROBLEM OF SUFFERING

The second element that Augustine brings to his theology of original sin is a profound reflection on the problem of human suffering and evil. Here Augustine had to steer a course between two extremes. The Pelagian position failed, in Augustine's estimate, to take the problem of suffering and evil with sufficient seriousness. Evil was merely a product of choice, tempted through a desire to imitate. On the other hand, there was the position of the Manichean sect with which Augustine had flirted in his youth. The Manicheans saw evil as substantial, a substance in its own right. Augustine eventually rejected this dualism because he felt it made good powerless in the face of evil. Between these two extremes of Pelagian optimism and Manichean pessimism, Augustine sought to develop his own understanding of suffering and evil.

Here Augustine's starting point is a reflection on human experience. He sees all of humankind living a life full of suffering through sickness, war, famine, death and so on. While many of us may not agree with such a proposition, that may be more a product of our own insulation from much of human suffering, made possible by the affluence of the First World. Living conditions in Augustine's day were more what we would associate with the Third World. Nothing illustrates this more clearly than Augustine's own account, in *City of God* (Book 22, Chap.8), of someone preparing to undergo surgery for a cancer of the bowel for a second time, without anesthetic.

Now clearly God is good and just. Surely a good and just God would not allow such a situation *unless we deserved it*. His conclusion was that all humankind lived under God's anger. We do in fact deserve all our human suffering as a result of our inherited sin from Adam. Indeed we often hear a spontaneous affirmation of Augustine's argument when people say "Why did the sickness happen to me? I don't deserve it!" Such a linking of suffering and punishment is quite common. Augustine is tapping into this spontaneous feeling and giving it voice.

In this way Augustine sought to avoid the Manichean position which saw suffering and evil resulting from an evil creative power in opposition to God. Rather all our suffering is a punishment for our original fall, all evil the result of an original human sin. This evil is not a substance in its own right but results from the choice of a lesser good when a higher good is available. Evil is simply a lack of a good which should have been.

This argument, while superficially appealing and quite logical, has lost some of its strength in recent times. It presumes a creation which is set up as perfect, in which there is no suffering, no evil. Any change from this initial state must be for the worse since the original condition is perfect. Now while such a position was accepted in the past, modern theories of evolution have thrown out the idea that the world was originally set up in a perfect static state. Rather we see the world as developing to higher and higher perfections, through a process of complexification of matter. On such a view suffering is not a punishment but the outcome of a world still in a dynamic, developing process of becoming. Finite being will always suffer as it comes up against its limits and seeks to overcome them.

CONCUPISCENCE

The third element that Augustine adds to his understanding of original sin is the notion of *concupiscence*. Concupiscence refers to the "lower" human passions, especially the sexual passions. For Augustine, such passions are intrinsically disordered since they are out of the control of the reasoning mind. Such a disordering cannot have been part of God's original creation which was perfect, so it can only have come about as the result of some evil. We all suffer from the effects of concupiscence because of Adam's sin. What is often not clear in Augustine's writings is whether concupiscence is the effect of original sin or is, in fact, original sin itself. This confusion will be reflected again in the Reformation debates on justification. The identification leads to problems because it becomes difficult to see how baptism frees us from original sin since concupiscence clearly remains. On the other hand, the Reformer's identification of concupiscence with sin led them to assert the position of *simul justus et peccator*, at once just and sinner.

Augustine generally identified concupiscence with sexual drive or libido. He saw human sexuality as dominated by passion, again speaking out of his own experience as related in *Confessions*. The sex organs are *pudenda*, "organs of shame". This is how Augustine reads the account of the fig leaves in the Garden of Eden (Genesis 3:7), needed to cover up the shame of disordered sexual desire. Here Augustine is tapping into strongly held Stoic beliefs, popular in his own culture. These beliefs saw all expressions of sexual desire as abhorrent, especially in women. Augustine was even not above exploiting feelings of shame over "wet dreams", again seen as a sign of concupiscence.[3]

However, there are occasions when the category of concupiscence is expanded to include all human rebellion against God, and not simply carnal passion. Hence Augustine can see avarice, hatred, greed, pride and so on, as signs of concupiscence. All human desires are now disordered, no longer subject to the control of reason. It is not even as if there is one single evil force within the person. Even our disordered desires compete among themselves for dominance, so that a person can be drawn simultaneously along many different avenues to sin. This is no simplistic account of a person torn between good and evil. Augustine is in touch with the potential chaos of human desires, each with a life of its own, running out of control. Evocatively he writes:

> Who can embrace wholeheartedly what gives him no delight? But who can determine for himself that what will delight him should come his way, and when it comes, that it should, in fact delight him?[4]

There is something unpredictable yet powerfully determining about our desires. Who can say that some deep and powerful desire will not spring up from within us and change our life—like the business executive who goes through a mid-life crisis, leaves his wife and family and runs off with a woman half his age? Who can say that there are not ancient childhood memories lurking within and waiting to bring forth pain and confusion into our present life?[5] It is this type of unpredictability, this sense of being "out of control", which indicated to Augustine the sinful reality of concupiscence.

The linking of concupiscence with disordered sexual desire gave Augustine an easy "explanation" as to how original sin gets transmitted. Since we are all conceived out of the concupiscence of our parents, we are all born with the stain of sin already upon us. We are literally born out of sin! Hence, for Augustine there is a necessity to Jesus' virginal conception. It is only through a virginal conception that Jesus can be free from original sin. (Such a position may, of course, be incompatible with the Catholic doctrine of Mary's own Immaculate Conception.) In fact, Augustine saw all sexual acts as sinful, though allowed in marriage as a lesser evil. Many have seen this negative attitude that Augustine had towards sexuality as a hangover from his Manichean past. Without doubt it has been a profoundly negative influence on Christian understanding of sexuality and sexual morality.

Augustine recognized the problems associated with the transmission of original sin. At the time there were two theories concerning the origin of the soul in a new baby. One theory, called creationism (not to be confused with modern, so-called scientific Creationism, which is based on nothing but a fundamentalist reading of the Bible) saw the soul as directly created by God and infused into the new life. The other, called traducianism, saw the soul of the child as formed out of the soul of its father, transmitted through the semen. Creationism created problems for Augustine since, if it is held, God must infuse a soul already stained with original sin. It then seems as if God is responsible for the transmission of original sin![6] On the other hand, while traducianism gives an easy account of the transmission of original sin, its quasi-materialistic understanding of the soul offended Augustine's Platonic spirituality.

Augustine saw concupiscence as a permanent disordering of human nature. As a result we are all born under God's anger, born in guilt. Through our own efforts we cannot become pleasing to God. All this fits in well with Augustine's pessimistic view of humankind. Without grace we are not able not to sin—*non posse non peccare*. Our freedom is in bondage to sin. While we are truly free to choose various courses of action, our freedom is only exercised in determining which sin we will commit. This is not to say that we are without hope. There is grace. Grace comes as God's free gift, to free us from our slavery to sin. However, it is only God's grace, which is primarily available through the sacraments of the one true Church, which can save us. Nothing else will suffice. Such grace brings about an inner transformation, healing the disorder of our passions and freeing us to do what is pleasing to God.

It would be a misreading of Augustine's understanding on concupiscence if one were to conclude that desires are to be repressed. Many, I fear, have drawn such a conclusion with detrimental effects for their spiritualities. Indeed such a repression is detrimental to our self-esteem since our spontaneous desires are part of our human nature. Repression of desire then becomes a form of self-hatred. The problem for Augustine is not desire but the disordering of desire. The same Augustine who speaks about concupiscence can also speak about our heart's desire for God, our great longing, the restlessness of our hearts waiting to rest in God. The solution is not to get rid of desire but to make sure you have the right desires, properly ordered. Moreover, Augustine is saying that the solution to disordered desires cannot come about by purely human means (e.g. putting in a greater effort, noses to the grindstone, pulling up our socks, more self-discipline) as Pelagius held. It can only come about as a gift from God, as grace.

These three observations, on infant baptism, the origin of suffering and the nature of concupiscence, are not the whole argument which Augustine brings to bear on the question of original sin. Another key piece of the argument is his analysis of Romans 5:12. Rather than deal with that here, I shall consider it in the next chapter dealing with the scriptural data on original sin.

THE CHURCH SPEAKS ON PELAGIANISM

In fact Augustine was able to turn the tide of ecclesiastical authority against Pelagius, despite an initial inability on the part of various authorities to see what the fuss was about. Pelagius' position was condemned at the Council of Carthage (418 AD). Canon 2 of the Council, which is essentially repeated in Canon 4 of Trent, focuses specifically on the link between original sin and infant baptism. It taught that original sin is "contracted by generation". While the Council condemned Pelagianism it did not fully adopt the Augustinian position. Indeed many of the darker aspects of Augustine's position arose again in the Reformation, with the Reformers pushing Augustine to the limit. At that time the Catholic Church felt the necessity to distance itself from such extremes.

The issues raised by the Augustinian–Pelagian debate emerged again in the battle over semi-Pelagianism, a weakened form of Pelagianism. The semi-Pelagians sought to maintain some form of human contribution by way of preparation for the process of justification. Again this was seen as lessening the total dependence of the person on God's grace for salvation. While the Catholic position has been willing to talk about co-operation, it is always co-operation with grace which God has already given. Semi-Pelagianism sought to speak of a co-operation prior to grace, which prepared the way for grace. This position was condemned at the Council of Orange (529 AD). This Council saw original sin as totally undermining human freedom so that we become slaves to sin. Such slavery can only be released through God's grace, and nothing else.

CONCLUSION

In this chapter we have gone over key elements in Augustine's argument for the existence of original sin. They are infant baptism, the problem of suffering and concupiscence. For Augustine original sin is a reality whose effects are writ large in human history. However it is important to keep in mind that Augustine's doctrine of original sin is only one side of a powerful theological stance. The other side, of course, is grace. One should only ever see the one as a counterpoint to the other. To separate his understanding of original sin from his understanding of grace is to warp the total picture. Unfortunately, this separation has often happened particularly at the level of the popular understanding of original sin. This link between the two is one of the driving forces behind this present book.

CHAPTER NOTES

Augustine has had much bad press in recent time. Some is deserved but most is the result of ignorance. Many of those who condemn him appear not to have even read him. My own appreciation of Augustine and his contribution to Christianity, both positive and negative, is largely the result of reading the excellent study by Peter Brown, *Augustine of Hippo* (Faber, London, 1967). Not only is this a scholarly work, it is a delight to read.

1 Cf. Peter Brown, *Augustine of Hippo*, p.343.
2 Ibid. p.385.

3 Ibid. p.388.
4 Ibid. p.155.
5 The case of Cathy Ann Matthews, already mentioned in Chapter 3, is a good example. She had completely suppressed memories of childhood abuse for most of her adult life until they burst back into consciousness.
6 Aquinas considers this objection and refutes it in *Summa Theologiae* 1a 2ae q83 a1.

CHAPTER ELEVEN

THE SCRIPTURAL WITNESS

In the previous chapter we considered the arguments that Augustine brought to bear in his position on the reality of original sin. There was one argument, however, which I did not pursue—his argument from scripture. As we shall see this argument has had a long and troublesome history and is surprisingly the weakest element of his position. In this chapter I shall also consider just what the scriptures do have to say about original sin. This will allow me to give an initial, heuristic definition of original sin.

AUGUSTINE AND ROMANS 5:12

What then was the scriptural basis of Augustine's position on original sin? While it is clear that Augustine draws heavily on the text of Genesis 3, it is Romans 5:12ff. which provides the key inspiration for his theology. Rarely have the personal limitations of one person had such a profound effect on the development of Catholic theology!

It should be noted that Augustine was largely a self-educated person. While he had a formal schooling, which he hated, it was predominantly the power of his own intellect which led to his attaining his position of pre-eminence amongst his contemporaries, at least in the Western Church. Given the nature of his education, there was one key element which he lacked in what would normally be considered a good education. Augustine could not read Greek well. For all his work with the scriptures, Augustine was dependent on the Latin translations of St Jerome and others and Latin translations of the various Greek Fathers of his own day. When Augustine turned to his Latin translation of Romans 5:12ff. to develop his theology of original sin, he read the following verse:

> Through one man sin entered into the world and through sin death, and thus death has passed into all men, *in quo omnes peccaverunt.*

The problem which faces the person seeking to understand this text is the significance of the "in quo". Following what he took to be a text from St Ambrose (which we now know was not written by Ambrose at all but by an unknown author whom we have labelled Ambrosiaster) Augustine took the "in quo" as a relative conjunction with its antecedent being Adam. Thus Augustine took the text to be saying that ". . . death has passed into all men, *in whom (Adam) all have sinned*". For Augustine this text was the clincher, the key text which "proved" scriptural support for his position on original sin. Here Paul seemed to be saying that all have sinned in Adam's sin; through some mysterious human solidarity, all are caught up in Adam's guilt. We all share in this guilt since we are all in some sense in him, in his loins, so to speak.

Such speculation about descendants being in their ancestors is not unknown in the scriptures. Hence in the Letter to the Hebrews 7:1–19 the author engages in a similar argument with regard to the relationship between the Levitical priesthood and the mysterious figure of Melchizedek in Genesis 14:17ff. The author of Hebrews is trying to solve the problem of how Jesus can be called a priest given that he was not a member of the tribe of Levi, the Jewish priestly caste. He solves it by saying that Jesus is a "priest of the order of Melchizedek". This order of priesthood is higher than that of the Levites since Abraham had offered tithes to Melchizedek. This established Melchizedek's superiority over the Levites since they were contained in the loins of Abraham (7:10). To modern ears such arguments sound quite esoteric, but to ancient ears they carried weight.

Let us now turn to a modern translation of Romans 5:12. If we consider a modern translation of the text we find the following:

> Well then; it was through one man that sin came into the world, and through sin death, and thus death has spread through the whole human race because everyone has sinned (TNJB).

Where is Augustine's "*in quo omnes peccaverunt*"? What has happened to the "in whom all have sinned"?

THE GREEK TEXT OF ROMANS 5:12

Fortunately we are able to turn to the Greek text, something which Augustine was not able to do. If we look at the Greek text we find the following:

> ... so death spread through the whole human race, *eph ho pantes hemarton.*

What is important here is the phrase, *eph ho*. It is this phrase which the Old Latin Bible had translated by *in quo*. In Greek the phrase *eph ho* means "because", or as we might say "in that". The Latin, *in quo*, could be considered a translation of "in that". The problem is that it is ambiguous. Thus Augustine could argue that *in quo* meant "in whom". Such a meaning, however, had never been drawn from the Greek text prior to Augustine. In fact Augustine was working from a misinterpretation of an ambiguous translation.[1] Moreover one can ask whether Augustine is giving the text an importance that Paul never attached to it.

Unfortunately the problem did not stop with Augustine. The same text, in the Latin and read through Augustinian eyes, found its way, as a proof text, into the canons of the Councils of Carthage (418), Orange (529) and Trent (1546). These Councils provide the classical sources for Catholic dogmatic teaching of original sin. Trent in fact goes out of its way to quote the Latin of Romans 5:12 in the face of a renewed Renaissance scholarship which was becoming aware, at last, of the difficulty caused by the Greek and Latin texts.

This serious flaw, both in Augustine's argument and in the dogmatic tradition, should not be underestimated. However, it is not clear that its consequences are fatal. As we saw, Augustine's argument for the reality of original sin rests on more than his exegesis of scripture. We have to allow for the possibility of people coming to a right conclusion even with a faulty argument. The stance of both Augustine and Church dogma may be weakened but they are not necessarily destroyed!

MODERN VIEWS ON THE SCRIPTURAL DATA

Though I have argued for the key place of Romans 5:12ff., it may be more helpful for the reader if I first consider the more familiar material of Genesis 3. For most people this is the place where the doctrine of original sin finds its source.

What does Genesis 3 say?

From a purely literary perspective, the purpose of Genesis 3 is to provide an etiological explanation for the origins of evil and suffering. All cultures are confronted with the problem of trying to explain why there is suffering, why there is evil. In cultures which have not developed a reflective philosophy or theology, for example those of the Old Testament times, such a question will be answered by telling a story—this is how it all happened, this is the beginning of the problem. Typically suffering and evil are seen as the result of some ancient calamity, either a war between the gods or through some human agency. The literary genre of such narratives is myth. In Genesis 3 we do not have an historical narrative relating the events of the first man and woman. We have an etiological myth which seeks to give meaning to a present experience of suffering and evil by reference to a mythical originating event, lost in the long gone past.[2] To speak of it as myth does not mean that it is a lie, or wrong. It simply identifies the literary form used by the author to convey a divinely revealed truth.

Since it contains divinely revealed truth there are key differences between the myth of Genesis 3 and the prevailing myths of the surrounding cultures at the time. One popular myth, the epic Babylonian story of Gilgamesh, saw the origins of suffering in the capricious acts of the gods. It is their evil and conflict which leads both to creation and to human suffering. The myth of Genesis 3 takes quite a different stance. It seeks to locate the origins of evil, not in some cosmic conflict beyond human reach, but "in history", in the concrete actions of human agents. Evil does not come from God or from some evil source. No, it arises from humankind's departure from God's will, from a misuse of human freedom.

Not only does Genesis 3 seek to locate the origins of evil in human history, it seeks to locate them from the very beginning of human existence. There has never been a time without evil and suffering. As soon as there are people there is sin. Though there are elements of the "myth of the golden age" in the biblical account, in that Adam and Eve live in a garden with everything they need, it is a very short age. There is nothing in the account which could justify later theological speculation about the "original integrity" of Adam and his enjoyment of supernatural and preternatural gifts. While there is the presence of the Tree of Life, this is withheld not so much as a punishment but out of a strange fear on God's part that if they do eat of it they will truly become like God, living forever. This is a very primitive piece of anthropomorphic mythology.

The author of Genesis 3 does see this sin of Adam and Eve as having consequences for humankind. This is only natural since the author is precisely trying to explain the origins of suffering and evil. The major consequences are seen in the altered relationships between man and woman and between man and nature. Thus the sin of Adam and Eve introduces disharmony into the social and natural order. In the first place, birth will become a trial for the woman (an etiological explanation for the pains of childbirth). Secondly, woman becomes subservient to man, who will dominate her life (an etiological explanation for the low place of women in society). Thirdly, the man finds his relationship to the land disrupted, only able to produce enough food by plain old hard work (an etiological explanation for the difficulties of an agricultural life). The snake is, of course, also punished by having to eat dust (an etiological explanation for the snake's characteristic of flicking out its tongue).

Further, the author sees the sin of Adam and Eve as the start of a "snowballing" effect of sin in the world. Soon there is murder (the story of Cain and Abel) and later even greater calamities. It culminates in the mindless violence of Lamech (Genesis 4:23–24) who kills a boy for striking him. Indeed Genesis 3–11 is replete with stories which could have been used as etiologies for evil—Adam and Eve, Cain and Abel, Lamech, the Tower of Babel. The placing of all these stories in the one mythic context creates an overall impression of an explosion of evil. It is out of this moral chaos that God steps in to create order, through the creation of the Chosen People, in the call of Abraham (Genesis 12).

It is important to note the following points. In the first place, the terms "original sin" or even "fall" are not used. They are the product of a later theological development. Secondly, while the author is concerned with the "historical" origins of evil, he still gives us no account of how evil is "passed on". It just starts and keeps on going. This is not a theoretical position such as we find in the work of Augustine. It is simply an empirical observation that once evil begins it continues. Thirdly, once we take the account outside its mythological context, it fails to provide any really satisfactory answers. Most importantly, where did the tempting serpent come from? In God's good creation, where does a serpent come which inclines Adam and Eve to do evil? While a later Jewish and Christian mythology sees in the serpent the figure of the Satan (cf. Wisdom 2:24), there is no indication that this is the intention of the author of Genesis.

Further, if we adopt the classical theological position which sees Adam and Eve as being in a state of integrity, where the will is subordinated to God and the passions to the will, then there are increased problems. If they enjoyed such an integrity, how could they have sinned, how could they have been tempted?

What does Romans 5:12ff. say?

A reading of an accurate translation of Romans 5:12ff. reveals a point of view not dissimilar to that of Genesis 3. Paul acknowledges the sin of Adam as the first in an ongoing series of sins. With Adam's sin, death enters the world and passes onto all people since all, in fact, have sinned. As with Genesis 3 we have an empirical observation that sin has become the universal norm of human existence, touching each and every one of us. With sin comes a new meaning to death, death as alienation from God. Again as with Genesis 3, Paul posits no mechanism for the transmission of Adam's sin or guilt. There is no theory here of original sin as we find in Augustine but an affirmation of the universality of actual sin and the need in all for salvation.

However, to focus solely on the verse Romans 5:12 in isolation from the rest of the context, is to miss the point of what Paul is saying. Paul is not so much concerned with Adam, but with Jesus. Hence special note should be made of the *Christological* context of Paul's discussion. Paul has carefully constructed an opposition between the one man, Adam, and the one who was to come, Jesus, the Christ.[3] Whatever Paul's conception of the relationship between Adam's sin and human sinfulness, clearly Paul sees Jesus Christ as having saved us from it. Jesus is the source of an overpowering grace which reverses whatever was brought about in Adam:

> If death came to many through the offence of one man, *how much greater an effect the grace of God has had*, coming to so many and so plentifully as a free gift through the one man Jesus Christ! Again *there is no comparison between the gift and the offence of one man*. One single offence brought condemnation, but *now, after many offences, have come the free gift and so acquittal* (Romans 5:15–17) [emphasis added].

This is the most important thing Paul has to say about original sin.

A DEFINITION OF ORIGINAL SIN

On the basis of the discussion above, we can come to a first positive statement about the nature of original sin:

Original sin is what Jesus saves us from[4]

As it stands, such a statement is merely a heuristic device.[5] It names the unknown, let "x" be the unknown, let original sin be what Jesus saves us from. It puts the unknown, original sin, into relationship with another term, salvation in and through Jesus. As yet we may not know much about this salvation, but the definition tells that the more we know about the one, the more we will know about the other. To some it might seem as if this is an empty, hollow definition and in some ways it is. It still requires insights to fill in each term, in a self-correcting spiral of learning. However, the key is that we get our terms in the correct relationship initially.

There are a number of things which suggest that this definition does place the terms in their right relationship. In the first place, as I have already noted, it is the basic outlook of Paul set out in the quotation from Romans. Whatever Adam did Jesus has saved us from it. It also helps us understand a text which was discussed in the first part of this book, I Timothy 2:4, "God wants all people to be saved". The universality of the offer of salvation is intelligible only in the light of the universality of original sin. What does God's redeeming work in Jesus save us from? Original sin!

Secondly, we have already seen this definition in operation in the debate between Pelagius and Augustine. Pelagius, in as much as he talked about original sin saw it in terms of imitation: we all sin because we imitate Adam. The solution is provided to us by the perfect example of sinlessness given to us by Jesus. Augustine knew from his own experience that the example of Jesus was not enough to bring salvation. Inasmuch as Jesus' good example is not enough to save us, original sin is more than simply imitation. Salvation requires more than someone to imitate, it requires an inner change, a transforming grace.

Thirdly, it is able to account for the fact that the doctrine of original sin is a specifically Christian doctrine. As I have already noted, the Jewish scripture has the account of Adam and Eve sinning in Genesis 3 but they have no theological doctrine of original sin. Indeed, both Jews and Moslems reject the notions of original sin and of salvation through Jesus. Both argue, in essence, that the deeds of another cannot affect me with regards to my salvation. The sin of Adam cannot condemn me, the cross of Jesus cannot save me.

Finally, the following point needs to be made. Many would say that belief in original sin is in a crisis. Many find it unintelligible and some have even argued against it. I would agree that belief in the doctrine is in crisis. But the crisis cannot be solved by recourse to dogmatic authority. The crisis has its roots in experience. Where the Christian community is no longer fully mediating the experience of salvation that Jesus brings, then the doctrine of original sin will appear less and less meaningful. Where a real experience of salvation is present, then there will be no crisis.

The strength of the definition is that, once adopted, it makes it impossible to speak about original sin on its own. While it is true that the Church should and must preach the doctrine of original sin, it does so in the context of the good news that Jesus saves us from it. The preaching of original sin on its own, without relation to salvation, is a serious distortion. Just how serious we shall explore later. It is often said that Church dogmas are about mysteries, and this is true. However, there is a distinction that needs to be made. The mystery of the salvation which Jesus brings is too much for us to fully comprehend, a mystery hidden in the fulness of God's own being. The mystery of original sin is of a different type. Its mystery lies in a lack of intelligibility, a lack of meaning, since it is about the origins of evil. In some sense we shall never understand the mystery of original sin, because basically there is simply nothing that can be understood.

CONCLUSION

In this chapter we have considered the scriptural material on original sin, in particular, the ways in which Romans 5:12 has been misused as well as how it can be creatively used. Scripture does not and cannot provide us with unequivocal evidence of the reality of original sin. Nor can it totally support any particular theory of original sin. This should not alarm us since the same conclusion could be drawn about most Church dogmas. It took the Church three hundred years to affirm unambiguously the divinity of Jesus, with the opponents quoting just as many scripture texts as the supporters. Scripture is rarely sufficient in itself. In the next chapter I shall continue with an historical exploration of the developing position of original sin with a consideration of the theology of Thomas Aquinas. This will shed more light on our elusive prey.

CHAPTER NOTES

A key issue that this discussion raises is the relationship between scripture and defined dogma. For too long the dogmatic tradition of the Church has used scripture for its own purposes, seriously neglecting the context of verses and literary intention of their authors. With such a neglect it is quite possible to come to diametrically opposed views on key dogmatic issues, as the Church found in its early Christological and Trinitarian debates. Even when context and literary intention of authors are considered, it is doubtful if scripture alone is sufficient to determine dogmatic positions. Differences will still occur, not in the scriptures being interpreted, but in those who interpret it. In the dogmatic tradition concerning original sin, there is much in that tradition which cannot be critically grounded in scripture. The validity of such material does not rest on scripture alone. On the other hand its failure to find a grounding in scripture does mean that serious questions need to be asked regarding that tradition.

---

1 Joseph Fitzmyer notes that "in whom" is the "least convincing" interpretation. Further it was "unknown to the Greek Fathers before John Damascene". He gives a detailed examination of the variety of interpretations of the text in his commentary on Romans 5:12, in *NJBC*, p.845.

2 Gabriel Daly notes that "the most fruitful theological response to scientific and philosophical developments as they bear upon questions of creation and redemption has been to interpret the stories in Genesis 1–11 as aetiological myths, that is, as narratives which give symbolic account of how the world began and of what happened then to bring about the situation which we today experience", entry on Original Sin, in *TNDT*, p.728.

3 Cf. Brendan Bryne, *Reckoning with Romans*, Michael Glazier, Wilmington, 1986, pp.111–18.

4 This is, of course, not meant to deny that we are also saved from our personal sins. Its purpose is to focus attention on the relationship between original sin and salvation.

5 Augustine employs a similar device when he defines the term "person" as "what there are three of in the Trinity".

CHAPTER TWELVE

DID AQUINAS GET IT RIGHT?

While Augustine was the key figure in the development of the doctrine of original sin, he was not the only one. As we saw in a previous chapter, the Church adopted some, but not all of Augustine's positions on the matter. Further theological development was necessary to clarify what, if any, were the differences between Augustine's theology and what was to become the fuller position of the Church. In this process of development, the next significant input on original sin comes from the Scholastic period, in particular the contributions of Anselm (d.1117) and Thomas Aquinas (1225–1274). Here I shall consider the position of Thomas Aquinas.

The theology of Aquinas marks a turning point in the history of theology. The previously dominant Platonic theology, which had an implicit bias towards both a moral and ontological dualism, was to be replaced by an Aristotelean metaphysics which stressed the unity of created being. With the realization of this unity came a restored confidence in the goodness of human nature, in particular the goodness of reason, but also of all the human potentialities. This confidence in the goodness of human nature is well illustrated by the opposing views of Augustine and Aquinas on sexual pleasure. For Augustine, Adam and Eve would have experienced no sexual pleasure in the Garden since such sexual pleasure is the result of concupiscence. For Aquinas, on the other hand, sexual pleasure would have been heightened since it was not subject to the disordering influence of original sin and so would be more perfect.[1]

This confidence did not fall over into a naive Pelagian optimism. Aquinas remains, overall, fairly pessimistic about the human condition without grace. However, his confidence does prove too much for the later Reformers who see it as a selling out to Pelagianism. Their more rigorous Augustinian theology has no room for such confidence. We shall consider their response and the consequent response of the Council of Trent in the next chapter.

AQUINAS AND ORIGINAL SIN

As with Augustine, Aquinas' theology of original sin occurs against a backdrop of a theology of grace. Augustine's theology of grace was inspired and inspiring but it lacked a systematic speculative base.[2] As a consequence, his theology of original sin suffered from various ambiguities, as we have seen. On the other hand, Aquinas' theology of grace is a systematic masterpiece, using to the full the newly acquired (and significantly transformed) categories of Aristotle's metaphysics. For Aquinas grace is described in ontological categories as a supernatural elevation, an entitative habit of the soul. He proceeds with a detailed analysis of the potencies and habits which this elevation brings. This is the sort of analysis that Aquinas brings to his study of original sin.

Aquinas saw Adam, prior to the Fall, as not only free from sin but also as the recipient of special supernatural elevating graces. Such a precise formulation, absent from the thought of Augustine, was only possible in the light of Scholasticism's new-found and systematic distinction between grace and nature. The most significant of these graces was Adam's original integrity, the ordering of the will to God and the ordering of the passions to the will. Thus, prior to the Fall, human existence was harmonious but only as a result of this special grace of God. Technically, Adam was said to be in a state of *original justice*. Moreover Aquinas saw it as God's original intention that the whole human race be so graced in Adam. Adam was to have been the source of all grace for us all.

However, this original intention of God went unfulfilled when Adam sinned and lost God's grace. The immediate effect of Adam's sins was the disruption of his inner harmony, the loss of original integrity and justice. This loss of original justice becomes the central theme of Aquinas' understanding of original sin, a theme which Aquinas had himself taken from Anselm. Whenever he has to face some theological argument about original sin, it is this to which he returns—original sin is the privation of original justice. It is as a result of this loss of original justice that Adam suffered from a disordered concupiscence. Thus, for Aquinas, concupiscence is not original sin as is sometimes the case in Augustine's writings. Disordered concupiscence is a consequence of original sin, something which comes about in us all because of Adam's sin, but which cannot itself be identified with original sin. On the other hand, for Augustine, all concupiscence is disordered, a sign of our sinfulness.

In the metaphysical language of the day, Aquinas speaks of concupiscence as the material element of original sin, while the privation of original justice is the formal element (1a.2ae. q82.a3[3]). In less technical language what this means is that it is the privation of original justice which gives the material element of concupiscence the character or meaning of sin. Concupiscence has the meaning of sin because of the privation of original justice. Once the privation is removed, say through baptism, concupiscence may remain, but it no longer has its sinful meaning. However, there is another important consequence of Aquinas' theology. On the logic of this analysis, to experience concupiscence is not to be reduced to a state below nature but is part of the "natural" state of being human. For Aquinas, concupiscence is only absent through a special grace from God. Once that grace is gone as a result of sin, the natural state of concupiscence returns. Without the integrating influence of original justice, on the other hand, concupiscence becomes disordered.

On this analysis, concupiscence itself is morally neutral, part of our basic human nature. In general we may experience it as "inclining us to evil" but, more correctly, it should be seen as the resistance of our materiality to the urgings of our spirit, our will. It is the lack of integration between the two. While this lack of integration may make it harder to do good, it can also "resist" the doing of evil. Thus, as Rahner has pointed out, an involuntary blush when I tell a lie is also an example of concupiscence.[4] Similarly the galvanic skin response picked up by so-called "lie detectors" is a result of concupiscence. In both the body betrays the intention of the will to lie. It betrays the lack of integration between bodiliness and the will. Concupiscence is thus part of the "natural" structure of human limitation.

This disruption of human "nature", which the loss of original justice brings about, is then passed on to all Adam's descendants. It had been God's intention that all humanity be graced in Adam, passed along with Adam's human nature. However, Adam lost grace, firstly for himself, but then for all. All that Adam had to pass onto his descendants was human nature alone, without original justice. All humankind are thus born in a state of "privation of original justice". In this sense they are lacking something they "ought to" (Latin—*debere*) have. Thus they can be said to be "in debt" to God. It is as if an inheritance had been lost. All suffer from the foolishness of one.

While the notion of original sin as privation remains the central theme, there are times when Aquinas hints at something more. For example, when discussing whether original sin is a type of habit (1a2ae. q.82, a.1), he states that original sin is not purely a privation but also a corrupt habit "of sorts". There is not only a loss, but perhaps also a sense that something has been lost, as "a child may bear family disgrace because of a forbear's crime" (1a2ae. q.81, a.1). In that sense we are worse off having lost original justice than if we had never had it in the first place!

In this regard it is interesting to note that Aquinas argues that if God were to fashion someone miraculously out of human flesh, then that person would not contract original sin. Indeed, "they alone contract original sin who descend from Adam through the exercise of the active reproductive powers derived from him by way of origin" (1a2ae. q.81, a.4). He does not argue that such a person (he may have Jesus in mind) would be free from original sin because he/she has had original justice restored, but because he/she was not derived from Adam "through the exercise of the active reproductive powers". Such a person may not enjoy original justice, but they would not have any sense of loss since they are not from Adam. Also, given Aquinas' use of words, "active reproductive powers", one would wonder what he would make of a procedure such as cloning, which does not seem to involve such powers. It would seem that Aquinas might hold that a cloned person would not suffer from original sin!

More difficult is Aquinas' analysis of the guilt of original sin. Not only are we in a state of privation but we are also guilty through original sin. Here Aquinas invokes a sort of organic moral unity of the human race. He uses two analogies to describe the relationship between Adam and the rest of humankind. In one, Adam is seen as acting "on our behalf" just as the ruler of a country may act on behalf of his people. Thus he says that "even in political matters all belonging to one community are reckoned to be like one body, and the whole community like one person" (1a2ae. q.81, a.1). In a sense the people as a whole act and share in the responsibility of the leader. In the second he speaks of Adam's relationship to humankind as analogous to that of the will to the bodily members (1a2ae. q.81, a.3). Just as actual sin passes to the body's members by the influence of the will, so "original sin is passed on to all upon whom Adam exerts his influence by the impulse of generation".

Finally, for Aquinas, children who die in "original sin" are not destined for punishment in Hell as Augustine believed. For Aquinas, unbaptized babies who die are deprived of the vision of God. However, they are still in a state of natural bliss, since they did not even know they were being deprived. Thus develops the Scholastic teaching of *limbo*. It was never anything more than a theological solution to a problem caused by the theology of original sin. It never attained any status in official Church doctrine, though it became a popular part of Catholic imagination. It was obviously more humane than Augustine's position, but still strikes us as contrived. Even within the Scholastic synthesis it caused problems since it was not clear what happened to those in limbo at the final judgment.

POSITIVE ASPECTS

Unlike Augustine, Aquinas held that human nature was not totally corrupted by the Fall. For Aquinas our natural inclination to good was still operative in the human soul. Indeed, for Aquinas, this natural inclination was part of the definition of being human. If it had been destroyed in the Fall we would simply have ceased to be human. Here we see some of Aquinas' confidence in human nature showing through. Again his thought is supported by a systematic framework. As long as we remain human, human nature is present with all its potentialities for good. But now our natural inclination to good is in conflict with our other desires and passions. It must continually compete with them for the attention of our will. Thus our desire for good is no longer able to achieve its goal in a consistent manner. It was because of this that Aquinas still held Augustine's pessimistic view of human freedom, that we are unable not to sin without the help of God's grace. In the end Aquinas held that human nature was not corrupt but "sick", so that he speaks of it as a "sickness of nature", in need of healing. This healing was brought about by God's grace which was both healing and elevating.

It was this confidence in the remaining powers of the soul which was strongly attacked during the Reformation. Luther held that not only was the will totally corrupt but so was the intellect. All human acts were sin. All human reasoning was specious. This not only attacked the conclusions of Aquinas, but more radically brought into question his whole methodology. If human reasoning is suspect then the whole metaphysical framework used by Aquinas is also suspect and thus to be thrown away.

Finally, Aquinas' adoption of Anselm's definition of original sin in terms of the privation of original justice established it as the major element in all subsequent debate about the nature of original sin. It is this privational notion which adds clarity to the ambiguous position of Augustine. It is also this privational understanding which Luther firmly rejected. Luther returned to a position which identifies original sin with concupiscence. Given concupiscence remains after baptism and justification, Luther could speak of the person as at once just and sinner—*simul justus et peccator*. In response, the privational definition was all but adopted by Trent and became firmly entrenched in post-Tridentine theology.

NEGATIVE ASPECTS

While Aquinas' theology represents an advance on the theology of Augustine, there are still aspects which are obscure or require further examination. In the first place, the reasons for the "transmission" of the guilt of original sin remain very hazy. The analogies he offers are not compelling. What is this mysterious moral organic unity between us and Adam? Moreover, if Adam lost grace could not God have restored it to Adam's descendants and started the whole process off again? Indeed, if we are not careful, the Catholic doctrine of the Immaculate Conception, that Mary was born free from original sin, can read as if God could have restored the whole race to original justice. If God could do it for Mary, why not do it for everyone, right after Adam's Fall? We should note, however, that Aquinas had serious reservations about the doctrine of the Immaculate Conception of Mary. There is a real danger that the process of transmission of original sin appears as some type of arbitrary decree on God's part, arbitrarily lifted for Mary, but applied for the rest of us.

Secondly, what does it mean to say that it was God's "original intention" that all humankind was to receive grace from Adam? In Christian theology the source of all grace is Christ. Would Adam have been "Christ" if he had not sinned? Further, what does it mean to talk about God's "original intention"? God's creative act is one and encompasses all of creation from beginning to end. As Lonergan pithily remarks, "There are no divine afterthoughts".[5] God does not say, "Well Plan A has gone off the rails, time to adopt Plan B"! There is only one divine "plan", one total encompassing providence, as I argued in Chapter 5.

To address such an issue Scholastic theologians used to ask such questions as "if there were no Fall, would Jesus still have come?". Some said "No, there would be no point to it!". Others said "Yes, as crown of God's creation". Of course, such hypothetical questions have no answer. As I argued in Chapter 5 on providence, God's creative act is one and the unity of this creative act includes the Incarnation (cf. esp. Ephesians 1:3ff. and Colossians 1:25ff.). This is the only created order we know. Sin does not destroy God's providence but is encompassed within it. Within that total providential plan the Incarnation has always been central. Thus Rahner can argue:

> ... God's saving will directed from the start towards Christ as its historical culmination was (freely) absolute, even in the face of sin ... [S]in ... was only permitted by God because transcended by his grace.[6]

Thirdly, it is clear that Aquinas' account rests on a literal reading of the Genesis account. In particular, he sees Adam as the unique progenitor of the human race. This assumption of monogenism is vital in his account of the transmission of original sin to the rest of humankind (though it should be noted that it is not so much monogenism, one set of first parents, but one first father, since for Aquinas it is only Adam who transmits original sin). The deprivation of original justice is passed on since the deprived (not depraved) nature is all that Adam had to pass on to his descendants. The guilt of original sin is passed on due to our organic moral unity which results from Adam's headship of the human race. While it is naive to criticise Aquinas for such an assumption, is it really viable today? And if it is not, what becomes of Aquinas' theology? Can it survive if monogenism is rejected?

It is interesting here to draw a parallel between Aquinas' acceptance of monogenism and his acceptance of another theory which has been shown to be scientifically incorrect. A reading of his account of the transmission of original sin shows that it rests heavily on a mistaken understanding of the role of semen[7] in human reproduction. The ancient world knew nothing of the role played by the woman's ovum in conception. For them the male semen provided all that was required of human nature, given an environment (the womb) in which to develop. Time and again Aquinas refers to the role of the semen in the transmission of original sin. Indeed, he goes so far as to say that if only Eve, and not Adam, had sinned we would not have lost original justice (1a2ae, q.81, a.5)! The change in scientific knowledge that has occurred about the process of conception would require a total rewriting of Aquinas' account of the transmission of original sin. Would it survive a similar rewriting if monogenism was rejected?

This is the challenge which polygenism puts before us. Within

Aquinas' framework the original personal sin and guilt of Adam became the original sin and guilt of all. The most pressing problem then is that if there is no Adam, in the sense of an original unique progenitor, where is our original personal sin and guilt? Can original sin be stripped of its originally personal nature and remain meaningful? Or is monogenism an essential element in the doctrine of original sin, as it is an essential element in the theology of Aquinas?

CONCLUSION

In this chapter I have explored key elements in Aquinas' theology of original sin. Aquinas makes a considerable contribution to our understanding of original sin but there are still unanswered questions. Perhaps what is needed is an open acknowledgement of the limits of what can be answered. The key difficulty above revolves around the transmission of original sin. Can such a difficulty be resolved? In the end is it not about the mystery of the origin of evil in me? Perhaps in the end such a question has no answer, it is a brute fact without any totally satisfactory answer. In the next chapter we shall further our historical investigation with a consideration of the Reformation debates on original sin. When that is done I shall be in a position to develop a more complete synthesis.

CHAPTER NOTES

For this account of the theology of Thomas Aquinas I have drawn upon the study, *Original Sin: Two Major Trends in Contemporary Roman Catholic Reinterpretation*, by G. Vandervelde, as well as on the original text of Aquinas. Vandervelde gives a scholarly and concise account of the development of the theology and doctrine of original sin from the early Fathers to the present day in the first chapter of his study. For the serious student, however, there is no substitute for reading the work of Aquinas himself.

---

1 S. Duffy makes this observation in "Our Hearts of Darkness; Original Sin Revisited", *Theological Studies*, n.49 (1988), p.605, n.10.

2 *See* for example Lonergan's comments in *Grace and Freedom*, pp.2–5.
3 This accepted shorthand notation refers to the first part (*prim*a) of the second part (*secund*ae) of the *Summa Theologiae*, question 82, article 3.
4 *See* his *Theological Investigations*, Vol.1, pp.347ff.
5 Cf. *Insight*, p.695. The statement occurs in Lonergan's discussion of the divine solution to the problem of evil.
6 *See* Rahner's entry on "Salvation" in *Encyclopedia of Theology*, K. Rahner (ed.), Burns & Oates, London, 1975, p.1521.
7 The term *semen* is itself misleading. Semen means seed, which the man was seen as providing, while the woman provided the environment for growth, like soil for a seed. In fact biologically the male does not provide seed but rather, in keeping with the plant-like analogy, pollen! In general the term semen has fallen from scientific favor and the term sperm is used in its place.

CHAPTER THIRTEEN

REFORMATION, TRENT AND AFTER

The theology of Thomas Aquinas was a major achievement in both the areas of grace and original sin. While it was a dominant stream of thought in Catholic theology up to the Reformation there remained a significant theological pluralism on various questions in the area. However, this pluralism remained within the bounds of an orthodoxy established by the Councils of Carthage and Orange. This orthodoxy was largely unquestioned until the time of the Reformation. While the Reformation began as a protest against the abuses of the system of indulgences rampant in the Church, it rapidly became a theoretical critique of the Church's perceived theology of grace. Such a critique had many consequences for other areas of theology and for Church practice, so that in the end the Reformers saw themselves as having no alternative than to start from scratch and form their own Churches established on a renewed theology of grace.

While the central issue of the Reform was that of grace, it should not surprise us that the topic of original sin also became an area of dispute. The two are related as cure to disease, as light to the darkness of the human condition. Anything said in one area will affect the other and vice versa. While the spotlight was on the area of grace, a no less serious debate occurred on the topic of original sin.

LUTHER AND ORIGINAL SIN

In reading Luther on grace and original sin, it is always important to recall his own Augustinian origins. Luther was an Augustinian monk, steeped in the theology of Augustine. Augustine never developed a systematic account of grace or original sin, so that there are many positions which could be drawn from his writings. Luther represents one such position, one judged extreme by the Catholic Church at the time.

Luther rejected what he understood of the Scholastic notion that original sin was merely a lack or privation of original justice. To accept such a position would:

> ... give occasion for lukewarmness and a breakdown of the whole concept of penitence, indeed to implant pride and presumptuousness, to eradicate fear of God, to outlaw humility, to make the command of God invalid, and thus condemn it completely.[1]

These are clearly fighting words. For Luther, original sin is not merely a privation of original justice but more a positive inclination to evil. It is:

> ... a propensity towards evil ... a nausea towards the good, a loathing of light and wisdom, and a delight in error and darkness, a flight from and abomination of all good works, a pursuit of evil ...[2]

This is, of course, much more in line with the Augustinian identification of original sin with concupiscence and the understanding of concupiscence as inherently disordered. Luther was not concerned with the fact that concupiscence remained after baptism since he held that the baptized person was *simul justus et peccator*, at once justified and sinner. The persistence of concupiscence in the baptized person was further evidence for what has been called Luther's notion of imputed righteousness. For Luther, Christians enjoy an imputed righteousness. They are not really righteous, but God treats them as if they are since he imputes to them the righteousness of Christ.

At the time of writing his commentary on Romans, Luther maintained the Augustinian understanding of Romans 5:12, "*in quo omnes peccaverunt*". He recognized ambiguity, present even in Augustine's writings, as to what is meant by *in quo*, but claimed that the notion that all sinned *in* Adam remains valid—"a sinner can beget nothing but another sinner like himself"! (ibid.) This is significant if only because around this time Erasmus was pointing out to anyone who would listen, that Augustine's interpretation of Romans 5:12 could not be supported by the Greek text.

THE COUNCIL OF TRENT

In its response to the attacks of Luther and the other Reformers, the Catholic Church established a Church Council which was to rule authoritatively on the issues raised. The Council, held at Trent in Italy, was to address not only the dogmatic issues raised by the Reformers, but also the many areas of Church practice which the Reformers had criticized. These ranged from eucharistic practice to the training of priests. In calling the Council, its conveners stated clearly that they did not want the Bishops debating differences of opinion within accepted Catholic schools of thought. They wanted addressed only those issues which were raised by the Reformers. To some extent this had the effect of papering over differences among those schools and presenting a unified face. This appearance of unity was further strengthened by the decision not to allow access to the actual debates, which were stored in the Vatican archives. The documents of this debate were only released at the end of the nineteenth century.

The intention of the Council not to debate points of difference among accepted schools had an effect on the debate on original sin. There were, in fact, significant differences among the schools as to the nature of original sin. Since there was no unanimity on the point the Council sought only to speak of the effects of original sin rather than give an account of its nature. However, there are some points where it significantly departs from this policy.

In its deliberations on original sin, the Council of Trent gives us the most definitive teaching of the Catholic Church on the matter. It not only reiterates the positions of the earlier Councils of Orange and Carthage. It also goes beyond them, adding new clarity to the issue. This does not mean, however, that it is without limitations of its own. The Council, for example, simply repeats elements deriving from a pre-scientific world view without critically analyzing them. It assumes the view of the day which saw all humanity as springing from original first parents. Such issues were simply not being questioned by the Reformers and so should not be seen as being necessarily defined by Trent. This is not a criticism of Trent. It would be unrealistic to suppose that the bishops of Trent could have totally transcended the cultural assumptions of the day. Today, though, one must be aware of such limitations or one may do violence to the central intentions of the Council.

THE DECREES OF TRENT

I shall now turn attention to the actual decrees of the Council to see what it is they say. In some cases I have not given the whole of the text, but only that part of the text which is most significant.

> 1. If anyone do not confess that Adam, the first man, by his transgression of God's commandment in Paradise immediately lost the holiness and justice in which he had been constituted, and by the offense of this sin drew upon himself the anger and indignation of God and the death with which God had threatened him, and with death, captivity in the power of him who had the empire of death, that is to say the devil (Hebrews 2:14), and that the whole Adam by the offense of this sin was changed in body and soul for the worse, let him be anathema.

In this canon the Council comes closest to asserting the privational view of original sin. It speaks of Adam losing "the holiness and justice in which he had been constituted". This phrase was hotly debated within the Council and its wording was chosen so as to avoid taking a position among competing theological schools. In particular, reference to *original* holiness and justice was avoided. The canon is also largely a restatement of the first canon of the Council of Orange.

In general this canon declares that original sin has a radical effect on the whole person. Not only does Adam lose holiness and justice, he brings upon himself the anger and indignation of God, death, captivity to the devil and is worse in both body and soul. Interestingly, however, the canon avoids one aspect of the first canon of the Council of Orange by not referring specifically to the damage done to human freedom. Perhaps this is due to the Lutheran stress on the captivity of human freedom to the point where all human acts are sinful.

> 2. If anyone asserts that Adam's sin injured himself alone and not his descendants and that the holiness and justice received from God which he lost was lost for himself alone and not also for us; or that stained by the sin of disobedience he passed on to all humankind death and bodily punishment but not sin as well which is the death of the soul, let him be anathema. For he contradicts the words of the Apostle:

> "Wherefore as by one man sin entered the world and through sin death; and so death passed upon all men, *in quo omnes peccaverunt*" (Romans 5:12).

This canon basically repeats the second canon of the Council of Orange, though with some modification. It hints at the privational view of original sin in asserting that Adam's sin resulted in the loss of holiness and justice for all humanity. However, it should be noted that this phrase represents an insertion into what was said by the Council of Orange. Thus the privational view sits alongside, and perhaps uneasily with, more positive descriptions of original sin as death of the soul.

What is clear is that this canon sees original sin as being passed on to all people, not just as death as a punishment for sin, but as *sin*. All are caught up in the sin of Adam. In support of this the Council quoted the text, Romans 5:12, "and so death passed upon all men, *in quo omnes peccaverunt*". The significance of this will be discussed later.

> 3. If anyone asserts that this sin of Adam, which is one by origin and is passed on by propagation not by imitation and which is in each and proper to each, is taken away by the powers of human nature or by any other remedy than by the merits of the one mediator, our Lord Jesus Christ who reconciled us to God by his blood, "made unto us ... justice, sanctification and redemption" (I Corinthians 1:30); or denies that this merit of Christ Jesus is applied to adults and to infants, in the sacrament of baptism duly administered in the form of the Church, let him be anathema ...

In this canon the Council declares the proper remedy for original sin, which is obtained by the merits of Christ and is applied to us through baptism. Thus it reaffirms the link between baptism and original sin which was established by Augustine in his debate with Pelagius.

Indeed the Pelagian debate is also in mind in the assertion that original sin is passed on "by propagation, not imitation". So it sees the problem of original sin as intrinsic, not extrinsic to the human situation. It is tied in with the very fact of being human, not just in some decision to imitate another in sin. In explicitly rejecting imitation this canon goes a little further than the Council of Orange which just has "by generation".

One should also note the exclusivist tone of the canon. Original sin can only be remedied through the merits of Christ which are applied in Christian baptism. Does Trent then teach that only Christians duly baptized can be saved? One cannot draw such a conclusion. The salvation of non-Christians was not on the agenda for the debate. To use Trent to draw such a conclusion would be to lift it out of its historical context and have it answer questions it never intended to address. As in all such cases, this is not valid.

> 4. If anyone denies that children newly from their mothers' wombs should be baptized, even though they come from baptized parents; or says that they are baptized for the remission of sins but bear nothing of the original sin from Adam which must be expiated in the bathing of regeneration to obtain eternal life, so that for them the form of baptism, "for the remission of sins", is understood not in a true but a false sense, let him be anathema. Because the words of the Apostle "Through one man sin entered the world and through sin death and so death passed on to all men, *in quo omnes peccaverunt*" is not to be understood otherwise than the way in which the Catholic Church which is spread over the whole world has always understood it . . .

This canon largely restates the second canon of the Council of Carthage, the first council to address the Pelagian–Augustinian controversy. It deals with a key issue of that debate, the place of infant baptism. As we have seen, the practice of infant baptism was a major plank in Augustine's argument concerning the reality of original sin. With Carthage, this canon affirms the validity of infant baptism, even in the case where both parents have already been baptized, a significant addition to the position of Carthage. Such a baptism is necessary, even for infants, if they are to obtain eternal life. As with the previous canon there is an exclusivist tone to this canon.

From this canon we can see that original sin is seen as being present even in newborn infants. Note however that nowhere does the Council speak of original sin from the first moments of conception or some other yardstick of the beginning of life. I have already mentioned this earlier in Chapter 11. Indeed the Latin text is quite unusual in that it speaks of children *newly from their mothers' wombs (parvulos recentes ab uteris matrum)*, an awkward form of expression. It could more easily have said "newly born" (*parvulos mox nati*).

The other interesting feature of this text is its use of the controverted text, Romans 5:12. Indeed it particularly asserts an understanding of this text which is "not to be understood otherwise than the way in which the Catholic Church . . . has always understood it". Such assertions create many difficulties. The Fathers of Trent were aware at this stage, due to the work of Erasmus, that the Greek text could not support the Augustinian understanding. Their use of the text was a repudiation of

Erasmus' claim that the text had nothing to do with original sin. However, it is difficult to know what is the way in which this text has *always* been understood. It is clear that Paul, who wrote the Greek text, did not understand it as Augustine did. Neither did many of the early Greek Fathers of the Church. Perhaps, however, such things only create difficulties for those who see in such dogmatic statements the paradigm of truth and faith which contain no possibility of error even on factual questions.

> 5. If anyone denies that the guilt of original sin is remitted by the grace of our Lord Jesus Christ conferred in baptism, or even asserts that everything having the true and proper nature of sin is not taken away but is only brushed over or not imputed, let him be anathema . . . The Holy Council however knows and confesses that there remains in the baptized concupiscence or the inclination to sin; but since it is left to provide a trial it cannot harm those who do not consent and who manfully resist it by the grace of Jesus Christ . . . Of this concupiscence, which the Apostle sometimes calls sin (Romans 6:12ff.) this Holy Council declares that the Catholic Church has never understood it to be called sin in the sense of real and actual sin in those reborn, but only as coming from sin and inclining to sin. If anyone thinks the contrary, let him be anathema.

This is the only canon of Trent on original sin which does not simply reaffirm teaching of previous councils. As such it is specifically directed towards the teaching of the Reformers on the matter. The canon thus rejects Luther's notion that the righteousness of the baptized is only imputed. Their sin is not just covered over, but truly removed. Hence it asserts that nothing having the true and proper nature of sin remains in them. In doing so it explicitly rejects the notion that concupiscence is sin in the proper sense of the word. This marks a significant break from the Augustinian tradition which Luther represented. Indeed the superior of the Augustinian order, Seripando, fought within the Council against the rejection contained in this decree. It was one of the few areas in the Council where the Council Fathers took a stand with regard to an issue which was subject to debate within the various Catholic theological schools.

In this canon a clearer picture emerges on the relationship between baptism, original sin and concupiscence. Baptism is seen as removing the guilt of original sin but not its consequences. One of the consequences of original sin is concupiscence which is not to be identified with original sin nor with personal sin since it clearly remains after baptism. This is a rejection of any type of positive conception of original sin which simply identifies it with concupiscence. On the other hand one could argue that there is identification between original sin and the "guilt of original sin". Baptism removes the guilt so that the baptized are truly free from original sin.

POST-TRIDENTINE THEOLOGY

The decrees of Trent set the scene for all later developments in the theology of original sin. It allowed:

> Bellarmine (1542–1621) and others to determine the precise nature of original sin . . . in the following manner: since the remedy for original sin is the sacrament of baptism, and since by the sacrament sanctifying grace is infused, original sin must entail the privation of sanctifying grace.[3]

Vandervelde goes on to comment that:

> . . . by one ingenious stroke, the laborious procedure of determining the nature of original sin that had become prevalent in scholastic theology is obviated. That of which man is deprived in the condition of original sin need no longer be derived by tenuous speculation regarding that which man possessed in his *original* state, but can be derived from the ecclesiastical teaching regarding that which he possesses in his *present* (sanctified) state.[4]

From this time onward, the notion that original sin is the privation of sanctifying grace plays a dominant role in Catholic theology. One is left to wonder whether this privational view does full justice to that which Augustine sought to express.

MODERN DEVELOPMENTS

Modern thought on the question of original sin has swung between two poles. One has been described as the situationalist, the other sees original sin in terms of the universality of personal sin.

The situationalist position is exemplified by Karl Rahner. Using his distinction between the transcendental and the historical Rahner sees original sin in terms of the deprivation of sanctifying grace which was meant to be mediated historically by the first man, Adam, taken here as representative of the first human beings. This failure in the historical mediation of grace results in a sinful situation into which all human persons are born. This is the way in which original sin is propagated.

There is much to commend this position and I shall adopt elements of it later. It is *not* to be thought of as a capitulation to the Pelagian position of imitation, since much more than imitation is involved. The effects of our sinful situation derive from more than a mere imitation and indeed involve guilt. I shall consider this again in Chapter 17.

However, there is also something a bit neat about the distinction between the transcendental and the historical. The two are both poles of the one human existence and each conditions the other. The insistence from Augustine to Trent on the intrinsic nature of original sin points to a "transcendental" aspect to original sin which is mediated by our historical, sinful situation. I shall discuss this in Chapter 15.

The other position, which sees original sin in terms of the universality of actual sin, has been championed by the Dutch theologian, Alfred Vanneste. The universality of sin is simply a brute fact which finds no extra explanation in terms of a prior condition or inclination to sin in the person. Personally I cannot see how such a position adds to our understanding of original sin.

In a recent article on original sin, entitled "Our Hearts of Darkness: Original Sin Revisited",[5] Stephen Duffy discerns a third approach emerging in this area. Drawing on the work of such people as Paul Ricoeur[6] and Sebastian Moore, he sees a possibility of analyzing the myths of original sin, in the psychoanalytic sense, to help uncover the reality involved. Such a process involves both a deconstruction (hermeneutics of suspicion) and a reconstruction (hermeneutics of recovery) of the doctrine.[7]

> The aim of this process . . . is to open up a way between the naive historicism of fundamentalism and the bloodless moralism of rationalism, lest the treasure hidden in the Adamic myth and the Augustinian rationalization of it be squandered. The reconstruction proposed . . . revolves around personalistic and situationalist axes which derive from modern philosophical, psychological, sociological and theological insights. With these insights we can fathom not the pseudo clarity of the classical doctrine but *its dark symbolic richness, through which we may better articulate, though never with total lucidity, what is wrong with us and why* [emphasis added].[8]

This is the approach which I will be using in the following chapters.

CONCLUSION

In this chapter I have briefly considered the dogmatic and theological developments concerning original sin arising from the Reformation up to the present era. The main purpose of this and the immediately preceding chapters has been to give the reader some historical perspective on the questions which the doctrine raises, and to see the key issues as they emerged in their historical context. Without such a contextualization, positions can take on an absoluteness which was beyond the limits inherent in any historical situation. This is not to deny the possibility of coming to some definitive dogmatic position in, say, a Church Council. But it is to recognize that even in definitive teachings there are elements which remain limited by their context, questions which were not asked, assumptions which were simply made uncritically. A theologian must perform the difficult, and often thankless task, of seeking to sort out what is definitive from what is historically limited. It is this sorting process that I shall attempt in the next chapter.

CHAPTER NOTES

1. Again in this chapter I have drawn heavily on the study of Vandervelde. His work remains a standard reference in the area but sadly is not very accessible outside academic circles.

2. Steven Duffy's paper is the most helpful I have read in its assessment of the traditional expression of the doctrine and modern attempts to come to grips with it. Though I have developed my approach independently of his work, I have found in it a much more thorough expression and detailed justification of the approach than I could have hoped to give.

---

1 *Lectures on Romans, Luther's Works*, Vol.25, H. Oswald (ed.), Concordia Publishing House, St Louis, 1972, p.299.
2 Ibid. p.300.
3 G. Vandervelde, *Original Sin: Two Major Trends in Contemporary Roman Catholic Reinterpretation*, p.41.
4 Ibid. pp.41–2.
5 Cf. *Theological Studies*, #49, (1988), pp.597ff.
6 In particular Ricoeur's *Symbolism of Evil.*
7 On hermeneutics of suspicion and recovery, *see Introducing Contemporary Theologies*, p.20ff.
8 S. Duffy, op. cit., p.609.

CHAPTER FOURTEEN

PIECES IN THE "ORIGINAL SIN PUZZLE"

In the previous five chapters I have given an overview of the historical development of the doctrine of original sin. From its beginnings in the thought of Augustine to its definitive dogmatic exposition at the Council of Trent, the doctrine of original sin has been both controversial and precarious. I have already noted the repeated use of the misinterpretation of Romans 5:12—*in quo omnes peccaverunt*. This repeated use in both theological argument and dogmatic assertion must give us all cause for concern about the validity of the tradition. When coupled with the pre-scientific world view used to express the doctrine, one can wonder whether the doctrine has anything really to say to us today.

On the other hand, the alternative to upholding some such doctrine of original sin is to rewrite the whole of Christian theology, in particular those areas touching on grace and redemption. This would really require a "leap of faith" since it is not clear that at the end of such a process we would have anything even faintly resembling Christianity as we now know it.

In light of this, the basic position which I will take is that there is a "reality" which can be identified with what the tradition calls original sin.[1] Moreover, within the tradition there is the broad outline of what is meant by this term. My task as a theologian, is, as I see it, to try and make sense of the tradition, to be faithful to it. The alternative, to simply reject it as nonsense, seems to me a far more precarious path.

The Augustinian position claimed that we should believe so as to understand—*credere ut intelligere*. To simply reject the doctrine would be to run the risk of rejecting something we have not even tried to understand. Often it is only in belief that we find the commitment to continue investigation into something which tradition claims to be of vital importance for human living.

THE ORIGINAL SIN PUZZLE

The statement of belief that there is a reality called original sin does not mean that uncovering what it is will be in any way easy. What the tradition has handed down is little more than an outline, or more like the pieces of a puzzle. The task is to try to see how the pieces fit together, how they can fit into a unified whole. We should not expect a modern attempt to fit the pieces together to come up with the same sort of picture that, say, Aquinas had. Our different world view will give us a different slant on some, if not all the pieces. Pieces which before fell into place now seem curiously misplaced. Pieces which previously were forced into place can now be seen, in a different light, to fit elsewhere. The task is made more difficult by the very nature of the mystery under investigation, the mystery of the origin of evil. The topic itself tends to elude our grasp, as we shall see.

What then are the key pieces of the puzzle that need to be integrated into a systematic account of original sin? The following list is not meant to be exclusive. Hopefully however, it does include the major points which can be stated at this time.

1. Original sin is what Jesus saves us from

This is the basic heuristic device which we noted in Chapter 11. There I verified it by considering the scriptural data and other elements of the tradition. Here I should add that the whole history of the development of the doctrine of original sin has gone hand in glove with the developing doctrine of grace. Moreover the various doctrinal statements about original sin always relate it to the salvation won through Jesus' death and resurrection which is communicated to us through baptism.

Thus, any theology of original sin must make intimate contact with a theology of grace (dealt with in the first part of this book) and with a theology of salvation. If we make a statement about the nature of original sin, we must be able to say how it is that Jesus saves us from it, how it is that grace heals us of it. To some extent a theology of original sin must give way to a doxology, a word of thanksgiving, "yes there is this reality called original sin but, thanks be to God, through Jesus Christ we are saved from it".

This intimate connection between original sin, grace and salvation means that in some sense the first part of this book on grace has already conditioned the investigation given here. This will become more evident later.

2. *Original sin is distinct from personal sin*

As we have seen in the previous chapters, the tradition discusses original sin in relation to infants, newly from their mothers' womb. Such infants are clearly in no position to have committed personal sin. Their freedom has not sufficiently formed to the point of sinning, or of doing good, for that matter.

Some care then, has to be taken with the word "sin" in discussing original sin. Most of our use of the term "sin" refers to personal sin and so our understanding of sin derives from personal sin. Thus, when we use the word "sin" with regard to original sin, its use must be in some sense analogous. Personal sin always arises out of my freedom, yet this is the element specifically missing from original sin. It may arise from the freedom of another but it does not involve my freedom, so that it is not "personal" in that sense.

Finally, while recognizing the difference in terminology, it is important to see in original sin the precondition of our personal sinning. It is as a consequence of original sin that we experience our inclination to sin. In analyzing this inclination we can come closer to understanding the nature of original sin itself.

3. *Original sin relates to our human nature as a whole*

According to Thomas Aquinas, original sin is a sin or sickness of *nature*. It is not a matter of who we are, as arising out of our freedom, but a matter of what we are. It is to do with human nature itself. It is this nature which we have inherited from Adam and with it, says the tradition, we have inherited death and bodily punishment. Through original sin human nature is changed body and soul for the worse, so that the whole person is affected. Further, because it is a sickness of nature, human nature itself is insufficient to save us from it. As the Scholastics would say, to do (*agere*) follows to be (*esse*)—whatever we do is tainted by the sickness of what we are. Something beyond human nature, beyond human powers is required to free us from this original sin.

4. *Original sin involves guilt*

Canon 2 of the Council of Trent states that it is not just the death of the body which is passed on but sin as well. This sin is "in each and proper to each" (Canon 3). There is a real "guilt of original sin" (Canon 5) which is removed in baptism. Each of us is caught up in Adam's sin to the extent of a real guilt resulting from it.

However, we need a word of caution here. Guilt is a tricky category to use. In its fullest sense guilt is a feeling of personal failure due to a personal moral fault. Here, it is clear that there is no personal moral fault. Moreover, we know from experience that people can feel no guilt for the most heinous crimes, while others can feel great feelings of guilt for things totally beyond their control. In the first, there is a real personal failure but due to distortion of character, there is no feeling of guilt. In the second, there is a feeling of guilt but no reason for it. While the first is the bane of the moralist, the second is far more common and just as damaging. To some extent we all mildly suffer from the second, but in its severe forms it can lead to crippling anxiety and neurosis. It would be wrong and misleading to speak of these two cases as involving objective and subjective guilt respectively, as if the first is real while the second is not. Both are real, but neither is the full reality of guilt which is only appropriate for personal sin.

Further, the term used by Trent, "the guilt of original sin", does not specify what type of guilt is involved.

5. Original sin is passed on by "propagation not imitation"

This is closely tied in with the comment that original sin involves human nature. In line with the Council of Carthage, the Council of Trent stated that original sin is not passed on by imitation, a basic anti-Pelagian position. However, it added that original sin is passed on "by propagation". Strictly, this term is only defined by its opposition to imitation.

On an Augustinian position, propagation would mean the very act of sexual intercourse through which we are conceived, but it is not clear that this is what is meant by the Council. It certainly does not define it as such. Moreover, the only bench mark that Trent, or any other dogmatic definition, gives concerning original sin is that of newly born infants. Further, Canon Four uses the contrasting images of generation and regeneration, of birth and rebirth. Prior to birth, nothing is said.

There is, of course, something very commonsensical in not saying anything about original sin prior to birth. Since baptism is seen as the only remedy for original sin and baptism is impossible to apply prior to birth, it would seem most difficult to speak of original sin prior to birth. I Timothy 2:4 does **not** say "God wants everyone to be saved, except those who die in utero, for whom there is no possibility of salvation".

Thus, I would argue that propagation need not mean the act of conception. Propagation can mean more than that since the process by which I become a human being is more than the process of joining ovum and sperm. With Trent I will take birth as a significant bench mark in the process of propagation. Nor should we necessarily see the process of propagation as ending with the birth of the child.

6. Original sin is tied to our understanding of baptism and hence of the Church

Historically the first seeds of the doctrine of original sin were planted in the dispute between Augustine and Pelagius on the place of infant baptism. As part of its response to this dispute, the Council of Carthage, in its second canon, specifically linked the doctrine of original sin with infant baptism. This canon was essentially repeated by Trent in its Canon 4. The links between original sin and baptism are firmly established in the whole history of the doctrine.

The link, however, is no justification for the development of a magical understanding of baptism or the sacraments in general. An extrinsicist theology of grace can always assert anything it wants about grace and original sin since they are realities not accessible to human experience. Original sin means we begin life with a negative balance and baptism is our first deposit to put us into the black. However, once we reject such an extrinsic account of grace this magical account of the relation between baptism and original sin must be expelled.

Baptism is a sacrament with a specific effect. That effect is primarily an initiation into a Christian community, into the Church. Any account of original sin must tie in with the fact that it is entry into this community which frees us from original sin. It is in this community that we experience the mediated grace of Jesus' death and resurrection. Once we insert grace into the real experiences of human living, so too our account of original sin must draw on very real human experiences. If we fail to do this then we will of necessity fall back into a magical understanding of baptism in relation to original sin.

7. For our own age any account of original sin should attempt to be independent of the hypothesis of monogenism

Critically, for our modern understanding we must be able to separate our understanding of original sin from any hypothesis that the human race descended from an original pair of first parents. This may involve removing our understanding of original sin from any personal act of a unique progenitor e.g. Adam. However, we must still be able to locate the origins of original sin at the origins of humankind.

As we have seen, the assumption of monogenism is deeply embedded in the theology of Aquinas and is the unquestioned assumption of the dogmatic tradition. There had never been any serious reason to question it. It has only been since the development of the theory of evolution in the late nineteenth century that any alternatives have suggested themselves. Now from a scientific point of view monogenism seems a most unlikely hypothesis.

This does not mean, however, that we can separate our understanding of original sin from the origins of human existence. It seems clear from the doctrine that there has never been any time when the human race has been free from sin. Even the first human beings knew sin. Thus, when I consider the origins of original sin, I shall seek them not in the first human couple but in the conditions surrounding the first human beings, however many.

8. God is not to blame for original sin

The doctrine must be formulated so as to remove any type of arbitrariness on God's part. It is not simply something which God has arbitrarily decided, it is not a divine decision to stack the cards against us. In fact, God does everything possible to save us from original sin, even to the point of sending his Son, who dies on the cross for us. God is not to blame for original sin.

It is important to note the ways in which we have sought to blame God for our human condition. Why me, God? Why us?! As Rosemary Haughton notes:

> So there is, I think, a tendency to reduce the description of an "original" sinful choice to a failure in some kind of arbitrary test set up by God, because that makes it all "exterior" and manageable ... Even in trying to *think* about original sin we are actually tending to choose a way of thinking which enables us to *blame* God for setting things up that way and depriving us of a privilege to which we have some kind of right.[2]

Such a blaming is not simply to miss the point, it is to miss the point in a very calculated way. It shifts attention from us to God. It is a failure to accept responsibility. There can be no repentance for any sin, even original sin, unless there is a clear acknowledgement of responsibility on our part.

More is involved than a denial of responsibility. The very

denial itself is a symptom of the condition. The very shift tells us something about original sin—"The woman made me do it ... the snake made me do it". As Haughton notes, "Our imagination is itself conditioned by the sinfulness we are trying to understand and is resistant to ... clarification".[3]

9. Some account needs to be given of the "myth of the golden era"

A persistent element in the tradition is the "myth of the golden era", the belief that things were better in the beginning. This element is present in the theologies of Augustine and Aquinas and the dogmatic formulations of Carthage, Orange and Trent. Somehow things were better for Adam. He enjoyed an original sanctity and justice which we have never known. This is an element for which an account needs to be given.

I have already noted that there is little evidence in the scriptural material for such an element. It develops more in the patristic reflections on scripture and finds its way into dogmatic statements. Its mythic quality is attested to by the large number of cultures which have similar myths. It would seem that there remains, deep in the human consciousness, a profound sense of nostalgia, a sense of longing for the way things were. Things were simpler in the past, the truth was clearer. Now everything is confused, everything is up for questioning. How we long for a return to that simple past! Of such longings myths are born.

The term "myth" here is not derogatory. It simply refers to a type of consciousness, a type of communication which differs from our assumed rational consciousness. Myth arises out of imagination. Myth employs symbols within a narrative structure to speak of what cannot be spoken, to hint at what cannot be said. In many ways myth is a more effective form of communication since it frees our imagination and evokes our feelings in a way which purely rational discourse tends not to do.

10. Some account needs to be given of the role of the devil, the Satan

One persistent element in the account of the Fall is the role of the Satan. Even in the Old Testament the serpent is taken to be the Satan (cf. Wisdom 2:24). In the early Church the identification is simply taken for granted. Again this position finds its way into dogmatic definitions. We must be able to say something about this.

This is not the place to attempt some metaphysical account of the nature of purely spiritual beings and the possibility of such beings choosing evil and becoming demons. Nor is it the place to trace the ways in which such beings enter into the biblical imagination through Persian dualist mythologies. Certainly by the New Testament era the existence of demons, and a key Devil, is simply taken for granted by Jesus and his contemporaries. All such accounts have their place and validity[4].

However in this account, as always, I shall focus on the human experience which has led to the belief in such a being. This shall not be an account of extraordinary phenomena such as supposed acts of demon possession.[5] If such things happen, they appear to be rare and not of general significance. Original sin, on the other hand, is universal and of great general significance. The role of the Satan will be found in very common human experiences which tell us something about the nature of original sin.

11. Any account must recognize the difficulty of speaking about the mystery of the origin of evil

I have already noted this point before in Chapter 12. It is a reminder of just how far we can expect to go in any account of original sin. Somewhere our account must break down. If we were too successful in giving an account of original sin, it would all seem too reasonable. It might end up that it would be impossible to conceive of the world in any other way. If it all seems too reasonable then evil is reasonable and in truth the battle is lost! Evil becomes just something we all have to live with, even accommodate. But evil is not reasonable and the world can be different. Grace can abound.

We cannot allow ourselves to "think" evil away, as if it were insignificant, as did Pelagius. Nor can we allow ourselves to "think" it into our system so that it is always there, either from God or some anti-God, as does Manichean dualism. There can be no theoretical solution to the problem of evil, only a practical solution of living in God's forgiving grace. At some point an account of the origins of evil must break down since, in fact, evil has no "origin", no cause. It will always confront us with a mystery which has no full explanation.

These are the basic pieces of the puzzle as I see them.

A HERMENEUTIC PRINCIPLE

How are we to find our way around these various pieces? While some seem relatively straightforward, others come to us from a different world view, a different consciousness. The medieval world simply took the literal truth of Genesis 2–3 and incorporated it into their theology. Now this is no longer an option. As a way forward in this situation I would propose the following:

KEY HERMENEUTIC PRINCIPLE

> Any interpretation of scriptural, magisterial and theological material on original sin must be aware of the mythic dimensions of such material prior to any attempt at a systematic synthesis. All such material reflects something of a mythic consciousness coming to grips with the origin of evil.

As I have already said above, the term "myth" does not have any derogatory connotation in this context. In a rationalist context such a principle would lead one to suspect that all such statements are to be dismissed as "mere mythology". This is not what I am proposing. What I am proposing is that such statements cannot be analyzed as products of a purely rational consciousness but must be analyzed according to the canons of mythology. In this regard it will be the depth psychologies of Freud and Jung which will provide useful categories and insights leading to a meaningful analysis. The basic assumption of such a principle is that myth holds its power over us because it mirrors basic psychic processes common to all humankind.

Such a position is almost forced upon us since we are dealing with the mystery of the origin of evil for which no purely rational account can be given. Myth is perhaps the only approach which can express the origins of evil adequately. While our rationalistic minds have produced any number of theodicies, i.e. theoretical justifications of God in the light of the problem of evil, none of which ultimately satisfy, simpler cultures have told stories about the origin of evil. These stories, such as that of Adam and Eve, continue to exert a powerful influence on our approach to the world. While the various myths about creation and the origins of the world, culture and primitive technology have fallen beneath the march of science, myths about the origin of evil still have something to say to us.

Indeed we can be a little more precise with regard to the above hermeneutic (i.e. interpretative) principle. Above, I noted Haughton's suggestion that many of the ways we think about original sin tend to be ways of blaming God for our situation. This diversion of blame suggests that an appropriate hermeneutic is a hermeneutic of suspicion. Such a hermeneutic assumes that the myths involved not only reveal truths but also seek to systematically conceal truths. Truths are concealed which would lead to a real insight into the human condition. For example, we blame God when it is really us who are at fault. Uncovering such a process of systematic distortion of communication in dreams led Freud to develop his theory of psychoanalysis for the treatment of neurosis. A similar approach can be applied to the myths surrounding original sin.

Once such a hermeneutic principle is applied to discussion about original sin, it soon flows over into various soteriological schemes as well. Christian theology has developed a number of theologies of salvation (soteriologies). Many of these display the same mythic features found in theologies of original sin. This is to be expected since salvation comes as salvation from original sin. The myths of original sin and the myths of salvation are thus interlocking. I shall consider these later.

Finally, as I noted in the introduction to this part of the book and, as I have argued above, a purely rational account cannot be given concerning original sin. At times language will begin to break down and a different literary form is needed to express the inexpressible. I take it that the reader is sufficiently sensitive to be able to recognize the various shifts in literary form that take place.

CONCLUSION

In this chapter I have spelt out the various elements in the theology of original sin which I feel a contemporary account must try to integrate. I have further spelt out the type of hermeneutic which I intend to adopt in developing such an account. As my account unfolds I hope to be able to bring in each element as required. The success of this venture is not assured and is clearly speculative. It is in the classical sense, faith seeking understanding. The reader should remain aware, as I am, of the limits such a venture entails.

CHAPTER NOTES

The idea of using a hermeneutic of suspicion with regard to original sin is not new. In his study, *Moses and Monotheism*,[6] Freud gives an interesting analysis of original sin which employs such a method. However Freud is suspicious, not of evil, but of religion and so his account is quite different from that which will be given here.

Freud attempts to read the story of original sin in a radically historical manner. Using the evolutionary approach of Darwin he considers the situation of the first group of primal humans. On the basis of comparisons with social groups of apes he postulates the existence of a dominant male who had access to all the females to the exclusion of the younger males. In frustration the young males murder and cannibalize the dominant male and take his females for themselves. Caught up in the guilt of what they had done, they "divinize" the dead dominant male and place a taboo on murder and incest. They then pass on to their descendants their sense of guilt as a neurosis in the form of religion. In one swoop Freud "explains" patriarchal religion and the origins of our most ancient taboos. Religion is dismissed as neurosis which with the help of psychoanalysis, we can grow beyond. It is little wonder that Freud upset the Churches in his day!

Freud's account fails to address the question of the origin of evil. That was not his concern. However it does point out the weakness of any attempt to see the "fall" as a purely historical event. The further away we get from it, the less plausible it seems that it should affect us. For Freud it was about time we all grew up and put religion behind us. Any account which sees original sin simply in terms of something which happened in the dim distant past will be troubled by the same complaint, unless it seeks refuge in some purely extrinsicist account of grace and sin.

---

1 The guarded use of the term "reality" is deliberate. "Datum" would be a more accurate term, since in a very real sense original sin is an "unreality".
2 R. Haughton, *The Passionate God*, p.105.
3 Ibid.
4 For a brief account of these questions, *see* the entry on Demons in *TNDT*, p.275ff.
5 For a measured account of such phenomena, *see People of the Lie* by Scott Peck.
6 *See* the Pelican Freud Library, Vol.13, *The Origins of Religion*, p.239ff.

CHAPTER FIFTEEN

SYNTHESIS ON ORIGINAL SIN

In this chapter I shall begin an attempted synthesis on the question of original sin. The key elements in this synthesis have been given in the previous chapter, together with the type of approach I shall use. Such an approach is not new and in many ways I am indebted to the work of Sebastian Moore for providing the basic leads which I follow through in this and later chapters. I have found Moore's own psychological reading of original sin to be extremely helpful, though I think I take his approach a bit further than he does.

THE MYTH OF THE GOLDEN ERA

I have already noted the place of the "myth of the golden era" as an element requiring synthesis in our account. Since it is perhaps the most obviously mythic element it would seem like a good place to start our synthesis. What can be said about this myth?

An initial response would be to say that clearly there was no such "golden era". Humankind evolved from a more primitive state in primitive conditions. The first human beings lived primitive lives as hunter gatherers, the prey of faster, stronger animals, yet perhaps able to use their newly developed intelligence to overcome some of their predators. Hardly an idyllic situation.

This is too rationalistic an approach, trying to extract history from myth. Myth does not give us a direct account of how things were in the exterior world, more how things felt in the interior world. If myth is tapping into such a significant inner reality through symbol and story, perhaps the question we could ask is—what was the conscious experience of the first human beings like? What was the original condition of human consciousness? What was it like to "become human"?

Prior to the development of human consciousness the pre-human animal beings lived a life dominated by instinct. Animal consciousness was dominated by the biological concerns for survival, food, rest and reproduction. Instinctive survival was the name of the game. The eruption of human consciousness within prior animal consciousness, however, placed new demands on the evolving animal. Our newly-human being had to move out of an animal consciousness dominated by biological concerns into a fuller human consciousness, into a human world of intended meaning and value. This is a movement out of the simple instinctive world of the animal into the new demands and tensions of being and becoming human. What am I to do? What am I to become? Instinct alone cannot answer such questions.

In such circumstances would not the simple instinctive world of the animal appear, from the complexities of human existence, to be a "golden era" of simple perfect existence? Things were so much better then, none of the worries which now dominate consciousness, a simple world where action follows immediately along the well-worn paths of instinct. Prior to the development of a human consciousness, the animal existed in a state of primal undifferentiated union, a state which was simply given. With the development of human consciousness, unity must be achieved. It is not simply given, but comes about through moral struggle to do what is right.

In the face of this moral struggle comes an implicit awareness of the divine, the source of all moral being. The development of a moral consciousness brings with it the first taste of the transcendent, the implicit horizon of all our deciding. The sense of the transcendent becomes the new unity for which one strives, an elusive goal of union with the ground of all being. This is not a withdrawal into the primal union of the animal consciousness. It lies forever ahead, not a retreat but an advance into an open-ended future. The path back to the simple state of animal consciousness is no longer an option. Something definitive has happened, something new has occurred in the creation of a human consciousness. The union now to be sought is not the primordial union of the animal but the unity of a fuller human integration—hence the symbol of the cherub guarding the way back with a flaming sword. There is no return.

Moore has captured this event in the newly developed human

consciousness as reflected by the myth of Genesis in the following terms:

> We have been, alas, profoundly influenced by a theology of original sin that *fails* to interpret, in any serious sense, the story of the Fall. Instead of seeing the story as our primary myth, describing the *birth* of self-awareness with its attendant trauma, traditional theology has taken the story literally in the fatal particular that *before* the crucial event, the couple are self-aware and God-conscious beings. Thus the way was effectively blocked against seeing the Fall as the birth of our consciousness *and* the beginning of our God-consciousness *as* we lost the preconscious, primordial union, *to* which we are now drawn *as* conscious beings. In other words, the revelatory mirror to our condition was rendered opaque by monkish thinkers. And it has taken ... Darwin for us to realize that *not* to believe in original sin is *not* to believe in evolution.[1]

Such an account is clearly independent of any hypothesis of monogenism. It takes its stand not on an original pair of first parents, but on the original condition of an evolving human consciousness, however many may have been involved.

This eruption of human consciousness also has implications for the development of sexual identity. In an animal, sexual identity is instinctive. Animals just do what nature tells them to do, following powerful forces within them. This is not the case with human beings. In the human person sexual identity too must be achieved. The growing child must take on male or female social roles as part of its sexual identity. In various ways things can go astray. Our thinking can and does affect our sexual identity—psychologists often say that our most important sex organ is our brain! Despite their biologically determined gender, homosexuals can seek out the company of their own sex, transexuals can identify with the opposite sex. Simple biology is not enough to determine sexuality. Sexual identity is not just gender.

One clear difference between animal and human sexuality concerns the incest taboo. Animals have no incest taboo. Blood ties are of no significance. Human society, even from its earliest days, does. Here Moore reflects on the Genesis account of Adam and Eve—"Bone of my bone, flesh of my flesh" (Genesis 2:23). The paradisial experience of sex is incestuous. The primordial unity has been transcended by the breakthrough of human consciousness. Once such a breakthrough occurs, incestuous relationship offers an alluring path back to such a primordial unity. However such a path is a dead end, a return to an animal existence. It is directly opposed to the new human consciousness.

THE MYTH IN PRESENT EXPERIENCE

A myth will speak powerfully not simply because it is some type of species memory. If original sin is simply to do with such original experiences then perhaps we should say with Freud that it is time we grew up. However the myth remains powerful since, in some sense, the original crisis is relived in each individual in an analogous manner. Can we identify similar crises in the life of each individual?

In fact Moore identifies two crises in the life of the individual.[2] In the first place he notes the separation crisis between the child and mother. This occurs at about the age of twelve months. Prior to this time the child psychically identifies itself with the mother, without recognizing distinction. At this time the child begins to establish a separate identity from the mother. There are forces released within it which move the child beyond its dependence on the mother to seek out independence. In doing so it must move away from the security of union to new independence, with the promise of a richer union to come in real human relationship. This is analogous to the evolutionary situation discussed above.

Secondly Moore notes the "Oedipal" crisis through which the child establishes its sexual identity. Here, for the male child for example, there will be a suppression of the sexual opposite, the anima. This involves a rejection of his own "female" aspects, a rejection of some part of his own psychic make-up. The gain of a newly formed sexual identity is paid for by the cost of this suppression. A parallel process takes place in the female psyche. Moore argues that it is from this that the incest taboo arises. Members of one's own family are too easily identified with one's own anima. This is the rejected path back to primordial union. One should also note that homophobia, fear of homosexuals which is still powerful in society, tells us more about the cost of this struggle to establish sexual identity than any sense of inherent moral outrage.

Perhaps we can push back even further. Here we may recall the expression of Trent in speaking about original sin. It speaks of infants "newly come from their mother's womb" (*parvulos recentes ab uteris matrum*). This is a rather clumsy expression considering that it could have simply said "newly born". Such clumsiness could easily conceal a psychic clue whose power perhaps lies in the reference to the "mother's womb". Are we picking up here a reference to the birth trauma, the original breaking out of consciousness from the oceanic consciousness of the womb, the original "garden of Eden"? As I argued earlier, the basic reference point of Trent is the birth, not the conception, of the child.

What each of these events has in common is the breakthrough into a new horizon of human existence. In each there are barriers to be transcended, limits to be overcome. The dynamism for change is part of the human nature we have. We cannot remain within the womb, we cannot remain tied to mother's apron strings (the psychic equivalent to the umbilical cord), we cannot remain sexually undifferentiated. Each change opens up for us a new horizon, a new set of opportunities, but also new hazards. How do we respond to these crises of human development?

ORIGINAL SIN IN ORIGINAL EXPERIENCE

These crises in human development even in our original ancestors are not what is meant by original sin. At this stage all we have spoken about is the nature of the crisis itself, something of how it feels from the inside. However, of itself, there is nothing wrong with any of this. Original sin cannot be seen as a necessary and automatic consequence of our evolutionary and developmental circumstances. To do so would be to make sin, and hence evil, necessary. We would then either fall over into a metaphysical dualism or simply fail to take evil seriously. Something more has to be said, something else which goes wrong in the process. To consider this we must look more closely at our response to these crises.

Such crises are not comfortable. They involve struggle, suffering. In suffering, we do not feel good. Somehow we feel that it is not just our circumstances that are changing but that we must be doing something wrong. But what we are doing is being driven by powerful forces for growth within our nature, something over which we have little control. Something is wrong we feel, not with what we are doing, but with us. What was originally an experience of growth is experienced as a "fall". We begin to tell ourselves that something has gone terribly wrong. There is a longing to return to the prior trouble-free state. As such, there is an implicit rejection of what we have become. There is a *felt* rejection of our own *nature*, a radical disvaluing of self, a feeling bad about being *what* we are. The forces within us become alien, dangerous, something to be feared. All the negative aspects of concupiscence are born.

Moreover, these feelings are not just the spontaneous product of an isolated consciousness. They are reinforced, indeed mediated, to the person by those around who create the environment in which we all develop. Out of their own sinfulness parents respond to the developing child with anything from mild rejection to outright hostility. Further in the broader social environment there are any number of forces at work telling us that we are inadequate, that we don't measure up, that we have to be other than we are to be accepted, to be of value.

In "feeling bad about being what we are" we are rejecting our "creaturely status". As in the myth of Adam and Eve we seek to "become like gods", either through a return to the "divine" primordial union of animal consciousness or through utter rejection of our "animal" past through continually seeking to overreach our finitude. In this we can see the origin of a manic depressive cycle. In the depressive stage one slumps back into a despair at the limitations of human existence, grounded in our animal nature. In the manic phase one spurts ahead, ignoring the demands of the body, seeking to do anything and everything in one's near divine powers (or so one imagines!).

Typically both nature and society conspire to identify these two responses with different genders. As a result, the male is expected to overreach, in career, in sport, in battle. In response a male-created and male-oriented theology saw the root of all sin in pride. The female, on the other hand, closer to the natural world through her bodily cycles and through childbearing, is expected to hold back, to develop a nurturing role to comfort the burnt-out male. For women the danger is not pride but submissiveness, an oppressive inability to break out of male-defined social roles. While men die of heart attacks, women suffer from depression as both live out the consequences of our original self-disesteem.

What can we say about this response of self-disesteem? In the first place, it is unreasonable and unnecessary. Since, in fact, what we are is not bad there is no reason for so feeling. God has created us good (cf. Genesis 1:31). God does not make junk. Yet we continue to feel as if we are junk. Secondly, it involves feelings of guilt. We feel guilty since we feel we must be doing something wrong. There is indeed a real feeling of guilt associated with such disesteem. Thirdly, it is conceivable within a child. Even quite young children can show symptoms of such a disesteem. It is displayed in an inability to trust the world, an anxiety that seeks to control the world, a fear in breaking out of familiar patterns.

Finally, this lack of feeling of self-worth is the precondition for personal sin and is confirmed in each personal sin. When one feels bad about oneself it is easy to be convinced that one is not good enough to do the right thing. In for a penny, in for a pound—you're already no good so what does it matter if you commit this sin? Already the defenses are weakened and are easily breached by temptation. Moreover, when we do sin, it merely confirms for us what we already believed—see, I was right; I am no good.

From the above discussion I would argue that such an original self-disesteem is what is meant by original sin in us. It relates to what we are, a felt rejection of our human nature prior to any exercise of our freedom. As such it conditions our freedom by establishing a distorted horizon into which we enter.

One can ask as to the theological nature of such a claim to identify original sin with an original self-disesteem of our human nature. Basically such a claim only makes sense within the systematic which I have developed. As I noted previously, the description of grace as transcendent value sublating our self-esteem already conditions any discussion of original sin. Grace comes as a solution to the problem of original sin. Transcendent value restores our damaged self-esteem and further protects it from attack. However, in this systematic, the state of original sin is more than the mere deprivation of grace. In the absence of grace my self-esteem becomes the natural principle of my horizon. Of itself this would be of no concern. What I have argued above implies that, given original sin, self-esteem is not in its "natural" state. Thus we "enter" the world with our self-esteem already damaged.

At this stage I have only briefly mentioned the issue of the transmission of such an original sin. This shall be discussed further in Chapter 17.

THE SATAN

At this stage it might be worth saying something about the figure of the Satan concerning the above suggestion on original sin. I shall begin by noting what the term "Satan" means. In the Hebrew language the term "Satan" means the Adversary or the Accuser.[3] In legal language the Accuser is the one who puts before the court the accusation against the accused. In the perspective developed here the Accuser is the voice within continually undermining our self-esteem, running us down with a multitude of accusations, loading us with false guilt. Using this we can attempt to uncover some of the mythology about this figure.

If we turn to the Genesis account we find Adam and Eve listening to the voice of the Accuser. The Satan's temptation "you shall be like gods" (Genesis 3:5) is not only a temptation. It is an implied criticism "you want to be like gods and you should be like gods, *but you're not*"! The Accuser is getting under the skin of Adam and Eve, taunting them with their finitude—"There is something wrong with you, something wrong with just being human".

In her description of neurosis, Karen Horney picks up a similar tale. She describes how the neurotic is driven by their "shoulds"—"I should do this, I should have done that". At the heart of this drivenness is a self-esteem dominated by guilt. She states:

> But when trying—anxiously—to measure up to [his shoulds] he feels most of the time that he falls pitiably short of fulfilling them. The foremost element in his consciousness is therefore self-criticism, *a feeling of guilt for not being the supreme being* [emphasis added].[4]

In this description of neurosis we see the work of the Satan undermining identity through a series of baseless accusations. Yet who among us would claim to be free from such an inner voice? Surely such a description as that given by Horney is applicable to us all to a greater or lesser extent? Such a bondage to the Satan is not some spectacular phenomenon such as is given in accounts of "possession". It is much more real, more common and more dangerous.

We should also consider the Christian myth concerning the origin of the Satan. In Christian mythology the Satan was originally a good angel, the Lucifer or bearer of light.[5] He was indeed the highest angel of the heavens. However in pride he overreached himself and so fell from heaven and became the Accuser, the Satan attacking humankind. What can be made of this mythology?

In psychological terms the light within each of us is our conscience. Vatican II describes conscience as our most secret core, a sanctuary where we can be alone with God.[6] The role of the Lucifer can be interpreted as that of bearing the light of conscience, to illuminate human actions by the timely and accurate pronouncement of accusations. This was indeed a god-like task and involved an intimacy with both God and the human person. However the Lucifer overstepped the boundaries of the task. Not satisfied with a god-like task within conscience he wanted to be the whole of conscience. He ceased being the Lucifer and became the Satan, the Accuser who stands before our God accusing the brethren night and day. The Satan is a false conscience which leads to the false consciousness that is sin. Only God can quieten the accusations of such a conscience (I John 3:19–21).

The problem with the accusations of false conscience is that they always carry a certain amount of plausibility. Whatever good we do, we could always have done something better if only circumstances were a bit different, or if we had stretched ourselves a little or a lot. A career, once chosen, precludes many possibilities for doing good. If I am a teacher I cannot be a doctor and save lives. If I marry I cannot be a priest; if a priest I cannot have children (at least in the present circumstances). There are always goods left undone or even undoable, which in turn produces a rich field of possibilities for the accusations of the Satan.

Moralists are generally worried about the type of false conscience which tells us that something is good when it is really bad. While such a problem is not uncommon, the opposite is far more common. Not only is it more common, it is far more disorienting in the moral sphere. When we do wrong and it is condoned by a false conscience, it is simply rationalizing what we have already decided to do. However when we have done nothing wrong, yet find ourselves accused by a false conscience, we are totally undermined. It leads us to doubt ourselves and all our moral judgments. Nothing makes sense any more. Even repentance does not help since there is really nothing from which to repent. Such a confused state will quickly lead to real moral faults.

Indeed the accusations of the Satan, the feelings of guilt which he plays upon, lead to a serious weakening of our sense of evil. When we are confronted with an evil situation we already feel guilty about it. We feel as if we may already be compromised by it. Since we feel already compromised we do not and, in fact, cannot afford to see the evil as bad as it really is. We get sucked into its framework—it's really not so bad! The freer we are from such a pervasive sense of guilt, the more clearly we see evil for what it is. Indeed no-one sees evil with as much clarity as Jesus, who sees it in all its ugliness.

Finally we should note that the Johannine Jesus refers to the Satan as the Father of Lies (John 8:44). The biggest and most damaging lie is that there is something wrong with us, that we are not loveable, that God wants nothing to do with us, that God is angry with us before we have even done anything. Yet these are the lies that the Satan tells us and we believe him.

To live in the life of grace does not mean that one no longer hears the voice of the Satan. This voice never dies away. It is always present, hoping to get our attention with some new accusation. The voice does not die. It is drowned out by a stronger voice, the powerful and primal shout of "Yes" given by Jesus. Jesus affirms human existence, my existence. Hence Paul can say, even though he had never met Jesus, that Jesus "loved *me* and gave himself up for *me*" (Galatians 2:20). Grace is the stronger voice saying "yes, I love you, you are precious to me" (cf. Isaiah 43:4). Nothing can come between us and such a love from God (cf. Romans 8:38–39), certainly not the voice of the Accuser.

THE VOICE OF ORIGINAL SIN

From the perspective above it is possible to read Augustine's arguments for original sin in a new light. In particular, I shall consider the arguments on suffering and the nature of concupiscence.

Augustine argues that the human experience of suffering points to the reality of original sin. Since God is good and just, human suffering must be a punishment for some original sin in which we all share. While I previously criticized this as being based on a static view of the universe, it would be wrong to ignore the psychological significance of this analysis.

The spontaneous link made between suffering and moral evil is very common.[7] People caught in great suffering exclaim "Why me?!", as if their suffering is meant to be a punishment for some unknown wrong. "I don't deserve this", or worse still "I must deserve this", they say, as if suffering is "just", and hence deserved, only as a punishment. Yet ontologically, suffering has no connection with punishment or moral evil, *per se*. All finite being suffers in as much as it comes up against its limits. Thus bones break when pushed beyond their capacities. Bodies convulse when chemical and biological limits are reached within them. People cease to function when pushed beyond their psychological limits. Suffering is part of any finite existence. In a very real sense there is simply no way to avoid such suffering.

Yet we continue, as did Augustine, to spontaneously make such a link. It is not difficult to see in this link the work of the Satan, the voice of original sin. In the experience of suffering the accusation arises, "this is your fault, this is a punishment for your wrongdoing". Since my finitude is part of my ontological structure as human, the accusation is saying that there is something wrong with being human, with being a finite being. It is telling us we should feel guilt about being human!

Even in the systematic account of Aquinas we get something of the same process. The privational view of original sin sees that state of original sin as humankind being left simply in a state of nature, without the aid of original justice. Again, there is a strong sense that something is wrong with simply being human. Simply being human is a dis-grace. In fact this strong sense that something is wrong with being human is precisely what original sin is all about!

Augustine's argument concerning concupiscence has a similar structure. From the Scholastic viewpoint concupiscence is part of the ontological structure of human nature. It is part of the structure of human finitude. Yet Augustine evokes in us a sense of guilt about concupiscence. To quote again from Karen Horney, we can develop a real "*feeling of guilt for not being the supreme being*".

This is not to be too critical of Augustine. Augustine's genius was to give voice to a very real human experience. It was only the depth of his own interiority, his spirituality which enabled him to be so sensitive to what is present but unarticulated in us all. Indeed it was a necessary first step in understanding the nature of original sin. However it is only a first step and one should remain aware of its ambiguities. I shall consider these again in Chapter 17.

CONCLUSION

In summary, we can note that this model of original sin makes contact with the following pieces of our puzzle:

* it distinguishes original sin from personal sin.
* it relates to our nature.
* it involves feelings of guilt.
* it is free from any assumption of monogenism.
* the unintelligibility is located in us, not God.
* it accounts for various mythic elements.
* it says something about "Satan".

There are still other elements that need to be addressed, in particular questions about salvation and the relationship between original sin and baptism. This I shall attempt to do in the next two chapters.

CHAPTER NOTES

It is interesting to note that Satan makes his first appearance in the Old Testament in the Book of Job. Here he is described as one of the sons of God. While he only makes an explicit appearance at the beginning and end of the book, the whole thrust of Job's so-called comforters is to incarnate the role of the Accuser.

Each of Job's friends levels accusations of sin against Job who strenuously denies the charges. The depth of Job's faith in God and himself is shown in his refusal to submit to such accusations. It is interesting to note that the early Fathers saw Job as a type for Christ. It is also interesting to note how the book of Job incorporates both immediate (the Satan) and mediated (Job's "comforters") aspects of the human predicament.

---

1 S. Moore, "Original Sin, Sex, Resurrection and Trinity", *Lonergan Workshop*, Vol.4, p.88.
2 *See* his *Let this Mind be in You*, pp.71ff.
3 E.g. John McKenzie, *Dictionary of the Bible*, Geoffrey Chapman, London, 1968, p.774.
4 *See* Horney's *Neurosis and Human Growth*, p.76.
5 The term "lucifer" arose from the Vulgate translation of "morning star" in Isaiah 14:12. The early Fathers took this as a reference to "the prince of demons", however the text originally referred to the death of a king of Babylon, probably Nebuchadnezzar, cf. the footnote to Isaiah 14:12 in TNJB.
6 *Gaudium et Spes*, n.16:

> His conscience is man's inner most secret core, and his sanctuary. There he is alone with God whose voice echoes in his depths. By conscience, in a wonderful way, that law is made known which is fulfilled in the love of God and of one's neighbor.

7 *See* for example, Scott Peck, *People of the Lie*, p.45.

CHAPTER SIXTEEN

DEATH, RESURRECTION AND SALVATION

In the previous chapter I sought to correlate original sin with the experience of a radical self-disesteem, a felt disvaluing of our very humanity, a feeling bad about being human. This understanding helps make sense of some of the things said about original sin as well as some of the distortions of the doctrine. One very significant question which remains is that of salvation—how does the death and resurrection of Jesus save us from such a radical self-disesteem? In this chapter I would like to explore some of the soteriological schemes offered to explain the work of Jesus. Here, as in the previous chapter, I am picking up hints in the writings of Sebastian Moore whom I have found most helpful in these matters.

As with the material on original sin in the previous chapter, what is of significance here is not so much the positive accounts given in the tradition, but the distortions which have crept into those accounts. Such distortions have entered into our theology of salvation in such a way as to hide the very things that were meant to be revealed. Not only do we find it difficult to think clearly about original sin, we also find it difficult to think clearly about salvation. It is interesting to note that the Church has never formally defined any doctrines in the area of salvation.[1] Perhaps this arises precisely from this difficulty. While the scriptures and liturgy are full of rich images and symbols for salvation the systematic expression of these is fraught with difficulties.

THE SOTERIOLOGY OF MOORE

How does Moore understand the process of salvation? Moore begins his analysis of the human condition with a positive account of the role of human self-esteem. My self-esteem is my most basic question addressed to the world—am I of significance? Does my life have meaning? This places my self-esteem in an intersubjective context. For Moore the most basic human need is the desire to be desired by significant others, be they parents, friends or lovers. Ultimately this desire extends to God—am I desirable to the very source of my being? This is Moore's reading of Augustine's saying: "Our hearts are restless, my God, until they rest in you". This positive account of self-esteem has already been explored in Chapter 3.

On the other hand, Moore understands our basic condition of original sin as a radical disvaluing of self, a disaffection with creaturehood. This leads to an emotional ambivalence towards life. Our sense of our own goodness becomes not just a search, but a desperate plea, "*Am I good?!*". Our self-esteem is always subject to a nagging doubt that really we're no good, that basically there is something wrong with being what we are. In the previous chapter I identified this with the voice of the Satan, the Accuser. This gives rise to an ambivalence which lies at the heart of the human tragedy.

How does a person caught in such ambivalence experience God? On the one hand God is the source of a possible affirmation which can sustain me beyond the grave. God's "yes" to my most basic question would be nothing less than heaven. On the other hand, in the light of my disesteem God seems to stand over me like a dominating parent, punishing me for my failings, ready to pounce on me for the slightest fault. If God's "yes" is heaven, God's "no" would be hell. From the position of my disesteem, God stands as the ultimate put-down, infinite being forever taunting me in my finitude. We experience ourselves as "under God's anger". In fact, from a psychological point of view, such anger is nothing but our projection of our own anger at God, our anger at being what we are, finite, hurting beings.

In a weakened sense we experience something of this ambivalence we feel towards God when we see someone who is very good. While we feel drawn to such a person because their goodness is so attractive, we can also feel a bit repelled. Their goodness can, we feel, put us in a bad light. Such tall poppies should be cut down to size, or at least we feel they should. They can make us feel bad in the light of our own felt inadequacies. Such an ambivalence colors all our relationships.

In this regard, Moore asks us to consider the experience of Jesus' disciples. On the one hand the disciples are drawn to Jesus because his goodness shines through. In following Jesus they experienced the greatest possible affirmation of their being. Jesus is Good News, he is good to be around. In his pure goodness, Jesus reveals a God of love who stands waiting to affirm and forgive us all. On the other hand, the disciples are still uncertain, a bit afraid, of what is being asked of them. Their basic resistance remains, their doubts about God cannot be so easily shifted. God (and Jesus, as God's emissary) is still seen as the ultimate threat.

What then happens in the death of Jesus on the cross? In the crucifixion the disciples experience the "death of God". The threat of God/Jesus is destroyed. Yet with the death of Jesus, the God which Jesus revealed as affirming and loving appears powerless in the face of evil. The affirmation which they had experienced appears like an illusion. With Jesus' death goes any hope for the affirmation which their hearts desire. For Moore, this is the experience of desolation, a dying without death, an emptiness of the heart which only God can restore to life. And this is what happens at the resurrection. In the resurrection the disciples experience the rebirth of their desire, a restoration of life. However, it is a new life, a new desire, free from the distraction of anger at God. The risen Jesus does for them what only God can do—he forgives them of their original sinfulness. In a very real sense, the resurrection is not just the restoration of Jesus to new life, but also the restoration of the disciples.[2]

This model of salvation offered by Moore has great explanatory power. In what follows I would like to pick up some of the themes present in Moore's analysis and push them a little further.

JESUS' DEATH AS A SACRIFICE

Moore's soteriology helps us understand some of the classical soteriologies which sought to explain how the death of Jesus saves us. One of the most widely accepted soteriologies is that of Anselm. Anselm saw the sin of Adam, as representative of the human race, as an offense to God. Since the measure of the offense is taken from the one offended, sin is an infinite offense to God. To satisfy divine justice an appropriate reparation needs to be made. However, since humans are only finite they cannot make up for an infinite offense. In his mercy God sends his Son, Jesus, who as human can offer satisfaction on behalf of humanity and whose satisfaction has infinite value since he is God incarnate. Those who picked up Anselm's model often extended it by speaking of Jesus' death on the cross as a substitutory sacrifice needed to appease God's anger.

While not questioning the basic structure of Anselm's model, the extension made by others, and often accepted in popular thought, requires some examination. What sort of God are we talking about who would require the gruesome death on a cross of his beloved Son? Such a God is more like a monster, more like a demon. Indeed it seems more like the demands of the Satan. Lonergan has claimed that such notions of God "cannot easily be distinguished from blasphemy".[3] Yet how could it be that such strange notions have become such a popular part of Catholic piety? Again we see evidence of the sort of systematic distortion which conceals truth rather than reveals it.

Many, in response to this, have suggested that the language of sacrifice should be dropped as inadequate, or even barbaric. Others have suggested, with greater sensitivity, that the language be transformed into the language of self-sacrifice. Jesus' death on the cross is a self-sacrifice out of love, as parents would sacrifice themselves for a child, as a symbol of the depth of Jesus' love for the world. While this suggestion has obvious merit, I would like to stay for a while with the darker aspects of the terms which, at first sight, are so "blasphemous".

If we pursue the question of sacrifice then we are drawn to ask "to whom is the sacrifice offered? who demands Jesus' death?". The rationalist approach reads the mythic language of sacrifice literally and answers "God the Father". Such an answer is blasphemous so the question is rejected as meaningless. However, a basic structure of myths is the way they work both to reveal and to conceal key truths. The question remains valid, "who demands Jesus' death?". But the answer is to be sought by analyzing (in the psychoanalytic sense) the myth. If the answer is not God (or Jesus), the only remaining character in the mythological drama is humankind. As is often the case, myth inverts key relationships. Jesus' death is then a sacrifice in the primitive sense, not to God but to us. Thus we arrive at the position of Moore above. Jesus is the sacrifice to our anger which destroys the god who is experienced as a threat to our being, and reveals a God of unbounded love and forgiveness.

There is indeed a necessity about the death of Jesus but the necessity of the death of Jesus—"the Son of Man *must* die" (Mark 8:13)—is not some divine necessity but simple human compulsion. Jesus is too good to be around, too much of a threat to us. We see the same "necessity" at work in the deaths of Gandhi and Martin Luther King. To some extent we all hide from the light which uncovers our weaknesses. Such a hiding has a compulsive force and such compulsion is the very antithesis of freedom.

It is easy to see why such a reality is suppressed in myth. It is a shocking truth about the depth of evil in the human heart. In the death of Jesus we seek to rid ourselves of God once and for all. As Moore claims:

> The causal connection of sin with the death of God [in Jesus] is sin's requirement of the death of God for its absolving, such is sin's depth ... As people involved in the primal guilt [i.e. original sin], we call, in a way we hardly understand, for the death of God.[4]

As Freud discovered, the male child's desire for the mother and wish to kill the father, the so-called Oedipus complex, is too shocking a truth to bring to consciousness. It must be buried in the subconscious where it gives birth to appropriate myths. So too the desire to kill God is too shocking a truth to reach full consciousness and thus gives rise to a myth about God demanding a pure and spotless victim in order to leave us in peace.

THE WHY OF JESUS' DEATH

One of the weaknesses of Anselm's soteriology is the way it abstracts from the actual historical circumstances of Jesus' life and death. On that basis what Jesus actually says and does in his earthly ministry are of no consequence. All that is important is that Jesus, through his death on the cross, offers satisfaction to the Father. To some extent the same could be said of the soteriology suggested by Sebastian Moore.[5] All that is necessary is that Jesus provoke our anger and this is done simply by the structure of our ambivalent response to his goodness. This still remains somewhat abstract. However it is not sufficient to say that Jesus went about doing good. We must consider the specific type of good that Jesus did. This can further help us in our consideration of Jesus' death as sacrificial.

It is significant in this regard to recognize that Jesus' public ministry, especially in the many miracles he performs, is directed towards those who are victims of social structures of sacrifice. Any and all of us are victims of the petty shortcomings of our neighbors, friends and lovers. However the specific type of good that Jesus does is not just directed to people on that individual level. Jesus seeks out those who are victims at the social level—the lepers, the prostitutes, the tax collectors, all those who were ostracized from proper society, put down, expelled, marginalized. Through these actions Jesus is seeking to restore Israel to its original charter of justice and equality for all.[6]

In his ministry Jesus identifies with the victims of society's compulsive need to sacrifice. On the cross that identification becomes complete and total. Jesus becomes the Victim, the pure Sacrifice. It is important to remember that Jesus' death is not brought about by some poor individual annoyed by Jesus' action—a one-off assassination. Jesus' death is an execution by the state. As Caiaphas says in John's Gospel, "... it is to your advantage that one man should die for the people, rather than that the whole nation should perish" (John 11:50). Jesus dies because of his subversive identification with society's victims—"whenever you do this to the least you do it to me" (cf. Matthew 25:40,45). This identification is too painful a reminder of the suffering we as a society have caused. Jesus *must* die, must himself become a victim.

We can find this same recognition of the social significance of Jesus' sacrificial death in the eucharistic dispute in the Church of Corinth. By reintroducing social distinctions into their eucharistic celebration, the people of Corinth are negating the reality the eucharist proclaims. I have already discussed this in Chapter 6.

THE RESURRECTION OF JESUS

Moore's analysis of the saving power of Jesus' death and resurrection rests on the experience of emotional ambivalence that is experienced by the disciples with regard to Jesus, and ultimately with regard to God. While Moore focuses on the ambivalence as present prior to Jesus' death, it would be wrong to conclude that Jesus' death, of itself, removes such an ambivalence. Indeed if anything, Jesus' death gives extra power to that ambivalence. We can see this by a consideration of Freud's classical analysis of the taboos associated with the dead.[7]

Freud finds that such taboos arise out of an attitude of emotional ambivalence towards the dead person. He notes that when a loved one dies "it not infrequently happens that the survivor is overwhelmed by tormenting doubts ... as to whether she may not herself have been responsible for the death". He goes on at length:

> We find that in a certain sense these obsessive self-reproaches are justified, and that this is why they are proof against

> contradictions and protests. It is not that the mourner was really responsible for the death . . . Nonetheless there was something in her—a wish that was unconscious to herself—*which would not have been dissatisfied by the occurrence of death* and which might actually have brought it about if it had had the power . . . [W]e find that *behind the tender love there is a concealed hostility* in the unconscious. This is the classical example, *the prototype*, of *the ambivalence of human emotions.* [emphasis added]

Such hostility cannot be allowed to come to the surface. It needs to be suppressed as a defense against overwhelming feelings of guilt. While Freud distinguishes between the form of defense as found in the neurotic, and that of the so-called "primitive", we should be slow to say that such responses are not found in us all. Indeed it seems to me that many modern horror films reflect such feelings with their themes of "the return of the living dead". Of the "primitive" Freud states:

> The defence against [the hostility] takes the form of displacing it on the object of the hostility, on the dead themselves. The defensive procedure . . . is known as "*projection*". The survivor thus denies that he has ever harboured any hostile feelings against the dead one; the soul of the dead harbours them instead and seeks to put them into action during the whole period of mourning.

Further:

> It is no longer true that they are rejoicing to be rid of the dead man; on the contrary, they are mourning for him; but, strange to say, *he* has turned into a wicked demon ready to gloat over their misfortunes and eager to kill them.

Moreover, he notes "the survivors who have most to fear will be those who were formerly its nearest and dearest".

It is not difficult to imagine Jesus' disciples in the situation depicted by Freud. They had deserted Jesus at his moment of greatest need. One had betrayed him, another denied him, all had left him to his fate. The feelings of guilt and powerlessness must have been overwhelming for them as they sought out mutual solace after his death. It was almost like a bad dream and there is a real sense of relief that perhaps they can put it all behind them—"Simon Peter said 'I'm going fishing'. They all replied 'We'll come too'" (John 21:3). Let's go back to what was familiar and safe, and pretend it all didn't happen.

To people caught up in such feelings, news of the resurrection does not bring unalloyed joy. In the face of desertion, denial and betrayal, what is a Jesus returned from the dead going to do? Will he come as an avenging angel, a "wicked demon ready to gloat over their misfortunes and eager to kill them", as Freud suggests? Such a prospect, of a resurrected Jesus, is likely to bring not joy but fear, even blind terror.

It is not difficult to find evidence of such a fear in the accounts of the resurrection. It comes through most clearly in Mark's gospel where the women greet news of the risen Jesus by running away, "frightened out of their wits" (Mark 16:8). However, all the gospels mention fear, fear of the Jews (John 20:19), fear among the Jewish high priests (Matthew 28:62–66), fear of ghosts (Luke 24:37). It is clear that fear was in the air. The disciples are repeatedly being told not to be afraid, cf. Matthew 28:5,10; Mark 16:6; Luke 24:36–38; John 20:20–21. Yet the very inconsistency of identifying who was afraid and of what they were afraid, points, psychologically, to the difficulty in acknowledging the real emotional ambivalence that was felt by the disciples about the resurrection of Jesus.

If this psychological reading of the texts is correct, the emotional ambivalence of the disciples towards Jesus extends into the resurrection encounters themselves. It is only in the resurrection encounters with Jesus that this ambivalence is lifted, and it is lifted precisely in the experience of forgiveness that comes from the risen Lord. Here we can agree with Schillebeeckx that the basic resurrection experience is one of forgiveness and conversion.[8] All the guilt-induced fears, all the subsequent projected hostility are shown to be phantoms. Jesus does not come back as an avenging demon spreading fire and wielding the sword. He returns as the one who still pours out his love, who still forgives. This is the good news, not that Jesus is risen, but that Jesus is risen *and forgiving*. It is this forgiveness which blasts away the prior emotional ambivalence and turns the disciples into men and women of courage and grace.

It is in this resurrection experience of Jesus' forgiveness that we can find the experiential basis for the author of I John saying "God is light; there is no darkness in him at all" (I John 1:5). There is no darkness in the risen Jesus, no malice, no seeking of revenge, no hardness of heart. It is in the resurrection of Jesus that his total innocence shines through. In the resurrection Jesus proves beyond doubt that he is the Just One. Further the resurrection of Jesus by the Father is God's own vindication of Jesus' innocence. And if this total innocence is true of Jesus, then equally it is true of God, his Father. The emotional ambivalence felt by the disciples towards Jesus is a real symbol of the emotional ambivalence we all feel towards God. If Jesus is no threat, even returned from the dead, then neither is God and we may approach God in confidence knowing that we will be "able to quieten our conscience in his presence" (I John 3:19).

It is this revelation that in Jesus, and hence in God, there "is no darkness at all"'that has power to break forever the emotional ambivalence we all feel towards God. It is this that gives Jesus' death and resurrection its *universal* saving significance. While, however, we do not share the direct experience of the disciples, we do enter into the dynamics of the saving event in the celebrations of baptism and eucharist and in the liturgical celebrations of Easter. In each eucharist Jesus again shows himself to be the giving one, pouring out his life, placing himself at our disposal with the defenselessness of unconditional love.

THE ONGOING SACRIFICE

Having thus interpreted the myth of Jesus' death as an appeasing sacrifice I would now like to further investigate the notion of sacrifice as applicable to our present situation.

In its primitive dark form the concept of sacrifice correlates with that of victim. For each sacrifice there is a victim sacrificed. Though one may note with a certain smugness that our present sensibilities do not allow for such primitive acts, when we look at our lives and our society we see that in fact we do sacrifice other people time and time again. Our lives and our society are littered with the victims we have sacrificed—out of anger, apathy, malice, anxiety, in order to maintain the status quo, etc. In our personal lives they may include our children, our spouses, our colleagues, our friends, even ourselves. In our society they include the unemployed, indigenous peoples, those on welfare payments. On a global scale they include the poor and starving of many nations whose plight we refuse to address because it may force us to reform our lifestyles. These are the many victims of the ideological distortion of the social order which we previously considered in Chapter 4.

Such people we sacrifice on the altar of our own inadequacy, our own lack of freedom, our own lack of self-esteem. We sacrifice them so that we may feel more powerful, we put them down to try to build ourselves up. It is not God who receives our sacrifice but the one who would be like God, the Satan, the Accuser, who harries us with our failures, taunts us with our finitude, demanding ever greater sacrifices which seem never enough. They can never be enough since in each case there is some justice in the sacrifices we make. Even if people are not guilty of the sins for which we sacrifice them we know that they, like us, have their faults, that they, like us, have sacrificed others in their turn.

In the case of Jesus there is no justice in the sacrifice we make of him. He is the spotless innocent victim, the *pure* sacrifice, with no underlying justification. With the sacrifice of Jesus the horror of the logic of sacrifice is laid bare. At last we have a victim who is equal to the depth of our anger, a victim who willingly takes on that anger, who bears our sins though innocent himself. We have vented our fury upon an innocent man and are left to contemplate the total futility of our actions. Easter Saturday has all the qualities of a calm before an expected storm—surely all hell will break loose! Yet what in fact breaks loose is not hell, but the justice of God. God meets human injustice with divine justice and raises up Jesus as the Mediator of divine love and forgiveness.

Here we have, I would argue, a basic structure of a fallen human existence, the structure of original sin. It is the structure of evil in the human heart, a structure which Jesus' death and resurrection seeks to overcome. In the death of Jesus the structure of evil, of sacrificing others, is met by the structure of love, to willingly sacrifice oneself for the sake of another. The drama of the crucifixion is of cosmic proportions, of the root of evil in conflict with ultimate good. As is often the case evil seems to win the day. Jesus dies and with him seems to go all hope. Just another brave but foolish man cast aside by the forces of the world who are determined to maintain their privileges and the ideologies which sustain them. But God has raised him up and vindicated the love that Jesus reveals. In the end, love *is* more powerful than death, good more powerful than evil.

This point of view may also shed some light on our traditional understanding of the eucharist as a sacrifice. In the eucharistic celebration we enter into the drama of divine sacrifice, touching again the reality of the man–God who hands himself over to us to do with what we will. It is not God who requires this sacrifice but us, so slow are we to learn the lesson of Calvary. In the eucharist Jesus is again present to us as the Victim who calls on us to renounce all victimizations. This is the lesson we must learn. As the Council of Trent so bluntly puts it, it is a sacrifice "such as *human* nature requires" DS 1739.

CONCLUSION

In this chapter we have considered how it is that Jesus saves us from original sin. I have argued that the structure of Jesus' death and resurrection gets to the heart of our original self-disesteem by freeing us from the necessity of sacrificing others. In a sense Jesus' situation is archetypal, bringing into the sharpest focus the futility of the logic of sacrifice by meeting it head-on with the power of self-sacrificing love. In the resurrection God reveals whose side God is on, to show once and for all that there is no darkness in God, only light. Such a God can always be approached with confidence. However the picture is not yet complete. It would be wrong to think of Jesus' death and resurrection as bringing salvation in some *deus ex machina* manner. Jesus' death and resurrection provide the archetypal pattern of salvation which we are all called to follow in our own lives, in the light of God's grace. To complete our analysis we must say something about the Church and original sin.

CHAPTER NOTES

1. It is not uncommon in theology to distinguish between soteriologies which focus on the death and resurrection of Jesus, and those which focus on the Incarnation. In the above analysis I have focused on the first type. However it is easy to see how the second type fits in, as well as seeing its shortcomings. If original sin is seen in terms of an original self-disesteem, a feeling bad about being human, then the Incarnation reveals that, in fact, there is nothing wrong with being human. If God has become human then human dignity is restored to the full.

While this is true there are two difficulties associated with it. The first is to ask whether we would ever know about the Incarnation if it were not for the death and resurrection of Jesus, where Jesus does for the disciples what only God can do and so reveals himself to be God. The second difficulty is more profound and perhaps more to the point. The problem with many ideologies is not just that they distort human self-esteem. In many cases they extend to a very denial of the humanity of those sacrificed. Thus the early Church Fathers would argue as to whether women really had souls—were they really human? Colonial racists denied the humanity of indigenous races and treated them as being mere animals. Those who argue for abortion deny the humanity of the newly conceived child.

This is why it is fitting that Jesus identify himself with those who are most marginalized, the very least. As Paul says:

> He did not count equality with God something to be grasped, but emptied himself, taking the form of a slave (Philippians 2:6–7).[9]

This is a much more subversive stand, an affirmation of the humanity and human dignity of those at the very bottom of society. A slave in Roman society had no legal rights and was to all intents and purposes a non-person. By identifying himself with the non-person, Jesus rejects any ideology which would seek to deny the human identity of such people.

It is interesting to note that so-called liberal theology often takes its stand on the Incarnation. The criticism levelled at liberal theology by political theology is that it fails to take seriously the issues of social evil and sin, which are highlighted by the plight of the non-persons of the world, the poor, the marginalized.

2. While Anselm's soteriological model has proved to be the most popular, the other popular model, which predates Anselm, is that of the ransom theory. It sees Jesus' death as a ransom paid to free us from our bondage to the devil who had gained certain rights over us. This model was popular among the early Church Fathers.

One difficulty which this model had was in deciding to whom the ransom was paid. It did not seem right that the ransom be paid to the devil, but it did not make sense that it should be paid to God. This confusion has led later commentators to claim that this is only an image which should not be pushed to the point of answering such meaningless questions.

From the psychological point of view the confusion over who gets the ransom is highly significant. It points to our basic confusion as to the identity of God—is God a God of life, or simply the devil in disguise? Our inability to distinguish between God and the Satan is a reflection of the basic experience of original sin. As I have noted above, it is in the disciples' experience of the resurrection that this confusion is finally and definitively clarified. God is a God of life in whom there is no darkness. In the resurrection the Satan is finally "driven out of heaven" and his place taken by the Son "who pleads for us at the right hand of the Father".

3. The approach taken in this chapter seems to have been anticipated in the thought of the second century theologian, Origen. In *Past Event and Present Salvation: The Christian Idea of Atonement*, Fiddes notes that "Origen employs the curious phrases that Christ 'propitiated the sinner' or 'propitiated sin' or 'propitiated men to God'" (p.79). Fiddes finds it curious "since [Origen] is not using it in the usual sense of appeasing God's anger". Indeed Origen seems to be saying that it is the sinner who is appeased, not God. Yet on the above analysis one could say that Origen said exactly what he meant to say!

1 A schema, basically on Anselmian lines, was drawn up for discussion at Vatican I, but the Council was interrupted before it could be discussed.
2 For a fuller account of Moore's theology *see Introducing Contemporary Theologies*, Chap.6.
3 *The Desires of the Human Heart*, p.207.
4 Cf. S. Moore, *The Fire and the Rose are One*, p.146.
5 In his latest work, Moore goes some way to meeting such an objection, *see* his *Jesus the Liberator of Desire*, pp.37–8.
6 *See* B. Meyer, *The Aims of Jesus*, SCM Press, London, 1979, pp.170–3.
7 "Totem and Taboo", in *The Penguin Freud Library*, Vol.13, *The Origins of Religion*. The material here is all taken from, pp.116–19.
8 *See* his *Jesus, An experiment in Christology*, pp.379–97.
9 Some translate the Greek *doulos* as servant rather than slave and see in it a reference to the suffering servant of Isaiah 53:12. Brendan Byrne comments that "although linguistically plausible, this [translation] disturbs the sequence of ideas", *NJBC*, p.795.

CHAPTER SEVENTEEN

WHERE DOES BAPTISM FIT IN?

The story of salvation does not end with the death and resurrection of Jesus. As the New Testament bears witness, the death and resurrection of Jesus is the beginning of a new era of salvation, the era of the Church. The Church has a mission to the world, the mission of mediating the transcendent value of Jesus to a world torn apart by sin. In this context we can address the question of the relationship between original sin and baptism.

ORIGINAL SIN AND BAPTISM

As we have already seen in Chapter 10, the question of baptism, especially infant baptism, has played a key role in the development of the doctrine of original sin. It was from the practice of infant baptism that Augustine argued that even newly born infants suffer from the sin of Adam. The doctrine of original sin provided the theoretical rationale for the praxis of the Church. Already in the African Church, to which Augustine belonged, there had developed folklore stories of children dying without baptism and being miraculously restored to life so that they could be baptized and saved from the pains of hell. There was, and still remains, a serious danger in this of seeing baptism as a quasi-magic rite, a magic incantation for removing a powerful curse. Many priests still experience people coming to the Church to have children baptized—people who have not entered the

Church since marriage—whose dominant motivation is a half-remembered catechism lesson about unbaptized children who die and go to limbo.

In recent theology there has, of course, been a real swing away from such a position. The recent development of the Rite of Christian Initiation for Adults (RCIA) has shifted the Church's focus onto seeing adult baptism as the norm. Baptism is now seen primarily as entry into the Church, an initiation into the life of the Christian community. On a superficial reading this may seem more conducive to the Pelagian understanding of the role of baptism, and one might get the feeling that Augustine is turning in his grave. Indeed, the new rite of baptism for children makes only one passing reference to original sin, and even that reference is optional.

Is the Augustinian perspective no longer valid? Or is it possible to reconcile the two positions outlined above? Is baptism primarily about freeing people from original sin or is it primarily about entry into the Church?

When the question is put in such a way, the presumption is that we are talking about two different effects of the one sacrament. Such a presumption is not valid. In order to overcome such a false dichotomy we need to realize that baptism "frees us from original sin" precisely because it is entry into the Church. Thus baptism does not have two effects—entry into the Church *and* the washing away of original sin. It has one effect since the two are one. In the community of the Church there is the mediation of grace which affirms the weakened sense of self-esteem present in the ungraced. The Church as community "frees us from original sin" through its overwhelming (in the Greek, *baptizo*, means to drown, or overwhelm, with water) love, which mediates the experience of transcendent value to the newly baptized person.

Such a position removes, once and for all, any notion of baptism being a magic rite. It is because of a very real entry into an identifiable community which has a clearly identifiable role to play that we can speak of the "removal of original sin". This position highlights the mutual responsibilities of both parties, both the baptized person and the Christian community into which he/she enters. If the baptized person has no further contact with the Church, through a personal decision or that of his/her parents, then it is meaningless to speak of the sacrament freeing the person from original sin. In classical language the sacrament is valid, but not efficacious. It may become effective at a later date when such a person renews meaningful contact with the Church.

The responsibilities are not all one way. Baptism frees us from original sin inasmuch as we enter into a community which mediates grace to us. If the community does not take such a responsibility seriously, if it shamefully neglects its new members to the point of even increasing their sense of alienation, then again the sacrament has not been effective. Normally, in the case of infant baptism, such a responsibility is discharged by the parents of a newly born child (or failing them, the godparents). However, the community cannot afford to neglect the duties that it has to its new members if it is to take its sacramental life seriously.

Indeed the baptized person has entered into a journey of freedom, a freedom which is meant to be sustained by the Christian community which mediates God's love and forgiveness. Baptism as a rite of initiation only marks the beginning of that journey, the beginning of a new freedom. While it is valid to see this freedom as a "freedom from original sin", it is also important to recognize that the freedom which the Christian community mediates is a growing freedom, a continual struggle against forces which seek to undermine that freedom. The voice of the Satan remains but it is countered by a new voice, that of God as mediated through the Body of Christ, the Church.

It is also possible to see how this "freedom from original sin" can be mediated outside of sacramental baptism and entry into the Church. Wherever people enter into a community which affirms their existence, which loves them so that they are no longer prey to the Accuser, then the grace of God can be effectively mediated by that community. Such a community can effectively overwhelm (i.e. baptize) its members with love. Within a traditional theology such people can be said to have experienced a "baptism of desire". Indeed Cajetan, the great Scholastic theologian of the sixteenth century, had already noted that "the prayer and desire of the child's parents might be seen as a vicarious baptism of desire".[1] This could easily be seen to be the case in a non-Christian setting. They have placed their trust in their own experience of transcendent value which has been mediated to them by their community and which Christian faith sees as fully affirmed in the person of Jesus.

THE TRANSMISSION OF ORIGINAL SIN

Given all that has gone before, it is perhaps now time to take up the vexatious question of the transmission of original sin. It is this question which has been at the heart of many modern debates about the whole doctrine. For Augustine original sin is transmitted in the very act of human conception. Sexual intercourse is always driven by concupiscence so that every child is born out of concupiscence and hence carries the stain of original sin. With Aquinas the picture shifts. Original sin is the privation of original justice. Adam passes on mere human nature, without original justice, and so original sin is passed on through natural procreation. Modern theology has found this linking of the transmission of original sin with procreation as troublesome and has sought various ways around the link. Any such attempt must face squarely the teaching of Trent, that original sin is transmitted by generation, not imitation.

I have already argued that the significant bench mark for original sin is the birth rather than the conception of the person. This obviously goes against the Augustinian position which sees the transmission of original sin occurring in the very act of conception. I would now like to further the argument on this point.

As we saw in Chapter 13, post-Tridentine theology argued in the following manner concerning the nature of original sin. The nature of original sin is revealed by the nature of its healing. Trent taught that baptism is the washing away of original sin, and that baptism gives sanctifying grace. Hence original sin is primarily the absence of sanctifying grace, a condition which baptism rectifies! While such a metaphysical argument has an attractive simplicity it fails in an important respect. Its abstract nature helps to hide from us the way in which baptism confers sanctifying grace since it overlooks the way in which the Church mediates grace to its new members. By focusing on the immediacy of grace, which is more easily handled by metaphysical means, it undercuts the mediational aspects which are more historical. As I argued above, baptism removes the guilt of original sin precisely because it brings about the historical event of entry into the Christian community.

Nevertheless, the structure of post-Tridentine theology's argument remains valid. The nature of original sin *is* revealed by the nature of its healing. Just as sanctifying grace has inseparably both immediate and mediated aspects, so too does original sin. The immediate aspect is seen most clearly in the work of the Satan, that distortion of conscience which harries us with accusations about the deficiencies of human nature. However, as with grace, this immediate aspect cannot be separated from the ways in which the experience is historically mediated.

Indeed it is not too difficult to see how the mediational aspects of original sin work. I am born into a world which is dominated by sin. The various ideologies which distort human society shape my consciousness even prior to any free decision on my part, prior to any hope of a conscious decision to imitate what I see around me. The power of such evil seduces me, undermines my self-esteem, warps first my feeling and then my thinking so that my horizon is distorted from the start.

Such a process is most clearly seen in the case of child abuse. To the young child the parent has a god-like status. In the normal course of events, the parent provides all its wants and needs and is seemingly omnipotent. Yet things can go terribly wrong. The parent no longer provides love and care but treats the child with, at best, indifference, at worst with violence. Such a situation causes intolerable damage to the child and the patterns of such damage are well documented. The child cannot relinquish its image of the parent as god-like.[2] The parent can do no wrong in the child's eyes. The child is forced to conclude that it must be at fault itself.

Children who experience such treatment will almost invariably grow up with an insurmountable burden of guilt. In fact they carry, in their own bodies, the guilt of their parents. The worse their treatment, the worse their own sense of guilt. Yet why should they feel guilty? They are the most innocent of victims, whose spirit has been all but crushed from their earliest moments. Unless something happens to break the cycle of violence, unless grace is mediated, such people tend to confirm their own sense of self-hatred with their own acts of violence towards others. This is not some form of mechanistic determinism, but an empirically verifiable correlation of a slavery to sin. There is a way out, but it cannot be achieved through human effort alone. It requires the grace of God.

Yet the question remains, why should the child feel guilty? It has not done anything. There is something fundamentally wrong-headed about such a feeling. Clearly we can correlate it with the interior accusations of the Satan. Yet why is this voice present? Is not the presence of this voice itself difficult to understand, as unintelligible as the exterior evil which gives such accusations their power. The origins of evil remain, as always, mysterious. It is important to acknowledge both immediate and mediational aspects as two poles in the one "reality" of original sin.

It is also important to note the role played by guilt in the above process. All of us experience, through the evil of others, a real sense of guilt. We feel guilt about things, even things which are totally beyond our control. Such a feeling of guilt distorts all our relationships, all our decisions. Most importantly it distorts our perceptions of evil. In such a confused state it does not take long before we confirm the guilt we feel by a real moral fault.

Further, it is significant that Trent sees baptism as freeing us from the "guilt of original sin". Baptism should free us from this sense of guilt. The affirming love of the Christian community frees me from such feelings, allowing me to see the reality of the limits of my guilt and responsibility. It also frees me to see evil as it really is, to name it as such, and so to take a prophetic stand against evil. While such guilt remains it cripples me, renders me powerless—*non posse, non peccare*! However to be freed from it is like being born again, putting on the new man and putting off the old (cf. Ephesians 4:22–24). Baptism frees me from the power of sin and death, bringing me to new life in Jesus Christ.

There remains the matter of Trent's insistence that the children of baptized parents must themselves be baptized (Canon 4). While there is a certain logic to the position that baptized parents cannot transmit what they no longer possess, there is a stark realism in Trent's insistence that the children of baptized parents also be baptized. In the first place, it reminds us that entry into the Church cannot be presumed, but is the result of a divine providential election. In the second place, even baptized parents will sin against their children and so assist in the transmission of original sin. Further, we all live in a world dominated by sin and no child can expect to be quarantined from it forever.

ONTOLOGY OR HISTORY?

The above departure from traditional understanding can gain further warrant by a consideration of theological method. I have already noted the difficulties Aquinas had with the question of the transmission of original sin. Scholasticism in general sought to provide a purely metaphysical account of the reality of original sin. Thus it saw original sin in terms of a privation, an ontological lack of original justice. It is questionable whether a purely ontological analysis of original sin is adequate.

In this regard it is interesting to note that Lonergan has suggested "that redemption was one of those categories that could not adequately be dealt with in Aristotelean categories, that it required a theory of history and historical categories".[3] If such is the case with redemption, then such is also the case, I would argue, with original sin. It has to be recognized that there were strong methodological limitations to Scholastic theology which did not allow it to think in such historical terms. As in the theology of grace, so too in the theology of original sin, history has to become an important category.

A TEST CASE—THE IMMACULATE CONCEPTION

No analysis of original sin can ignore the Catholic doctrine of Mary's Immaculate Conception, the belief that Mary was conceived free from original sin. This belief represents a serious test case for any analysis of original sin, since such an analysis must be able to give a meaningful account of Mary's situation.

At first sight the doctrine of the Immaculate Conception seems to deal a death blow to the analysis given above. It seems to focus attention on Mary's conception rather than her birth, whereas I have focused attention on birth as a major bench mark for original sin. Such a stance, however, needs to be questioned. The doctrine of the Immaculate Conception sought to define Mary's freedom from original sin. It was not the intention of the definition to define something about original sin itself. It adopted the not uncommonly held position that linked original sin with the conception, but as I have already noted, the only bench mark given by Trent is birth, infants newly from their mothers' wombs.

Indeed a similar misreading of the Immaculate Conception has been used to claim that the Church teaches that life begins at conception. The doctrine of the Immaculate Conception cannot be used to say that the Church teaches that life begins at conception since it was not the intention of the doctrine to address the issue. It simply assumed a common bench mark, that of conception, to note the beginning of life.[4] The Church cannot define a new doctrine about the beginning of original sin, or life, by accident. It must seek to explicitly address the issue.

The other difficulty is that the doctrine is regularly presented as a special privilege given to Mary, as Mother of Jesus, without reference to anyone or anything else. While it should be seen as a special privilege given to Mary, it should not be seen in isolation from the rest of salvation history. Mary's state should be seen as the mature fruit of a tree planted with the call of Abraham (Genesis 12). From the call of Abraham, through the exile in Egypt, the Exodus through the desert, and most importantly in the giving of the Torah (the Jewish law) God was working with his Chosen People, building up a history of grace mediated by the men and women of the Old Testament. Central to this history of grace was the building of a society built on justice, in which the orphans and widows, the strangers and outcasts would be fairly treated. This was the tireless message of the prophets.

This history of grace produced remarkable men and women

who were relatively free from the crippling effects of the history of sin. It is of interest to note that we spontaneously acclaim the mother and father of Mary to be saints, even though we have no reliable historical information about them. It is almost impossible to conceive how Mary could be free from original sin if her parents were not holy people. This is not to say, of course, that the holiness of the parents would be sufficient of itself without the freely given grace of God to Mary herself, and the profound workings of divine providence in her personal life.

This view of the Immaculate Conception removes it from the arena of being an arbitrary, random act on God's part to free Mary while keeping the rest of us bound. Mary's freedom from original sin is the culmination of thousands of years of history, of grace and human cooperation overcoming the effects of sin, reaching its apex in this one human person. It seems to me that this is a much more meaningful understanding of Mary's Immaculate Conception than one which sees it in isolation from the rest of salvation history.

A PITFALL FOR THE CHURCH

The doctrine of original sin, while part of the Church's deposit of faith, is not without its pitfalls for the Church. There is no question that the Church is called upon to preach the doctrine. The question is, how is it to do so?

It is important here to distinguish between empirical and normative viewpoints. It is one thing to say that this is the way things are, another to say this is the way things should be. While it is true, on an empirical, statistical basis, that men are more aggressive than women, this does not mean that men should be more aggressive. This is especially important to keep in mind when discussing original sin.

It was the genius of Augustine to give expression to a profound human experience, the experience of original sin. He gave voice to all the previously voiceless experiences of guilt and anger, ultimately anger at God. He called all this original sin and said we all suffer from it. This was a perfectly justified empirical observation. However, there is a shift which occurs from this empirical view to a normative one. It is one thing to say "you feel guilty", quite another to say, "you should feel guilty".

If we take the viewpoint of Moore, then we would conclude that most of what is said about original sin, particularly at the level of the popular imagination, is more to do with the "voice of original sin".

> Thus we get the bad situation that while the best psychologists and counsellors are coming to understand the root of our evil as a bad self-image, Christians tend to say to them, "You are leaving out original sin"—not realizing that these psychologists are, precisely, *pointing* to original sin.

Moore goes on to note that:

> So subtle is this "original sin" that it has managed to perform a brilliant trick ... It has persuaded religious people that the comment "And that's just the way it is", is the voice of God ...
>
> What has happened is that the *voice* of original sin ... has masqueraded as the *doctrine* of original sin. With the disastrous consequence that preaching the doctrine of original sin is reinforcing the voice of original sin![5]

It is in the preaching of the Church that my initial definition of original sin becomes most important: *original sin is what Jesus saves us from*. The Church cannot cut off its doctrine of original sin from the doctrine of salvation in Jesus. Once such a separation is made then the Church substitutes the doctrine for the voice. Instead of freeing us from original sin through its mediation of overwhelming love, it reinforces original sin. It becomes not a call to raise us up, but a further put-down, a further voice of the Accuser.

CONCLUSION

This concludes the discussion of the nature of original sin. In this chapter I have considered the relationship between original sin, Church and baptism. While the discussion has involved a departure from traditional theological positions on original sin, I have sought to show that such a departure is justified, indeed necessary. In the next and final chapter I would like to discuss two issues which touch at the heart of the nature of original sin, the issue of male domination of women, and the issue of human misuse of the natural environment.

CHAPTER NOTES

It is interesting to consider the symbolism associated with baptism, in both scripture and Church teaching and liturgy.

Paul speaks of those who are baptised as having died with Christ so that they may rise with him. Baptism is death without dying, death to the old ways dominated by guilt to the new ways of grace. Baptism is entry into the tomb with Jesus, it is being crucified with him, so that we can share in the resurrection. Baptism is entry into *new life* (Romans 6:1–11, also Colossians 2:12). Entry into our first life, birth, is entry into a world of ambiguity, affected by sin—we fall prey to the accusations of the Satan. Baptism is being *born from above*, not returning to the womb, but being born of the Spirit (John 3:1ff.) into a community of grace, free from the crushing guilt of original sin. Such people have been *begotten by God* (I John 3:9, 5:1).

The Dogmatic Constitution of the Church, *Lumen Gentium*, speaks of baptism as entry into a priestly community and incorporation into the Church. Baptism involves a *rebirth*, as sons and daughters of God.

All these images point to baptism as a *re-birth*, being *born* again into the new life, free from the ambiguities of our first birth. The New Testament data concerning something happening prior to birth is a sense of divine election, as when Paul proclaims that "God ... had specially chosen me while I was still in my mother's womb" (Galatians 1:15). Indeed such an election occurs at the very beginning—"Before the world was made, he chose us, chose us in Christ, to be holy and spotless, and to live in his presence" (Ephesians 1:4).

---

1 *TNDT*, p.585.
2 Indeed all of us, and abused children in particular, find it difficult to distinguish between our parents and our image of God. Cathy Anne Matthews notes the importance for her of the discovery that her abusive father was not God, cf. *Breaking Through*, pp.58ff.
3 "The Church", by Joseph Komonchak, in *The Desires of the Human Heart*, V. Gregson, (ed.), p.222.
4 On the question of when life in fact begins, see the thorough study by N. Ford, *When Did I Begin?*, CUP, 1988.
5 *See* Moore's, *Let This Mind Be in You*, pp.83–5.

CHAPTER EIGHTEEN

SOME SOCIAL CONSEQUENCES OF ORIGINAL SIN

In this chapter I would like to explore two areas of social concern which relate directly to what has been said about original sin. Though all sin relates to original sin, inasmuch as original sin is the root cause of all sin, still the two areas which I wish to consider are in a sense archetypal. They point to the very heart of the problem in a very clear and distinct manner. Indeed this archetypal quality is verified even in the biblical texts which see them as consequences of the first sin of Adam and Eve.

The two areas which I would like to explore are sexism and human relationship to the natural environment. Not only are these two areas of significant contemporary concern for society, but their close relation to original sin points to issues which should lie at the heart of the Church's mission to the modern world.

SEXISM AND ORIGINAL SIN

In the history of the Church the story of the Fall has done nothing for the cause or status of women in the Church. Even in the New Testament, the blame for the Fall is laid at the feet of Eve (I Timothy 2:14). The early Fathers of the Church expand on this notion blaming Eve, and with her all women, with seducing men from holiness, turning men away from God and generally making life difficult! Many saw women's subservience to men as a fitting punishment for Eve's part in the Fall—indeed they believed it would be wrong not to so punish women since it would undermine God's just and holy punishment!

While some balance was restored through the special place given to Mary in popular piety and eventually in Church teaching, in the end this only tended to polarize the situation. The Madonna–Whore typology was formed and since most women did not measure up to the Madonna, they were typecast as whores.

As it stands, it may look as if the doctrine of original sin has been a major cause of sexism within the Church and certainly not good news for women. For many feminists this fact alone is enough to question the validity of the doctrine. However, as I noted before, it is important here to distinguish between empirical and normative view points. As I hope to show, the connection between sexism and original sin is indeed very strong, though in the history of the Church it has been tragically inverted.

Let us begin with the story of Genesis 3. The story of the Fall concludes with curses associated with the main characters, Eve, Adam and the snake. I have already spoken briefly on these in Chapter 11. The curse against Eve is as follows:

> I will give you intense pain in childbearing, you shall give birth to your children in pain. Your yearning will be for your husband, yet he will dominate you (Genesis 3:16).

As I suggested before, the author's purpose in writing this is to give an etiological explanation for what he sees as a present disorder. Why is it that women suffer in childbirth? Why is it that men dominate women? Both these things are clearly seen as wrong, so why do they happen? In trying to understand the origins of these evils the author seeks to locate them in this first of all sins. The suffering and domination of women are the result of sin. This situation is not how God originally intended it to be.

It is here that the distinction between the empirical and the normative are most important. The author is saying "this is the way it is". The author is not saying "this is the way it should be". Indeed, he is trying to explain how the present evil situation came to be, so that in fact he is saying "this is *not* the way it should be"! It is not good that men dominate women in society since this is not God's original intention.

It was not uncommon for Jesus to draw upon this concept of God's original intention. In his teaching on marriage and divorce Jesus counters the then current practice of the Jews with the claim that "this is not how it was in the beginning" (cf. Matthew 19:1ff., Mark 10:1ff.).[1] Indeed, as has been pointed out by numerous authors, Jesus' own attitude to women in no way reflects the assumed male dominance present in Jewish society. Jesus speaks to women as equals, allows women to become his disciples, castigates his male disciples for not listening to the witness of women to his resurrection. In his actions Jesus lifts the curse of Genesis 3, treating women as equal partners in discipleship, restoring them to their original dignity. Thus Paul is able to proclaim, in Christ, "there can be neither male nor female" (Galatians 3:28).

The radical nature of this approach, together with the deeply ingrained nature of sexism, meant that its key insights were soon lost within the Church. Even within New Testament times there was a backing away from the radical equality of men and women, especially in the Pastoral Epistles. By the time of the early Fathers women are back in their place and all's well with the world! This process has been documented in the work of Elisabeth Schussler Fiorenza, *In Memory of Her* (Crossroad, NY, 1984). It is this ingrained nature of sexism which gives some indication of its connection with original sin.

As I have considered it, original sin is our original self-disesteem, a disesteem with our creaturehood, with our human nature as such. Human nature is caught in the dialectic of transcendence and limitation. Transcendence is the realm of the spirit, of the all-encompassing drive within human consciousness. Limitation is the realm of the body, of rootedness in the material. Our rejection of our creaturehood can be evident in one of two ways. One is to reject limitation, to overreach in transcendence without regard for the limitations of human nature, or of the world itself. The other is to retreat into limitation, to turn away from challenge, to be locked into the cycles of nature. Culturally men are identified with the first option. Men are seen as rational, dominant, thrusting forward. Women, on the other hand, are culturally identified with the second. Women are seen as caught up in feelings, subject to bodily rhythms, irrational.

This linking of women with materiality is even reflected in language. Both *material* and *maternal* have the same root in Latin, *mater*, the Latin word for mother. Indeed we speak of Mother Earth, and Mother Nature. It is through women that all human life comes in a manner which emphasizes our biological nature, and women's bodily rhythms are a constant reminder of our animal origins. Psychically then, women become symbols of human limitation, of all the forces which hold back the thrust towards transcendence, the life of the spirit. It is this psychic identification of women with limitation which lies at the heart of sexism.

Sexism arises out of our felt rejection of our human nature. Males, caught up in a one-sided thrust towards transcendence, reject any reminder of their basic limitations. Nothing is a greater reminder of limitation than women and men's own dependence on women. Such dependence becomes irksome and must be suppressed through developing social structures of domination. Domination seeks to mask the very real relationships of dependence upon women that all men have, as mothers, wives, lovers. Indeed it is in the area of sexual relations that things become most difficult. Nothing is a clearer reminder of our animal origins than the act of sexual intercourse itself. In intercourse our very bodiliness can overtake us and give expression to our most basic instincts. Such a powerful reminder of our animal origins must undergo an equally powerful repression, often flowing over into mindless sexual violence as repressed energies explode into consciousness. Women are labelled the cause of the problem, they are the seducers, the whores. Women who suffer the most violent of rapes are blamed for leading men on: "it's all the woman's fault, she asked for it". Men become unable to take responsibility for their own sexuality, placing the whole burden, be it for maintaining virginity or contraception, upon women. Men cannot take responsibility, for to do so would be to acknowledge their own bodiliness, to befriend it, to rob it of its compulsive power, to esteem themselves as they are, transcendent, yes, but still grounded in bodily limitation.

Women, too, are caught up in an ambiguity towards their own human natures. Their own bodily rhythms and society conspire to constantly remind them of their rootedness in the natural world. In their self-disesteem they identify with the roles they are given. Theirs is the job of nurturing, of bearing children, of making a home, and giving comfort to the man who ventures out "bravely" into the "real" world outside. Theirs is the secondary place, the lower place. Largely denied access to the realm of the spirit, of intellect, science, the arts, women can become depressed, despairing, isolated. The few who burst through into the "male" world of the spirit are seen as unfeminine, unnatural. Women's contributions to history, the arts, the sciences are relegated to footnotes, or simply forgotten altogether.

Sexuality again becomes distorted. It becomes a way of luring men, of trapping them into relationship so that women can enjoy the one source of fulfillment considered legitimate, the bearing of children. Women take on all the responsibility for the mundane tasks of family life—they see it as their lot in life, a fitting "punishment" for the guilt of being a female.

Such a situation is not life-giving to either men or women. Men have heart attacks while women suffer depressive breakdowns. Neither men nor women experience the saving balance of accepting both transcendent and grounded aspects of human nature. We can look at such a situation and truly say, "this is not how it was meant to be in the beginning". This imbalance is the result of sin. Indeed, it is a reflection of our most basic original sin, our rejection of our human nature. Grace comes to us as a healing power to overcome such an imbalance, to free us from such sin and restore us to wholeness.

If this is the case, if grace operates to free us from sexism at its very roots, then sexism cannot be seen as a peripheral issue for the Christian Church. Jesus died and rose again to free us from the power of sin, from the very source of sin itself, our original self-disesteem. For a Church which lives in the power of the resurrection, sexism is an intolerable sin. For the Church to perpetuate sexism in its own ranks, by the systematic exclusion of women from positions of responsible decision-making within the Christian community, is a denial of the saving message of Jesus. For as Paul reminds us, in Christ, "there are no distinctions ... between male and female" (Galatians 5:28).

ORIGINAL SIN AND THE ENVIRONMENT

The same general principles outlined above can be applied to the question of the relationship between humanity and the natural environment. While this relationship has not been the focus of as much attention from the Christian tradition as has been the issue of sexism, the recent growth of environmental consciousness has helped to bring it to the fore in Christian thinking.

While much attention has been focused on the text of Genesis 1:28, "Fill the earth and conquer it", a more significant text is again found in the account of the first sin. Just as Eve is cursed for her part in that sin, so too is Adam addressed by God. Yet significantly, it is not Adam who is cursed but the soil.

> Accursed be the soil because of you. Painfully you shall get your food from it as long as you live. It will yield you brambles and thistles, as you eat the produce of the land ... (Genesis 3:17–18).

Adam's suffering occurs *because the soil is cursed*! Again, the author is not saying that the soil should be cursed, that this is some punishment from God. Indeed it would be foolish to think of the soil as being punished! The author is attempting to understand the difficulties of his culture's present relationship to the soil, to the natural world. He reflects the sense that something has gone wrong in this relationship, something which is caused by sin. He then gives expression to this sense of dis-ease by an etiological explanation that the soil was originally cursed. In a way he is speaking with the voice of generations of farmers who, in their difficulties with the land, have cursed the soil many a time.

This sense that the soil is cursed is, as with sexism, archetypal of our situation of original sinfulness. The soil, the earth, is a powerful symbol of the limitations of human existence. The first human, Adam, is fashioned from the dust of the earth (Genesis 2:7). The very name "Adam" comes from a play on the Hebrew word for ground, "adamah", just as in English we could play on the words human and humus. He comes alive only with the life-giving breath of God, so that human existence is always a tension between the principle of transcendence, the spirit, and the principle of limitation, the material. We are beings whose heads are in the clouds, but whose feet are made of clay. Yet it is this very tension, which is part of human existence, which is rejected in original sin. Original sin is a sense that somehow, something is wrong with being human, with being caught between two worlds.

Again, as with sexism, the male, Adam, rejects any reminder of limitation. Just as the woman, a symbol of limitation, is cursed, so too is the soil. The soil is no longer something to nurture and value but something to dominate, to deprecate. Only that which is the product of human labor has any value. This was brought home to me very powerfully in one of David Suzuki's many documentaries on our relationship to the natural world. He pointed to a magnificent piece of forest land and said that to our eyes this land was "undeveloped". This forest, which in its own terms was beautifully developed, was simply seen as having no value. It would only take on value when it had been dominated, subdued and then molded to human requirements.

This radical dis-valuing of the land is clearly seen in our present global economic system. Primary products, such as grains, coffee, tea, fruit, dairy goods and so on, together with primary resources such as minerals, oil, coal and so on, are simply not valued. Only when they are processed, molded to the human will do they take on value. Such primary products are consistently undervalued on the world market, usually to the detriment of poorer, Third World nations. This undervaluing distorts economic production as such nations try to produce more and more for less and less return, pushing their soil to its limits, with the result that once productive land is turned into desert.

This has been the global pattern. Because limitation has been ignored, because the soil is not valued, the whole world is facing a major problem of desertification. Brendan Lovett reports that when the Americas were first inhabited by Europeans, the soil in the Central Plains of North America was sixteen feet deep. Half this has now been lost through overcultivation.[2] In North Africa the Sahara Desert is constantly expanding.[3] In South America and the Philippines, slash-and-burn agriculture can turn lush rain-forest into unproductive land within ten years.

This same repression of limitation can be seen in our treatment of the world's energy resources, which are also taken from the ground. World stocks of coal and oil, which took millions of years to form, are being consumed in the space of a few human generations without any sense of the limitation of such resources. The resultant release of millions of years of stored carbon dioxide into the atmosphere has now threatened to produce major and unpredictable changes to global weather patterns. The only solution offered by our technocrats is not to review our patterns of energy consumption, but to opt for nuclear power, which offers a legacy of death stretching for hundreds of generations.

Our whole attitude to the natural environment has been to see it as a cheap source of resources for our human consumption and a convenient dump of our waste. As a source we have raped the soil. As a dump we have poisoned our air, our rivers, our oceans. Yet all these are a necessary part of our *human* existence. Human *bodily* existence needs healthy soil, clean air and water if its biological being is to survive and flourish. But it is this very *biological* nature of our human existence which points to our limitation, limitation which we actively suppress. In failing to face up to the real limitations of human existence, we run the very real risk of making that existence impossible.

In earlier historical eras such a risk remained localized, and indeed we have seen cultures collapse because of an inattention to the limitations of nature. Northern Africa used to be the bread basket of the Roman Empire. Now it is largely desert. While such collapses remained localized they were salutary reminders to us of the risks we have taken. Now, however, the dangers are no longer localized. The effects on the environment are irreversibly global. Human activity has now reached the stage that every part of the globe is affected, even the most remote areas such as the Arctic and Antarctic poles.

In Chapter 8, I noted that there is a logic to sin and it is the logic of death, of destruction. To ignore limits is eventually to come up against them. To ignore the limits of life is eventually to come up against the limits of life. To ignore the limits of life on the entire planet is eventually to come up against the limits of life on the entire planet. The choice is ultimately one between life and death. To choose life means to accept that there are limits to human existence, that these limits are good and part of what it means to be human. Such an acceptance is saving, in the religious sense, since it means overcoming our original sinfulness, a sinfulness which involves a radical rejection of our human limitations, a rejection of our creaturely status.

CONCLUSION

These two examples, of sexism and environmental destruction, are closely linked. Both are consequences of the male-dominated or patriarchal structure of our society. The curse of Eve and the curse of the soil are both seen from the male perspective, a perspective which has psychically identified itself with the transcendent aspects of human existence. The solution to the problem, however, is not to opt for a matriarchal, natural world mysticism. Such a solution has its own problems, in its over-willingness to be subsumed into the natural world, its willingness to read the hand of God in natural disasters and disease. The solution to the problem cannot be found in opting for one or the other but in realizing that the very division is itself a sign of the problem. It is the division and separation between male and female, between human and natural, which lies at the heart of the problem. The solution is to be found in reconciliation, atonement i.e. in making all things one, at-one-ment.

Hence Paul can say:

> God was in Christ reconciling the world to himself (2 Corinthians 5:19).

The work of reconciliation is a divine task, a task of overcoming the divisions between men and women, between human and nature, between human and divine. It results in a new society in Christ in which there are no more divisions between Greek and Jew, slave and free, rich and poor, male and female. Even the natural world is caught up in this new society as it groans in one great act of giving birth, waiting with eagerness for the sons and daughters of God to be revealed (Romans 8:18ff.). It is this divine task that God invites us to partake in, living securely in his grace, at peace with ourselves and the world, no longer doubting the value of our existence.

The invitation is made to all people, to live as Jesus lived, to overcome the evil of division through a self-sacrificing love which evil can never overpower. This is the lesson of the resurrection. God raised up Jesus to new life, to become a new creation, to found a new society, to build the heavenly city. In this city the Satan has been expelled and the God of Life rules. In this society justice shall reign, no person shall be poor or alone. In this new creation the lion will lie down with the lamb; the earth will be bountiful and rich. In this new life, death has lost its sting and life wells up within to eternity. This is not just a promise for the future, but a mission for the present as we pray fervently, "your kingdom come ... *on earth* as it is in heaven".

---

1 *See* Ben Meyer, *The Aims of Jesus*, SCM Press, London, 1979, pp.137ff., for the significance of God's original intention for Jesus' ethical teaching.

2 *See* his *On Earth as in Heaven*, Claretian Publication, Quezon City, 1988, p.23.

3 *New Internationalist* reports that in the last fifty years "around 650 million square kilometres of farming land in sub-Saharan Africa have become desert ... and the process is accelerating" (June, 1990, p.16).

REVD DR JOHN CHRYSSAVGIS

ORIGINAL SIN—AN ORTHODOX PERSPECTIVE

FROM LIFE TO SURVIVAL

For Orthodox theology and spirituality, the "Fall" of humanity is the renunciation of the possibility of participating in true life, in personal relationship and in loving communion. The biblical account of the Fall refers to the initial choice of autonomy and self-sufficiency, as opposed to dependence upon and subsistence in God, the origin of life and love. This implies alienation from God and from oneself, fragmentation of the world and of human nature. The various needs of self-preservation become an end in themselves, and the Fall is ultimately *from the level of life to that of survival*. Thus the tragic words of J.-P. Sartre prove true: "my original sin is the existence of the other".[1]

The falling away is called "sin" (Gk, "αμαρτια"), which literally signifies "missing the mark" as to existential truth and authentic life, the only "end" of humanity according to the Eastern Church Fathers.[2] As for the term "original sin" (*originalis peccatum*), it is in fact not to be found in the Greek patristic tradition of the first millennium and it would, therefore, be inaccurate to apply it to the theology of the Eastern Church. Thus it is almost not surprising to find that the work of an Orthodox scholar, dealing with anthropology and the consequences of the Fall, in fact *nowhere* refers to "original sin" but only to the "transformation of ... the 'image' into 'garments of skin'", namely mortality.[3] The emphasis in the Orthodox tradition is upon life as dependent upon God. It is almost as if western writers concentrated intensely on the fateful *consequences* of the "first disobedience", and eastern theologians solely on the *way out* of the barrier of darkness towards the way of light. The overall dynamics then, are of life and death, not virtue and sin or blessing and fall. Sin is "subjection to passion and corruption and mortality",[4] while repentance is a *Pascha* from death to life, a reversal—"metanoia" actually means reorientation and redirection of mentality—of what has become the empirically "normal" development, namely the movement from life to death.

"ORIGINAL SIN" AND THE EASTERN FATHERS

The concept of "original sin" is the key to the understanding of many aspects of theology, such as salvation and anthropology.[5] In the Byzantine east, where Augustinian thought and polemics exercised little if any influence at all, the significance and implications of the sin of Adam—"the forebear's sin", as it is usually known—was understood along different lines. The extraordinary impact upon the west of the Augustinian controversy with Pelagius and Julian of Eclanum cannot be underestimated, however, and it is an oversimplification to dismiss eastern theology as being "semi-Pelagian". There is much more to it than this, and in fact the Greek patristic understanding of original sin differs sharply from the view of both Augustine and Pelagius. The eastern tradition developed its own views of purification from sin and life after death, seeing death less as *punishment for* than as divine *deliverance from* sin.

The most critical point of differentiation is the absence, among the Byzantines, of any notion of inherited culpability. The Eastern Church Fathers insist upon viewing sin as *personal* failure. Only a free, personal choice may commit sin and incur guilt. "Our salvation", writes Maximus Confessor, "depends on our will".[6] There can be no natural sin, or "sin of nature".[7] The Fall of Adam is not an ontological but an anthropological event. This in no way implies radical individualism; nor do the Byzantine theologians deny the unity of humanity. The Pauline doctrine of the two Adams refers, according to Gregory of Nyssa for instance, to the creation of humankind as a whole:[8]

> For as in Adam all people die, so also in Christ shall all be brought to life (I Cor. 15:22).

The sin of Adam is clearly related to all people, just as salvation by Christ touches everyone. Surely, however, neither original sin nor salvation may be effected in one's life without personal and free responsibility. Now the context of this passage is that of *death* in Adam and *life* in Christ, not of transgression and guilt. The distinction between the old and the new Adam is essentially one between death and life. The new Adam, Jesus Christ, is the model of existence, the source of life, the giver of salvation.

WHAT CONTEMPORARY ORTHODOX THEOLOGIANS ARE SAYING

Mortality and Sinfulness

For Cyril of Alexandria, humanity, after the sin of Adam, "fell sick of corruption". Cyril's opponents, the theologians of the School of Antioch, agreed with him on the consequence of Adam's sin. For Theodore of Mopsuestia, "by becoming mortal, we acquired greater urge to sin". The necessity of satisfying the needs of the body—food, drink, and other bodily needs—are absent in immortal beings, but among mortals they lead to "passions", for they present unavoidable means of temporary survival. Theodoret of Cyrus repeats almost literally the arguments of Theodore in his own commentary on Romans; elsewhere, he argues against the sinfulness of marriage by affirming that transmission of mortal life is not sinful in itself, in spite of Psalm 51:7 ("my mother conceived me in sin"). This verse, according to Theodoret, refers not to the sexual act but to the general sinful condition of *mortal* humanity: "Having become mortal, [Adam and Eve] conceived mortal children, and mortal beings are necessarily subject to passions and fears, to pleasures and sorrows, to anger and hatred".

There is indeed a consensus in Greek patristic and Byzantine traditions in identifying the inheritance of the Fall as an inheritance essentially of mortality rather than of sinfulness, sinfulness being merely a consequence of mortality. The idea appears in Chrysostom, who specifically denies the imputation of sin to the descendants of Adam; in the eleventh century commentator Theophylact of Ochrida, and in later Byzantine authors, particularly Gregory Palamas. The always-more-sophisticated Maximus the Confessor, when he speaks of the consequences of the sin of Adam, identifies them mainly with the mind's submission to the flesh and finds in sexual procreation the most obvious expression of man's acquiescence in animal instincts; but .... sin remains, for Maximus, a personal act and inherited guilt is impossible (John Meyendorff, *Byzantine Theology*, pp.144–5; quoted with permission from the author).

Ascesis and Theosis

When one believes that the principle of the immortality of the entire human person is the life-giving and incorruptible energy of the life-creating Trinity, and that death in man is due to his estrangement from the source of life, then it becomes apparent that the so-called mysticism of the Greek Church is not a supposedly platonist or decorative element but the very presupposition of the scriptural and patristic concept of man. An Orthodox Christian does not participate in the divine energies because he seeks union with God at the indication of philosophy .... On the contrary, the purpose is to oust the power of sin that reigns in death and corruption in order to reinstate in man the principle of immortality and return him to the way of perfection and *theosis* ....

Since the Greek Fathers have always taught that God did not create death and that the concepts of death, Satan and sin are closely interrelated, Orthodox piety has always been characterized by a heroic and martyric disposition, following in the footsteps of the Martyrs and Confessors for whom fear of and retreat before death signified falling into the hands of Satan and cutting off from the faith. Orthodox Christians have always sought to trample upon the sting of death and achieve freedom from all worldly care. "He who no longer fears death is beyond the tyranny of the devil .... He fears none, is above all and freer than everyone" (John Chrysostom, PG. 63:41–2). A characteristic feature of the Greek patristic tradition is the continual struggle against the tyranny of death, the devil and sin through the life of selfless love in Christ. Orthodox monasticism, the entire liturgical, hymnological and scriptural tradition of the Eastern Church, is imbued with this heroic and ascetical spirit (John Romanides, *Original Sin*, pp.156–8; author's translation).

Image and Likeness

Each new human being is born into a world where sin prevails everywhere, a world in which it is easy to do evil and hard to do good. Man's will is weakened and enfeebled by what the Greeks call "desire" and the Latins "concupiscence". We are all subject to these, the spiritual effects of original sin.

Thus far, there is fairly close agreement between Orthodoxy, Roman Catholicism, and classic Protestantism; but beyond this point east and west do not entirely concur. Orthodoxy, holding as it does a less exalted idea of man's state before the Fall, is also less severe than the west in its view of the consequences of the Fall. Adam fell, not from a great height of knowledge and perfection, but from a state of undeveloped simplicity; hence he is not to be judged too harshly for his error. Certainly, as a result of the Fall man's mind became so darkened, and his will-power was so impaired that he could no longer hope to attain to the likeness of God. Orthodox, however, do not hold that the Fall deprived man entirely of God's grace, though they would say that after the Fall grace acts on man from the outside, not from within. Orthodox do not say, as Calvin said, that man after the Fall was utterly depraved and incapable of good desires. They cannot agree with Augustine when he writes that man is under "a harsh necessity" of committing sin, and that man's nature was overcome by the fault into which it fell, *and so came to lack freedom*. The image of God is distorted by sin, but never destroyed; in the words of a hymn sung by Orthodox at the Funeral Service for the laity: "I am the image of Thine inexpressible glory, even though I bear the wounds of sin". And because he still retains the image of God, man still retains free will, although sin restricts its scope. Even after the Fall, God "takes not away from man the power to will—to will to obey or not to obey Him". Faithful to the idea of synergy, Orthodoxy repudiates any interpretation of the Fall which allows no room for human freedom.

Most orthodox theologians reject the idea of "original guilt", put forward by Augustine and still accepted (albeit in a mitigated form) by the Roman Catholic Church. Men (Orthodox usually teach) automatically inherit Adam's corruption and mortality, but not his guilt: they are only guilty in so far as by their own free choice they imitate Adam. Many western Christians believe that whatever a man does in his fallen and unredeemed state, since it is tainted by original guilt, cannot possibly be pleasing to God: "Works before Justification", says the thirteenth of the Thirty-nine Articles of the Church of England, ". . . are not pleasant to God . . . but have the nature of sin". Orthodox would hesitate to say this. And Orthodox have never held (as Augustine and many others in the west have done) that unbaptized babies, because tainted with original guilt, are consigned by the just God to the everlasting flames of Hell. The Orthodox picture of fallen humanity is far less sombre than the Augustinian or Calvinist view (Timothy Ware,

The Orthodox Church, Pelican, 1963, pp.228–9; reproduced by permission of Penguin Books Ltd).

The Fall of Adam

We must seek ways of interpreting the Fall other than by placing the blame on Adam for having exceeded the limits of his freedom. We shall have, perhaps, to abandon forensic categories of guilt. It may be more logical, more consistent with our view of the *imago Dei*, if we followed not St Augustine but St Ireneaus in this respect.

St Ireneaus took a very "philanthropic" and compassionate view of Adam's Fall. He thought of him as a child placed in Paradise in order to grow to adulthood by exercising his freedom. But he was deceived and did the wrong thing. What does this mean? It means that it was not a question of exceeding the limits of freedom. It was rather a question of applying absolute freedom in the wrong way. Now this is very different from saying that Adam should have adjusted his drive for freedom to his creaturely limitations. For had he adjusted his freedom this way, he would have lost the drive to absolute freedom, whereas now he can still possess it, though he needs to readjust and re-orient his freedom . . . .

If we look at what the story of Adam's Fall implies for creation, we notice that the most serious consequence of this Fall was death. This has normally—ever since St Augustine influenced our thinking—been taken to mean that death came to creation as a punishment for Adam's disobedience. This, however, would imply a great deal of unacceptable things. It would mean that God himself introduced this horrible evil which he then tried through his Son to remove. It would also seem to imply that before the arrival of man in creation there was no death at all. This latter assumption would contradict the entire theory of evolution in creation, and would also make it cruel and absurd on the part of the Creator to punish all creatures for what one of them did.

These difficulties lead us to the conclusion that the view of Irenaeus, Maximus, et al. is more reasonable on all counts, including the theory of evolution. Their view sees creation as being from the beginning in a state of mortality—owing . . . . to its having had a beginning—and awaiting the arrival of man in order to overcome this predicament. Adam's Fall brought about death, not as something new in creation, but as an inability to overcome its inherent mortality, (J. Zizioulas, in *King's Theological Reviews*, xiii, 1, 1990; quoted with permission).

THE HEART OF THE PROBLEM

The scriptural text which played a crucial role in discussions on original sin, not only of earlier centuries but to this day, is found in Romans, Chapter 5. This passage is given a centrality by Augustine which, I would argue, is not given by Paul himself. If one also takes into account the difficulty of verse 12 in particular, then one may well understand why it has led to such a sharp contrast of interpretation in the east from that in the west. In order to grasp more fully the meaning and depth of Paul's words, the text will be also quoted in the original Greek:

δια τουτο ωσπερ δι' ενος ανθρωπου η αμαρτια ετς τον κοσμον εισηλθεν	Therefore as sin came into the world through one man.

Up to this point, there is no controversy. The aforementioned fundamental unity of human nature is affirmed.

και δια της αμαρτιας ο θανατος	And, through sin, death [came into the world].

This too is an undisputed basic anthropological principle.

και ουτως εις παντας ανθρωπους ο θανατος διηλθεν	And so death passed on to all people.

It is here that the difficulty arises. Readers should, however, observe that the reference is to death, not sin. It is death that comes upon all people, not any inherited guilt. And Paul continues:

εφ' ω παντες ημαρτον	for that all have sinned.

The heart of the problem lies precisely in this phrase, and the issue is one of translation. The final four Greek words were translated into Latin as "*in quo* omnes peccaverunt", that is "*in whom* all have sinned", and this translation, in the final analysis a subjective *interpretation*, has led to the wholesale justification of the doctrine of guilt inherited from Adam. Yet the original Greek scarcely lends itself to such a rendering. The form "εφ' ω"—a contraction of "επι" with the relative pronoun "ω"—may simply be rendered as "because", a meaning acceptable to many scholars today but also to a number of Byzantine authors who saw nothing in this phrase beyond a moral similarity between Adam and his descendants, death being the normal "wages of sin" (Romans 6:23). Yet if we all die because we have sinned, then there is no original sin as such that is passed down. This interpretation, while still not implying that guilt is passed on to the descendants of Adam, unless they also sin as he sinned, nevertheless does not explain *how* death is "passed on". The translation "because" is grammatically suitable, but tends to blur the overall significance of the Pauline text. It appears that Paul's words are unqualified, almost incomplete. Perhaps his thoughts proceed more rapidly than his words. He begins to explain in later verses, but again without great detail: in v.13 the reference is to sin, while in v.14 one reads about death.

The second component, therefore, of the phrase "εφ' ω" may be a neuter pronoun, in which case it means "because", but it may also be masculine, as the Vulgate—and, even before that, the Old Latin—translation ("in quo") and the whole Western Church since Ambrosiaster understood it to be. The question is what the masculine pronoun refers to—is it Adam? He is not actually mentioned in this verse, and is only encountered in v.14 where we read that "death reigned from Adam to Moses". The pronoun may in fact refer to the other, much closer, masculine which precedes and substantiates the phrase, namely "death" (Gk. "θανατος"). If this is the case, then death is conceived as a cosmic reality that accounts for sinfulness in the world. Such a meaning would seem improbable to a reader trained in Augustine, but it is in fact the meaning accepted by the majority of the Greek Fathers.[9] The verse would thus read:

> Therefore as sin came into the world through one man and through sin, death; so death passed on to all people, and *because of death* all have sinned.

Death, or corruption, understood in a personalized sense, has in this way been viewed in the east as a cosmic, tyrannical disease that holds humanity and the whole of creation under its sway, both spiritually and physically. Mortality is the "murderer from the beginning" (John 8:44) which renders sin inevitable and "corrupts" nature.[10] The inheritance is of death rather than of sinfulness or guilt.[11] There is no denying the broader implication or causative uniqueness of Adam's transgression, but it is through death that sin is seen to exercise its power. Paul's theology is down-to-earth, based upon practical anthropological principles. According to the Greek Fathers death renders sin inevitable because one struggles in order to survive. If we were not threatened by mortality, then there would be no obligation, no overwhelming pressure to sin. The imminent threat of death forces us to sin in order to retain our existence.

Thus by the early fifth century, John Chrysostom is interpreting the Epistle to the Romans very differently and, in any case, not overemphasising the question of original sin. The bishop of Hippo, on the other hand, is at about the same time confronted with the Pelagian controversy and expounds his theory about infant baptism. Children, for Augustine, are born sinful and must be baptized "for the remission of sins". Yet his other contemporary, Theodoret of Cyrus, flatly denies that babies are baptized for their sins.

Baptism, for the Eastern Fathers, "remits" sins, especially in the case of adults, but its principal meaning is far wider and more positive: it is participation in Christ's Resurrection, communion in His victory over death, a Paschal mystery. Baptism is, therefore, the remission, not of original sin, nor primarily of personal sins, but of the necessity or propensity to sin. It delivers one from the inherited enslavement to and domination by sin, which through death became more congenial to humanity, and restores one to the integrity of free will. It is renunciation of Satan and regeneration in eternal life. All ancient baptismal rites underline these basic points. Such liturgical texts make reference to life and death, not to guilt and justification.

The only way out of the impasse in this world is identification with the Body of Christ in baptism and the eucharist. The jungle ethic that characterizes contemporary society is "eat in order to survive". The Christian ethic differs markedly: "Take, eat of this my body; drink all of you of my blood".

"REJOICE, I HAVE OVERCOME"

No one doubts that we constantly live in a state of tension. We are continually living in the world, yet are not of the world:

> I do not understand my own actions. For I do not do what I want, but I do the very thing I hate . . . . So then it is no longer I that do it, but the sin which dwells in me . . . . (Rom. 7:14–20).

St Paul tells us that somewhere, at sometime, something "went wrong", as a result of which the world fell into mortality. Consequently, due to "the reign of death" (Rom. 5:14), humanity resorts to sinful methods in order to survive, with a view to postponing death. Such a doctrine may appear existentially more pessimistic but it is *essentially more optimistic*. The existential fear is dispelled by Jesus Christ who alone is able to break the vicious circle:

> In the world you shall have tribulation. But rejoice, for I have overcome the world (John 16:33).

Christ utters these words immediately after informing His disciples of His death and resurrection.

Thus Christians are liberated from the fear of death and from the necessity of struggling for existence:

> Do not be anxious about your life, what you shall eat or what you shall drink, nor about your body, what you shall put on. Is not life more than food ...? (Matt. 6:25. cf. also I John 3:8–9).

The resurrection is the central doctrine that is the key to Christian spirituality (cf. I Cor. 15:14f.). For Jesus Christ "came that [we] may have life, and have it in abundance" (John 10:10).

---

1 *L' Etre et al Néant* (Paris 1943) p.321. See also *In Camera*, end of scene five, where Sartre says that "hell is other people".

2 Cf. Maximus Confessor, *Scholia* PG 4:384 C and 305 B.

3 Cf. P. Nellas, *Deification in Christ—The Nature of the Human Person* (St Vladimir's Seminary Press, 1987).

4 Maximus, *Quaest ad Thal.* PG 90:408BC.

5 *See*, for example, Athanasius of Alexandria, *De Incarnatione* 4 PG 25:104. The classical work in Greek on "original sin" is perhaps J. Romanides, *Original Sin* (Athens, 1956). Prof. Romanides also published an article in English entitled "Original Sin according to St Paul", in *St Vladimir's Seminary Quarterly* IV, 1–2 (1955). A concise, yet insightful analysis may be found in J. Meyendorff, *Byzantine Theology: Historical Trends and Doctrinal Themes* (Fordham 1974) pp.143–6. See also V. Lossky, *Orthodox Theology: An Introduction* (St Vladimir's Seminary Press, 1978) pp.79–94.

6 Cf. *Liber Asceticus* PG 90:953 B.

7 Cf. Photius, *Library* 177 and Maximus, *Expos. Or. Dom.* PG 90:905 A.

8. *De Opif. Hominis* 16 PG 44:185 B.

9. *See* J. Meyendorff, "*Eph. Ho* chez Cyrille d' Alexandrie et Theodoret", in *Studia Patristica* IV (1961) pp.157–161. Cf. also D. Weaver, in *St Vladimir's Theological Quarterly* 27,3 (1983) and 29,2–3 (1985).

10. Cf. Cyril of Alexandria, *In Rom.* PG 74:789 B; Theodore of Mopsuestia, *In Rom.* PG 66:801B and Theodoret of Cyrus, *In Rom.* PG 80:1245A. Curiously, although in disagreement on issues of Christology and Scriptural exegesis, Antiochenes and Alexandrians, at precisely the time of Augustine, are in total harmony on their interpretation of Romans 5:12 and in their understanding of original sin. Yet another contemporary of Augustine, who differs radically in his treatment of sin and baptism, is Mark the Monk: see his *De Baptismo* in Migne (PG 65).

11. This idea is found in John Chrysostom, *In Rom. Hom. 10* PG 60;474–475; Theophylact of Ochrid, *Exp. in Rom.* PG 124:404C; and Gregory Palamas, in J. Meyendorff, *A Study of Gregory Palamas* (London: Faith Press, 1962) pp.121–6.

SELECT BIBLIOGRAPHY

Material by or about Bernard Lonergan

B. Lonergan, *Grace and Freedom*, Darton, Longman and Todd, London, 1970.
—*Method in Theology*, Darton, Longman and Todd, London, 1972.
—*Insight*, Darton, Longman and Todd, London, 1958.
V. Gregson (ed.), *The Desires of the Human Heart*, Paulist Press, NY, 1988.

Material by or about Karl Rahner

K. Rahner, *Foundations of Christian Faith*, Crossroad, NY, 1982.
—"Concerning the relationship between grace and nature" *Theological Investigations*, Vol.1, Darton, Longman and Todd, London, 1961.
—"Some implications of the scholastic concept of uncreated grace", *Theological Investigations*, Vol.1, Darton, Longman and Todd, London, 1961.
—"Anonymous Christians", *Theological Investigations*, Vol.6, Darton, Longman and Todd, London, 1969.
L. Roberts, *The Achievement of Karl Rahner*, Herder and Herder, NY, 1967.

Material by Sebastian Moore

S. Moore, *The Fire and the Rose Are One*, Darton, Longman and Todd, London, 1980.

—*Let this Mind be in You*, Darton, Longman and Todd, London, 1985.
—"Original Sin, Sex, Resurrection and Trinity", in *Lonergan Workshop*, Vol.4, Scholars Press, Chico, p.85ff.

General theological material on grace and original sin

L. Boff, *Liberating Grace*, Orbis, NY, 1979.
G. Daly, *Creation and Redemption*, Gill and McMillan, Dublin, 1988.
J. Donceel, *The Searching Mind*, University of Notre Dame Press, Notre Dame, 1979.
S.J. Duffy, "Our hearts of darkness: Original Sin revisited", *Theological Studies*, 49 (1988) pp.597ff.
D. Edwards, *Human Experience of God*, Paulist Press, NY, 1983.
P. Fiddes, *Past Event and Present Salvation*, Darton, Longman and Todd, London, 1989.
R. Haight, *The Experience and Language of Grace*, Gill and Macmillan, Dublin, 1979.
R. Haughton, *The Passionate God*, Darton, Longman and Todd, London, 1981.
P. Ricoeur, *The Symbolism of Evil*, Harper and Rowe, NY, 1976.
E. Schillebeeckx, *Christ, the Christian Experience in the Modern World*, SCM Press, London, 1980.
—*Church, the Human story of God*, Crossroad, NY, 1990.
P. Schoonenberg, *Man and Sin*, Sheed and Ward, London, 1965.
G. Vandervelde, *Original Sin*, Rodopi, Amsterdam, 1975.

Psychological material

E. Becker, *The Denial of Death*, Free Press, NY, 1973.
S. Freud, "Totem and Taboo", in *The Origins of Religion*, Pelican Freud Library, Vol.13, Penguin, NY, 1985.
K. Horney, *Neurosis and Human Growth*, Norton, NY, 1950.
W. James, *The Varieties of Religious Experience*, Collier Books, NY, 1961.
C.A. Matthews, *Breaking Through, no longer a victim of child abuse*, Albatross Books, Claremont, 1990.
G. May, *Addiction and Grace*, Harper and Row, NY, 1988.
A. Meares, *The Door to Serenity*, Hill of Content, Melbourne, 1977.
M. Scott Peck, *The Road Less Travelled*, Rider, London, 1985.
—*People of the Lie*, Rider, London, 1985.

INDEX